Frommer's®

PORTABLE

Charleston
& Savannah

1st Edition

**by Darwin Porter
& Danforth Prince**

D0377772

Macmillan • USA

ABOUT THE AUTHORS

A native of North Carolina, **Darwin Porter** has also lived in South Carolina and Georgia and has explored extensively through the region's major cities and backwoods hamlets. A bureau chief of the *Miami Herald* at the age of 21, he has written numerous best-selling Frommer guides, notably to England, France, the Caribbean, and Italy. He still speaks with a Southern drawl, even after all his international travels. He is joined by **Danforth Prince,** formerly of the Paris bureau of the *New York Times*. Dan has lived in Georgia and traveled extensively in the Tri-State area.

MACMILLAN TRAVEL

A Simon & Schuster Macmillan Company
1633 Broadway
New York, NY 10019

Find us online at **http://www.mgr.com/travel**
or on America Online at Keyword: **Frommer's**

MACMILLAN is a registered trademark of Macmillan, Inc. FROMMER'S is a registered trademark of Arthur Frommer. Used under license.
ISBN 0-02-861422-4
ISSN 1090-154X

Design by Michele Laseau
Digital Cartography by Ortelius Design and John Decamillis
All maps copyright © by Simon & Schuster, Inc.

SPECIAL SALES

Bulk purchases (10+ copies) of Frommer's and selected Macmillan travel guides are available to corporations, organizations, mail-order catalogs, institutions, and charities at special discounts, and can be customized to suit individual needs. For more information write to: Special Sales, Macmillan General Reference, 1633 Broadway, New York, NY 10019.

Contents

List of Maps

An Invitation to the Reader

In researching this book, we have come across many intriguing hotels, resorts, restaurants, and shops, the best of which we have included here. We are sure that many of you will also discover appealing places as you explore Charleston and Savannah. Please don't keep them to yourself. Share your experiences, especially if you want to bring to our attention information that has changed since this book was researched. You can address your letters to:

Darwin Porter & Danforth Prince
Frommer's Charleston & Savannah, 1st Edition
Macmillan Travel
1633 Broadway
New York, NY 10019

An Additional Note

Please be advised that travel information is subject to change at any time—and this is especially true of prices. We therefore suggest that you write or call ahead for confirmation when making your travel plans. The authors, editors, and publisher cannot be held responsible for the experiences of readers while traveling. Your safety is important to us, however, so we encourage you to stay alert and be aware of your surroundings. Keep a close eye on cameras, purses, and wallets, all favorite targets of thieves and pickpockets.

What the Symbols Mean

✪ Frommer's Favorites

Hotels, restaurants, attractions, and entertainment you should not miss.

⑤ Super-Special Values

Hotels and restaurants that offer great value for your money.

The following abbreviations are used for credit cards:

AE	American Express	EU	Eurocard
CB	Carte Blanche	JCB	Japan Credit Bank
DC	Diners Club	MC	MasterCard
DISC	Discover	V	Visa
ER	enRoute		

Planning a Trip to Charleston & Savannah

*T*his chapter is designed to provide most of the nuts-and-bolts travel information you'll need before setting off for South Carolina or Georgia. Browse through this section before you hit the road to ensure you've touched all the bases.

1 Visitor Information & Money

VISITOR INFORMATION

Before leaving home, you can get specific information on South Carolina sports and sightseeing by contacting the **South Carolina Division of Tourism**, 1205 Pendleton St., P.O. Box 71, Columbia, SC 29202 (☎ **803/734-0122;** fax 803/734-0133). They can also furnish *South Carolina: Smiling Faces, Beautiful Places,* a detailed booklet with photos that covers each region of the state.

You can also contact the **Visitor Reception & Transportation Center** (VRTC), P.O. Box 975, Charleston, SC 29402 (☎ **803/ 853-8000**), for an advance copy of their comprehensive "Visitor's Guide" to Charleston.

When you come to South Carolina, look for one of the ten travel information centers located on virtually every major highway near borders with neighboring states.

If you have Internet access, a particularly useful resource for travel information is **CityNet (http://www.city.net)**, which provides links organized by location, then by category, to hundreds of other sites throughout the Internet.

For advance-planning information on Georgia, contact the **Division of Tourism, Georgia Department of Industry, Trade & Tourism,** P.O. Box 1776, Atlanta, GA 30301 (☎ **800/VISIT-GA** or 404/656-3590). Ask for information on specific interests, as well as a calendar of events (January–June or July–December).

A Georgia State Information Center is located near Savannah. It's open Monday through Saturday from 9am to 6pm and Sunday, noon to 6pm.

MONEY

It's becoming easier all the time to just bring along your ATM card and access your bank accounts while you're on the road. There are ATMs all over both Charleston and Savannah, even in supermarkets, but if you do need help in locating one, call **800/424-7787** for the Cirrus network, **800/843-7587** for the Plus system. Most ATMS will also make cash advances against MasterCard and Visa, but make sure that you've been assigned a PIN in advance.

Some people still prefer having the extra security associated with carrying traveler's checks. One major issuer is **American Express** (☎ **800/221-7282**).

2 When to Go

This is a mighty hot and steamy part of the country in summer—it's incredibly humid in July and August (sometimes June and September as well). But temperatures are never extreme the rest of the year, as shown in the average highs and lows noted below. Winter temperatures seldom drop below freezing anywhere in the state. Spring and fall are the longest seasons, and the wettest months are December through April.

Spring, which usually begins in March, is just spectacular. Delicate pink and white dogwoods and azaleas in vivid shades burst into brilliant bloom. Both Savannah and Charleston are heaven for gardeners (or anyone who likes to stop and smell the roses), so March and April are memorable times to visit. During spring and during Charleston's Spoleto Festival, hotel prices rise and reservations are hard to come by.

Charleston Average Temperatures in Degrees Fahrenheit

	Jan	Feb	Mar	Apr	May	June	July	Aug	Sept	Oct	Nov	Dec
High	59	61	68	76	83	87	89	89	85	77	69	61
Low	40	41	48	56	64	70	74	74	69	49	49	42

Savannah Average Temperatures in Degrees Fahrenheit

	Jan	Feb	Mar	Apr	May	June	July	Aug	Sept	Oct	Nov	Dec
High	60	62	70	78	84	89	91	90	85	78	70	62
Low	38	41	48	55	63	69	72	72	68	57	57	41

CHARLESTON, HILTON HEAD & SAVANNAH
CALENDAR OF EVENTS

February

- **Wormsloe Celebrates the Founding of Georgia,** Savannah. Wormsloe was the colonial fortified home of Noble Jones, one of Georgia's first colonists. Costumed demonstrations portray skills used by those early settlers. Call **912/353-3023** for details. Early February.

- **Low-Country Oyster Festival,** Charleston. Steamed buckets of oysters greet visitors to Boone Hall Plantation. Enjoy live music, oyster-shucking contests, children's events, and various other activities. Contact the Greater Charleston Restaurant Association, 185 East Bay St., Suite 206, Charleston, SC 29401 (☎ **803/577-4030**). Early February.

- **Southeastern Wildlife Exposition,** Charleston. More than 150 of the finest artists and more than 500 exhibitors participate at 13 different locations in the downtown area. Enjoy carvings, sculpture, paintings, live animal exhibits, food, and much more. Call **803/723-1748** for details. Mid-February.

- **Savannah Irish Festival,** Savannah. This Irish heritage celebration, complete with traditional music, dancing, and food, promises fun for the entire family. Call **912/232-6373** for details. Mid-February.

March

- **Festival of Houses and Gardens,** Charleston. For nearly 50 years people have been enjoying some of Charleston's most historic neighborhoods and private gardens on this tour. Contact the Historic Charleston Foundation, P.O. Box 1120, Charleston, SC 29402 (☎ **803/723-1623**). Mid-March to mid-April.

- **St. Patrick's Day Celebration on the River,** Savannah. The river flows green—and so does the beer—in one of the largest celebrations held on River Street each year. Enjoy live entertainment, lots of food, and tons of fun. Call the Savannah Waterfront Association (☎ **912/234-0295**) for details. St. Patrick's Day weekend.

- ✪ *Family Circle* **Magazine Cup,** Hilton Head Island. This $750,000 tournament draws the best women's tennis players on the island. Call **803/363-3500** for details. Late March to early April.

April
- **MCI Classic,** Hilton Head. This $1.3 million tournament brings an outstanding field of PGA tour professionals each year. The week-long tournament is held at Harbour Town Golf Links in Sea Pines Plantation. Contact Classic Sports, Inc., 71 Lighthouse Rd., Suite 414, Hilton Head, SC 29928 (☎ **803/671-2448**). Mid-April.

May
- **American Classic Tea Open House,** Charleston. America's only tea plantation welcomes the public for free tours—don't forget to buy some superb blends when you leave. Contact the Charleston Tea Plantation, 6617 Maybank Hwy., Wadmalaw Island, SC 29487 (☎ **803/559-0383**). Early May.
- **Savannah Symphony Duck Race,** Savannah. Each year the Savannah Symphony Women's Guild plays host as a flock of rubber ducks hit the water to go with the flow of the tides along Savannah's historic River Street. There's a $5,000 grand prize for the winning ducky. Contact the Savannah Symphony Women's Guild (☎ **912/238-0888**) for details. Early May.
- ✪ **Spoleto Festival USA,** Charleston. This is the premier cultural event in the Tri-State area. This famous international festival, the American counterpart to the equally celebrated one in Spoleto, Italy, showcases world-renowned performers in drama, dance, music, and art. Performances and exhibitions are held in various venues around Charleston. For details and this year's schedule, contact Spoleto Festival USA, P.O. Box 157, Charleston, SC 29402 (☎ **803/722-2764**). Late May through early June.
- **Memorial Day at Old Fort Jackson,** Savannah. A 21-cannon salute, flag-raising ceremony, and a memorial service pay tribute to America's fallen troops. The S guard for the ceremony is made up of members of the 1st South Carolina Volunteers re-enactment unit. Contact the Coastal Heritage Society (☎ **912/238-1779**) for details. Late May.

June
- **Juneteenth,** Savannah. This events highlights the contributions of more than 2,000 African-Americans who fought for their freedom and the freedom of all future generations. Contact the Coastal Heritage Society (☎ **912/278-1779**). Early June.

July
- **Thunderbolt Seafood Harvest Festival,** Savannah. A celebration of the harvest in a historic fishing village with food, fun,

games, entertainment, arts and crafts, and a parade. Contact the Thunderbolt Seafood Harvest Festival Committee (☎ 912/355-4422). Late July.

August

- **Savannah Maritime Festival,** Savannah. This celebration of the sea is competitive, educational, and entertaining. Experience a sailing regatta, the Tybrisa Ball, a sportfishing tournament, a 10k run, the Jet Ski Jamboree, the Beach Volleyball Classic, and a laser show with fireworks. Contact the Savannah Maritime Committee (☎ 912/236-3959) for details. Early August.

September

- **Scottish Games and Highland Gathering,** Charleston. This gathering of Scottish clans features medieval games, bagpipe performances, Scottish dancing, and other traditional activities. Contact the Scottish Society of Charleston, P.O. Box 31951, Charleston, SC 29417 (☎ 803/556-2417) for more information. Mid-September.

- **Savannah Jazz Festival,** Savannah. This festival features national and local jazz and blues legends. Don't miss the jazz brunch and music held at different venues throughout the city. Contact Host South (☎ 912/232-2222) for details. Mid-September.

October

- **MOJA Festival,** Charleston. The event celebrates the rich African-American heritage of the Charleston area with lectures, art exhibits, stage performances, historical tours, concerts, and much more. Contact the Charleston Office of Cultural Affairs, 133 Church St., Charleston, SC 29401 (☎ 803/724-7309) for details. Early October.

- **Corel Champions,** Hilton Head Island. In preparation for an end-of-the-year championship, world-class male tennis players compete in this $150,000 tournament. Call **803/842-1893** for details. Early October.

- **Tom Turpin Ragtime Festival,** Savannah. Tom Turpin, born in Savannah, was a major force in the development of ragtime. The festival honoring him includes concerts, seminars, parlor piano, and ragtime dance. Contact the Tom Turpin Ragtime Society (☎ 912/233-9989) for more information. Late October.

November

- **Festival of Trees,** Savannah. More than 75 uniquely decorated trees and wreaths festoon the area around the Marriott Riverfront

Hotel, and a special gift shop is set up to accompany the event. Contact the Parent and Child Development Services (☎ **912/ 238-2777**) for more information. Mid-November.

- **Crafts Festival and Cane Grinding,** Savannah. More than 75 crafts artists from four states sell and demonstrate their art. Music is provided by the Savannah Folk Music Society. Contact Oatland Island (☎ **912/897-3773**) for details. Mid-November.

December

- **Christmas 1864,** Savannah. Fort Jackson hosts the re-creation of its evacuation on December 20, 1864. More than 60 Civil War re-enactors play the part of Fort Jackson's Confederate defenders, who were preparing to evacuate ahead of Union General William T. Sherman. Contact Old Fort Jackson (☎ **912/232-3945**) for complete information. Early December.

3 Tips for Travelers with Special Needs

FOR TRAVELERS WITH DISABILITIES

The state of South Carolina provides numerous agencies to assist those with disabilities. For specific information, call the **South Carolina Handicapped Services Information System** (☎ **803/ 777-5732**). Two other agencies that may prove helpful are: **South Carolina Protection & Advocacy System for the Handicapped** (☎ **803/782-0639**) and the **Commission for the Blind** (☎ **803/ 734-7520**).

In Georgia, contact the **Georgia Governor's Developmental Disabilities Council** (☎ **404/657-2126**). **Traveler's Aid** (☎ **404/ 527-7400**) also offers assistance to visitors. The **Georgia Department of Industry, Trade & Tourism** publishes a guide, *Georgia On My Mind,* that lists attractions and accommodations with access for the disabled. To receive a copy, call **800/VISIT-GA, ext. 1903,** or write Tour Georgia, P.O. Box 1776, Atlanta, GA 30301.

The **Information Center for Individuals with Disabilities,** Fort Point Place, 27-43 Wormwood St., Boston, MA 02210 (☎ **617/ 727-5540**), provides travel assistance and can also recommend tour operators. **Mobility International USA,** P.O. Box 10767, Eugene, OR 97440 (☎ **503/343-1284**), offers accessibility information and has many interesting travel programs for travelers with disabilities. They also publish a quarterly newsletter called *Over the Rainbow* ($15 per year to subscribe). Help (accessibility information and more) is also available from the **Travel Information Service**

Getting Hitched in Charleston

Charleston is simply the most beautiful place in South Carolina for a wedding. With its historic homes, cobblestone streets, and age-old churches, there are many sites from which to choose.

The **Charleston Chapel for Weddings,** 22 Ashley Ave. (☎ **800/416-2779**), is located in the downtown historic district and is intimate enough for two or large enough for a party of 60.

Absolutely Wonderful Wedding Service, 25 Broad St. (☎ **803/723-9441**), features a number of romantic wedding locations throughout the city and will pick up your marriage license at the Marriage License Bureau for you at no additional charge. They have their own private Wedding Garden on historic Broad Street that will accommodate 15–20 people.

Other locations throughout the city include Thomas Bennett House (☎ **803/720-1203**), Charleston Landing (☎ **803/556-4450**), Dock Street Theatre (☎ **803/577-7400**), Lowndes Grove Inn (☎ **803/723-3530**), and the Old Exchange Building (☎ **803/727-2165**).

(☎ **215/456-9600**) and the **Society for the Advancement of Travel for the Handicapped** (SATH), 347 Fifth Ave., Suite 610, New York, NY 10016 (☎ **212/447-7284**).

A publisher called **Twin Peaks Press,** Box 129, Vancouver, WA 98666 (☎ **360/694-2462**), specializes in books for people with disabilities. Write for their *Disability Bookshop Catalog*, enclosing $4. One useful title is *Access to the World, a Travel Guide for the Handicapped*, by Louise Weiss, which can also be ordered from Henry Holt & Co. (☎ **800/247-3912**).

Accessible Journeys (☎ **800/TINGLES** or 610/521-0339) and **Flying Wheels Travel** (☎ **800/535-6790** or 507/451-5005) offer tours for people with physical disabilities. **The Guided Tour Inc.** (☎ **215/782-1370**) has tours for people with physical or mental disabilities, visual impairments, and who are elderly.

Amtrak (☎ **800/USA-RAIL**) provides redcap service, wheelchair assistance, and special seats at most major stations with 72 hours' notice. People with disabilities are also entitled to a 25% discount on one-way regular coach fares. Disabled children ages 2 to 15 can also get a 50% discount on already discounted one-way disabled adult fares. Documentation from a doctor or an I.D. card proving your disability is required. For an additional charge, Amtrak also offers wheelchair-accessible sleeping accommodations on long-distance trains, and service dogs are permissible and travel free of charge. Write for a free booklet called *Amtrak's America* from Amtrak Distribution Center, P.O. Box 7717, Itasca, IL 60143, which has a section detailing services for passengers with disabilities.

Greyhound (☎ 800/752-4841) allows a disabled person to travel with a companion for a single fare and, if you call 48 hours in advance, they will arrange help along the way.

FOR GAY & LESBIAN TRAVELERS

Gay hotlines in Charleston fall under the 24-hour crisis prevention network, at **803/744-4357.** In addition, the **South Carolina Gay and Lesbian Information and Community Center,** located in Columbia (☎803/771-7713), also functions as a conduit to other such organizations as the **Low Country Gay and Lesbian Alliance** (☎ 803/720-8088).

A free publication called *Etcetera Magazine* is available in virtually every gay-owned or gay-friendly bar, bookstore, and restaurant in Georgia, the Carolinas, Tennessee, Alabama, and Florida. It boasts a bona fide circulation of 22,000 readers a week, a figure qualifying it as the largest gay and lesbian publication in the Southeast. If you'd like a copy in advance of your trip, send $2 for a current issue to P.O. Box 8916, Atlanta, GA 30306. Or, when you arrive, call **404/525-3821** to find out where you can pick up an issue nearby. You can also call the same number for information on gay resources throughout the South.

4 Getting There & Getting Around

BY PLANE

You can fly into Charleston on **Delta** (☎ 800/221-1212), **Continental** (☎ 800/525-0280), **USAir** (☎ 800/428-4322), and **United** and **United Express** (☎ 800/241-6522).

You can fly directly into Savannah International Airport via **Delta** or **Continental.**

Another option is to fly into Atlanta's **Hartsfield International Airport.** From here you can get a connecting flight, or rent a car and easily drive to either Charleston or Savannah in a few hours. **Delta** is the major carrier to Atlanta, connecting it to pretty much the entire country as well as 32 countries internationally. Other choices include **America West** (☎ 800/235-9292), **American** (☎ 800/

433-7300), **British Airways** (☎ 800/247-9297), **Continental,** **Japan Airlines** (☎ 800/525-3663), **Kiwi** (☎ 800/538-5494), **KLM** (☎ 800/374-7747), **Lufthansa** (☎ 800/645-3880), **Northwest** (☎ 800/225-2525), **Swissair** (☎ 800/221-4750), **TWA** (☎ 800/221-2000), **United,** and **USAir.**

BY CAR

South Carolina has a network of exceptionally good roads. Even when you leave the highways for the state-maintained byways, driving is easy, and AAA services are available through the **Carolina Motor Club** in Charleston (☎ **803/766-2394**).

Interstate 95 enters South Carolina from the north near Dillon and runs straight through the state to Hardeeville on the Georgia border. If you're driving from the north, you can branch off onto I-26 to reach Charleston. The major coastal artery of South Carolina, U.S. 17, also runs through Charleston. The major east–west artery is I-26, running from the northwest corner of the state through Columbia, and then ending at Charleston.

South Carolina furnishes excellent travel information to motorists, and there are well-equipped, efficiently staffed visitor centers at the state border on most major highways. If you have a cellular phone in your car and need help, dial #HP for Highway Patrol Assistance. Also, in South Carolina vehicles must use headlights when windshield wipers are in use as a result of inclement weather. Remember that drivers and front-seat passengers must wear seat belts.

If you're coming to Georgia from the north or south, I-95 will take you right to Savannah. If you're coming from the northwest, I-75 runs into Atlanta and south toward Macon; from there you can pick up I-16 to Savannah. State-run welcome centers at all major points of entry are staffed with knowledgeable, helpful Georgians who can often advise you as to time-saving routes. The speed limit of 55 m.p.h. and the seat belt law are strictly enforced. In Georgia, you can call **404/656-5267** for 24-hour information on road conditions.

Before leaving home, it's a good idea to join the **American Automobile Association** (AAA), 12600 Fairlake Circle, Fairfax, VA 22033-4904 (☎ **703/222-6000**). For a very small fee, they provide a wide variety of services, including trip planning, accommodation and restaurant directories, and a 24-hour toll-free telephone number (☎ **800/222-4357**) set up exclusively to deal with members' road emergencies.

Leading car-rental firms are represented in both cities and in the airports. For reservations and rate information, call the following: **Avis** (☎ 800/331-1212), **Budget Car Rental** (☎ 800/527-0700), **Hertz** (☎ 800/654-3131), and **Thrifty Car Rental** (☎ 800/367-2277).

BY TRAIN

Amtrak (☎ 800/USA-RAIL) services both Charleston and Savannah. Its tour packages include hotel, breakfasts, and historic tours of Charleston at bargain rates. Be sure to ask about their money-saving "All Aboard America" regional fares or any other current fare specials. Amtrak also offers attractively priced rail/drive packages in the Carolinas and Georgia.

PACKAGE TOURS

Collette Tours (☎ 401/728-3805) offers an 8-day fly/drive tour, the "Charleston/Myrtle Beach Show Tour," which guides you through a day of Charleston's most historic sites, visits a Civil War–era plantation in Georgetown, and ends up in Myrtle Beach with dinner and entertainment at Dixie Stampede, Broadway at the Beach, and Magic on Ice.

Mayflower Tours (☎ 800/365-5359) runs a 7-day Myrtle Beach, Charleston, and Savannah tour that features an Atlanta city tour with Olympic sites and Stone Mountain, coastal touring on the Grand Strand in Myrtle Beach, Brookgreen Gardens, Pawley's Island, and Georgetown. It moves on to the historic city of Charleston where you will tour gracious homes, cobblestone streets, pre-Revolutionary buildings, the famous Battery, and the Old Market and Exchange. You'll stay the night after dinner for a Broadway-style variety show, *Serenade,* and travel to Savannah the next day, with tales of the stately mansions and well-kept gardens on board the Old Town Trolley.

FAST FACTS: South Carolina & Georgia

American Express   Services are available through Palmetto Travel Service, 4 Liberty St., Charleston (☎ **803/577-5053**), and at 5500 Abercorn St., Savannah, GA 31405 (☎ **800/528-4800** or 912/351-0770).

Area Code   In South Carolina, it's 803 for the entire state. Savannah's area code is 912.

Car Rentals   See "Getting There & Getting Around" earlier in this chapter.

Climate   See "When to Go" earlier in this chapter.

Drugstores   The most popular drugstore chains in the Carolinas and Georgia are Eckerd, Revco, and Rite Aid. Although none of these offer 24-hour service, Eckerd does have stores in the larger cities that remain open until midnight.

Emergencies   Dial 911 for police, ambulance, paramedics, and fire department.

Information   See "Visitor Information," earlier in this chapter.

Liquor Laws   The minimum drinking age in both states is 21. Some restaurants in South Carolina are licensed to serve only beer and wine, but a great many serve those plus liquor in minibottles, which can be added to cocktail mixers. Beer and wine are sold in grocery stores seven days a week, but all package liquor is sold through local government-controlled stores, commonly called ABC (Alcoholic Beverage Control Commission) stores, which are closed on Sundays.

In Georgia, you can buy alcoholic beverages in package stores between 8am and 11:45pm (except on Sunday, election days, Thanksgiving, and Christmas).

Newspapers and Magazines   The major papers in South Carolina are the *State* (Columbia), *Greenville News,* and *Charleston Post and Courier.* The *Sandlapper* is a local quarterly magazine. The *Atlanta Journal-Constitution* is Georgia's leading daily newspaper. *Southern Living* is a glossy publication concerned mainly with architecture, travel in the South, and gardening—profusely illustrated with color photography.

Taxes   South Carolina has a 6% sales tax, and Georgia has a 5–6% sales tax.

Time Zone   South Carolina and Georgia are on eastern standard time, going on daylight savings time in summer.

Weather   In South Carolina, phone **803/822-8135** for an update; in Georgia, call **900/932-8437** (95¢ per minute).

2

Charleston

*I*n the closing pages of *Gone with the Wind,* Rhett Butler tells Scarlett that he's going back home to Charleston where there is still a little grace and charm left in the world. In spite of all the changes and upheavals over the years, Rhett's endorsement of Charleston still holds true.

If the Old South still lives all through South Carolina's Low Country, it positively thrives in Charleston. All our romantic notions of antebellum days—stately homes, courtly manners, gracious hospitality, and, above all, gentle dignity—are facts of everyday life in this old city, in spite of a few scoundrels here and there, including an impressive roster of pirates, patriots, and presidents.

In spite of a history dotted with earthquakes, hurricanes, fires, and Yankee bombardments, Charleston remains one of the best-preserved cities in America's Old South. It boasts 73 pre-Revolutionary buildings, 136 from the late 18th century, and more than 600 built prior to the 1840s. With its cobblestone streets and horse-drawn carriages, Charleston is a place of visual images and sensory pleasures. Tea, jasmine, and wisteria fragrances fill the air; the aroma of she-crab soup (the local favorite) wafts from sidewalk cafés; and antebellum architecture graces the historic cityscape. "No wonder they are so full of themselves," said an envious visitor from Columbia, which may be the state capital but doesn't have Charleston's style and grace.

In its annual reader survey, *Condé Nast Traveler* magazine named Charleston as the fourth top city to visit in America, which places it ahead of such perennial favorites as New York, Seattle, and San Antonio. Visitors are drawn here from all over the world—it is now quite common to hear German and French spoken along with English on local streets.

Charleston is, and always has been, a city of culture, exemplified by the paintings of Elizabeth O'Neill Verner, the decorative ironwork of Philip Simons, or even Ira Gershwin's *Porgy and Bess*—and most definitely the internationally renowned Spoleto Festival USA.

And does this city have a modern side? Yes, but it's well hidden. Chic shops abound, as do a few supermodern hotels. But you don't come to Charleston for anything cutting edge. You come to glimpse an earlier, almost-forgotten era.

A LOOK AT THE PAST

When King Charles of England magnanimously gave eight of his loyal subjects the strip of land between the 29th and 35th parallels, these "lord proprietors" sent out colonists to settle Albemarle Point and the peninsula between the mouths of the Ashley and Cooper rivers.

By the mid-1770s, Charleston (originally named Charles Towne) was an important seaport. As desire for independence from Britain grew, Charlestonians threw out the last royal governor and built a palmetto-log and sand fort (Fort Moultrie, which remained a working fort right on through World War II) on Sullivan's Island. They repulsed a British fleet on June 28, 1776, and then sent couriers to the Continental Congress in Philadelphia. The British returned in 1780, however, and held the city until December 1782. It took more than 300 ships to move them out—soldiers, Tory supporters, slaves, and tons of loot.

In the 1800s, the economy of the South became ever more dependent on slavery and the plantation system, and grew ever more disaffected from the industrial North. Charleston gained a reputation as a center of gentility and culture, where wealthy rice and indigo planters pleasured themselves with imported luxuries and built stately townhouses (to which they regularly repaired for the summer to escape backcountry mosquitoes and malaria). These Southern aristocrats supported the first theater in the United States, held glittering socials, and invented the Planter's punch cocktail.

The election of Abe Lincoln, who won the presidency without carrying a single Southern state, proved to be the straw that broke the camel's back. Tensions boiled over in 1860, as the first Ordinance of Secession, passed in Columbia, was signed in Charleston. Soon thereafter, South Carolinians opened fire from Fort Johnson against the Union-held Fort Sumter, and the Civil War was off and running. Although attacked again and again during the war, the city remained a Confederate stronghold until February 1865.

After the war, Charlestonians simply did not have the money to rebuild as rapidly as Atlanta did. The demolition of old structures didn't begin until the 1900s—and by that time, fortunately, a preservation movement had developed. Many local families still own and live in the homes their planter ancestors built, and they still take pride in their well-manicured walled gardens. Charleston today remains a city without skyscrapers and modern architectural monstrosities.

Despite the ups and downs of family fortunes, Charlestonians manage to maintain a way of life that, in many respects, has little to do with wealth. The simplest encounter with Charleston natives seems invested with a social air, as though the visitor were a valued guest to be pleased. Yet, there are those who detect a certain snob-bishness in Charleston, and—truth be told—you'd have to stay a few hundred years to be considered an insider here.

1 Orientation

ARRIVING

Charleston International Airport is in North Charleston on I-26, about 12 miles west of the city. It's served by **Delta** (☎ 800/221-1212), **Continental** (☎ 800/525-0280), **USAir** (☎ 800/428-4322), and **United** and **United Express** (☎ 800/241-6522).

Taxi fare into the city runs about $24; the **airport limousine** has a $9 fare (☎ 803/767-7111). All major car-rental facilities, including Hertz (☎ 800/654-3131) and Avis (☎ 800/331-1212), are available at the airport. If you're driving, follow the airport access road to I-26 into the heart of Charleston.

If you're driving, the main north–south coastal route, U.S. 17, passes through Charleston; I-26 runs northwest to southeast, and ends in Charleston. Charleston is 120 miles southeast of Columbia via I-26 and 98 miles south of Myrtle Beach via U.S. 17.

Amtrak arrives at 4565 Gaynor Ave., North Charleston (☎ 800/USA-RAIL).

VISITOR INFORMATION

The **Visitor Reception & Transportation Center** (VRTC), 375 Meeting St., Charleston, SC 29402 (☎ 803/853-8000), just across from the Charleston Museum, provides maps, brochures, tour information, and access to South Carolina Automated Ticketing. The helpful staff will assist you in finding accommodations and planning your stay. Numerous tours depart hourly from the VRTC, and restroom facilities, as well as parking, are available. Be sure to allow time to view the 24-minute multi-image presentation "Forever Charleston," and pick up a copy of their visitor's guide.

The center is open from April to October Monday through Friday from 8:30am to 5:30pm and on Saturday and Sunday from 8am to 5pm; and from November to March daily from 8:30am to 5:30pm.

CITY LAYOUT

Charleston's streets are laid out in an easy-to-follow grid pattern. Main north–south thoroughfares are King, Meeting, and East Bay streets; Tradd, Broad, Queen, and Calhoun streets bisect the city from east to west. South of Broad Street, East Bay becomes East Battery.

Street Maps   Unlike most cities, Charleston offers a most helpful map—and it's distributed free. Called *The Map Guide—Charleston,* it includes the streets of the Historic District as well as surrounding areas, and offers tips on shopping, tours, and what to see and do. Maps are available at the **Visitor Reception Center**, 375 Meeting Place at John Street (☎ **803/853-8000**).

NEIGHBORHOODS IN BRIEF

The Historic District   In 1860, according to one Charlestonian, "South Carolina seceded from the Union, Charleston seceded from South Carolina, and south of Broad Street seceded from Charleston." The city preserves its early years here at its southernmost point, the conjunction of the Cooper and Ashley rivers. The White Point Gardens, right in the "elbow" of the two rivers, provide a sort of gateway into this area where virtually every home is of historic or architectural interest. Between Broad Street and Murray Boulevard (which runs along the south waterfront), you'll find such sightseeing highlights as St. Michael's Episcopal Church, the Calhoun Mansion, the Edmonston-Alston House, the Old Exchange/Provost Dungeon, the Heyward-Washington House, Catfish Row, and the Nathaniel Russell House.

Downtown   Extending north from Broad Street to Marion Square at the intersection of Calhoun and Meeting streets, this area encloses noteworthy points of interest, good shopping, and a gaggle of historic churches. Just a few of its highlights are the Old City Market, the Dock Street Theatre, Market Hall, the Old Powder Magazine, the Thomas Elfe Workshop, Congregation Beth Elohim, the French Huguenot Church, St. John's Church, and the Unitarian Church.

Above Marion Square   The visitor center is located on Meeting Street north of Calhoun. The Charleston Museum is just across the street, and the Aiken-Rhett Mansion, Joseph Manigault Mansion, and Old Citadel are all within easy walking distance of each other in the area bounded by Calhoun Street to the south and Mary Street to the north.

North Charleston   Charleston International Airport is located in this area, where I-26 and I-526 intersect. This makes North Charleston a transportation hub of the Low Country. It is primarily a residential and industrial community, lacking the charms of the Historic District. It is also home to the North Charleston Coliseum, the largest indoor entertainment venue in South Carolina.

Mount Pleasant   East of the Cooper River, just minutes from the heart of the Historic District, this community is worth a detour. Filled with accommodations, restaurants, and some attractions, it encloses a Historic District known as the "Old Village," on the National Register's list of buildings to preserve. Its major attraction is Patriots Point, the world's largest naval and maritime museum, and it's also home to the aircraft carrier *Yorktown.*

Outlying Areas   Within easy reach of the city are Boone Hall Plantation, Fort Moultrie, and the public beaches at Sullivan's Island and Isle of Palms. Head west across the Ashley River Bridge to pay tribute to Charleston's birth at Charles Towne Landing and visit such sightseeing highlights as Drayton Hall, Magnolia Gardens, and Middleton Place. One of the area's most popular beaches, Folly Beach County Park, is also west of the Ashley River.

2 Getting Around

BY CAR

If you're staying in the city proper, park the car and leave it for day trips to outlying areas. You'll find parking facilities scattered about the city, with some of the most convenient at Hutson Street and Calhoun Street, both near Marion Square; on King Street between Queen and Broad; and on George Street between King and Meeting. The two most centrally located garages are at Wentworth Street (☎ **803/724-7383**) and at Concord and Cumberland (☎ **803/724-7387**).

Leading car-rental companies in town and at the airport include: **Avis Rent-a-Car** (☎ **800/331-1212** or 803/767-7038); **Budget Car and Truck Rentals** (☎ **800/527-0700** or 803/577-5194); and **Hertz** (☎ **800/654-3131** or 803/767-4552).

BY BUS

City bus fares are 75¢, and there's service from 5:35am to 10pm (until 1am to North Charleston). Between 9:30am and 3:30pm, senior citizens and the handicapped pay 25¢. Exact change is required. For route and schedule information, call **803/722-2226.**

BY TROLLEY

The **Downtown Area Shuttle** (DASH) is the quickest way to get around the main downtown area daily. Fare is 75¢, and you'll need exact change. A pass good for the whole day costs $2. For hours and routes, call **803/724-7368.**

BY TAXI

Leading taxi companies are **Yellow Cab** (☎ 803/767-6565) and **Safety Cab** (☎ 803/722-4066); each company has its own fare structure. Within the city, however, fares seldom exceed $3 or $4. You must call for a taxi; there are no pickups on the street.

FAST FACTS: Charleston

Airport   See "Arriving," earlier in this chapter.

American Express   The local American Express office is at 956 Provincial Circle, Mount Pleasant (☎ 803/881-9339), open Monday through Friday from 9am to 5pm.

Camera Repair   The best option is **Focal Point,** 4 Apollo Rd. (☎ 803/571-3886), open Monday through Thursday from 9am to 1pm and 2 to 5pm, Friday 9am to noon.

Car Rentals   See "Getting Around," earlier in this chapter.

Climate   See "When to Go," in chapter 1.

Dentist   Consult the **Orthodontic Associates of Charleston,** 86 Rutledge Ave. (☎ 803/723-7242).

Doctor   For a physician referral or 24-hour emergency-room treatment, contact **Charleston Memorial Hospital,** 326 Calhoun St. (☎ 803/577-0600). Another option is **Roper Hospital,** 316 Calhoun St. (☎ 803/724-2970). Contact **Doctor's Care** (☎ 803/556-5585) for names of walk-in clinics near you.

Drugstores   See "Pharmacies," below.

Emergencies   In a true emergency, dial 911. If it's not a life-threatening situation, call **803/577-7077** for fire, **803/577-7434** for police, or **803/747-1888** for an ambulance.

Eyeglass Repair   Walk-in repairs for glasses are available at **Lenscrafters,** 7800 Rivers Ave. (☎ **803/764-3710**), North Charleston. Hours are Monday through Saturday from 9am to 9pm, Sunday from 1 to 5pm.

Hospitals   Local hospitals operating 24-hour emergency rooms include: **AMI East Cooper Community Hospital,** 1200 Johnnie Dodds Blvd., Mt. Pleasant (☎ **803/881-0100**); **River Hospital North,** 12750 Spelssegger Dr., North Charleston (☎ **803/744-2110**); **Charleston Memorial Hospital,** 326 Calhoun St., Charleston (☎ **803/577-0600**); and the **Medical University of South Carolina,** 171 Ashley Ave., Charleston (☎ **803/792-2300**).

Hotlines   Crisis counseling is available through **800/922-2283** or 803/744-HELP. The **Poison Control Center** is at **800/922-1117.**

Information   See "Visitor Information," earlier in this chapter.

Liquor Laws   You must be 21 years of age to buy or consume alcohol.

Maps   See "Orientation," earlier in this chapter.

Newspapers/Magazines   The *Post & Courier* is the daily newspaper in the metropolitan area.

Pharmacies   Try **Revco Drugs,** Wanda Crossing, Mt. Pleasant (☎ **803/881-9435**), open Monday through Saturday from 8am to midnight and Sunday from 10am to 8pm.

Post Office   The main post office is at 83 Broad St. (☎ **803/577-0688**), open Monday through Friday from 8:30am to 5:30pm, Saturday 9:30am to 2pm.

Rest Rooms   These are found throughout the downtown area, including Broad and Meeting streets, Queen and Church streets, and Market Street between Meeting and Church streets, and at other clearly marked strategic points in the historic and downtown districts.

Safety   The downtown area of Charleston is well lit and patrolled throughout the night to ensure public safety. People can generally walk about Charleston in the evening without fear of violence, though that's less true as the night wears on. The local trolley system, DASH, closes down at 10:30pm. After that, it's better to call a taxi than to walk through darkened streets late.

Taxes   The local sales tax is 6%.

Taxis   See "Getting Around," earlier in this chapter.

Transit Info   Contact the **Charleston Area Convention Visitor Reception & Transportation Center**, 375 Meeting St. (☎ **803/853-8000**), for information.

Weather   Call **803/744-3207** for an update.

3 Accommodations

Charleston has many of the best and most historic inns in America, even topping Savannah. The opening and restoration of inns and hotels in the city has been phenomenal, although it's slowing down somewhat (after all, the market can only absorb so many hotel rooms). However, Charleston now ranks among the top cities of America for hotels of charm and character.

The hotels and motels are priced in direct ratio to their proximity to the 789-acre Historic District; if prices in the center are too high for your budget, find a place west of the Ashley River and drive in to town for sightseeing.

Bed-and-breakfast options range from historic homes to carriage houses to simple cottages, and they're found in virtually every section of the city. We've reviewed our top choices below. One central reservation service to contact is **Historic Charleston Bed and Breakfast**, 60 Broad St., Charleston, SC 29401 (☎ **800/743-3583** or 803/722-6606), which represents other choices as well.

During the Spring Festival of Houses and the Spoleto Festival, rates go way up, with owners charging pretty much what the market will bear. Advance reservations are essential.

When booking a hotel, ask about any package plans that might be available. It pays to ask, because deals come and go; they're most often granted to those staying 3 to 4 days.

The **Charleston Trident Convention and Visitors Bureau,** P.O. Box 975, Charleston, SC 29402 (☎ **803/853-8000**), offers a Courtesy Discount Card giving the holder from 10% to as much as 50% off certain hotels, restaurants, tours, and even purchases, from the middle of November to the middle of February. This is the ideal time to visit Charleston if saving money is important to you.

Most of the recommendations below include a complimentary continental breakfast and parking in their rates.

In a city with rooms of so many different shapes and sizes in the same historic building, classifying hotels by price is difficult. Expensive places might in fact have many rooms that are moderate.

Moderately priced hotels, on the other hand, might have some special rooms that are expensive. So it depends on what room you get.

THE HISTORIC DISTRICT
VERY EXPENSIVE
✪ Charleston Place Hotel

130 Market St., Charleston, SC 29401. ☎ **800/843-6664** or 803/722-4900. Fax 803/724-7215. 403 rms, 47 suites. A/C TV TEL. $230 double; $250–$900 suite. Seasonal packages available. AE, DC, MC, V. Parking $8.

Charleston's premier hotel, with far better amenities and facilities than its leading competitor (the Mills House Hotel), this landmark rises eight floors in the Historic District. Behind a brick exterior, looking like a postmodern French château, it is big-time, uptown, glossy, and urban—or at least Prince Charles, a former visitor, thought so. Some hoteliers claim this 1986 hotel represents the New South at its most confident, a stylish giant surrounded by a neighborhood of B&Bs and small converted inns. Acres of Italian marble grace the place, leading to plush bedrooms with decor inspired by colonial Carolina.

Dining/Entertainment: The premier restaurant, Louis' Charleston Grill, is reviewed in section 4, "Dining." There's also a more casual café.

Services: 24-hour room service (brought on fine china), babysitting, laundry.

Facilities: Whirlpool, men's steam bath, aerobics studio, and sundeck.

EXPENSIVE
✪ Anchorage Inn

26 Vendue Range, Charleston, SC 29401. ☎ **800/421-2952** or 803/723-8300. Fax 803/723-9543. 17 rms, 2 suites. A/C TV TEL. $105–$184 double; $155–$229 suite. Rates include continental breakfast and afternoon tea. AE, MC, V.

There's no garden, and other than a heraldic shield in front, few concessions to ornamentation on the bulky exterior of this warehouse, originally built in the 1840s to store cotton. It functioned as an office building for many years until 1991, when a team of investors radically renovated and upgraded the interior. The inn boasts the only decorative theme of its type in Charleston: a mock Tudor interior with lots of dark paneling, references to Olde England, canopied beds with matching tapestries, pastoral or nautical

Charleston Accommodations

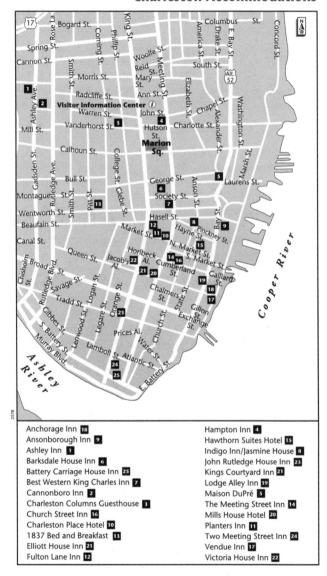

Anchorage Inn 18
Ansonborough Inn 9
Ashley Inn 1
Barksdale House Inn 6
Battery Carriage House Inn 25
Best Western King Charles Inn 7
Cannonboro Inn 2
Charleston Columns Guesthouse 3
Church Street Inn 16
Charleston Place Hotel 10
1837 Bed and Breakfast 13
Elliott House Inn 21
Fulton Lane Inn 12

Hampton Inn 4
Hawthorn Suites Hotel 15
Indigo Inn/Jasmine House 8
John Rutledge House Inn 23
Kings Courtyard Inn 21
Lodge Alley Inn 19
Maison DuPré 5
The Meeting Street Inn 14
Mills House Hotel 20
Planters Inn 11
Two Meeting Street Inn 24
Vendue Inn 17
Victoria House Inn 22

engravings, leaded casement windows, and in some places, half-timbering. Because the hotel is immediately adjacent to unremarkable buildings on either side, the architects designed all but a handful of rooms with views overlooking the lobby. Light is indirectly filtered inside through the lobby's overhead skylights, which can be a plus during Charleston's hot summers. Each room is uniquely shaped, and the most expensive units have bona fide windows overlooking the street outside. A genteel afternoon tea is included in the price.

Battery Carriage House Inn

20 South Battery, Charleston, SC 29401. ☎ **800/775-5575** or 803/727-3100. Fax 803/727-3130. 11 rms. A/C TV TEL. $149–$179 double. Rates include continental breakfast. No children under 12. AE, DISC, MC, V.

In one of the city's largest antebellum neighborhoods, this inn offers bedrooms in a carriage house behind the main building (constructed as a private home in 1843). In other words, the owners save the top living accommodation for themselves but have restored bedrooms out back according to a high standard. Don't stay here if you demand an inn with lots of public space. That you don't get, but you can enjoy the location, a short walk from the Battery—a seafront peninsula where you can easily imagine a flotilla of Yankee ships enforcing the Civil War blockades. Recent renovations have added four-poster beds and a colonial frill to the not overly large bedrooms. Unfortunately, if you call, you're likely to get only a recorded message until the owners are able to call you back. Despite the inaccessibility of the main house, and the difficulty of reaching a staff member, this place provides comfortable and convenient lodging within a desirable neighborhood. Breakfast, during nice weather, is served in a carefully landscaped brick courtyard.

Church Street Inn

177 Church St., Charleston, SC 29401. ☎ **800/552-2777** or 803/722-3420. Fax 803/853-7306. 31 suites. A/C MINIBAR TV TEL. $125–$185 suite. Rates include continental breakfast. AE, MC, V.

Adjacent to the City Market, this all-suite hotel has more charm and style than its nearby rival, the all-suite Hawthorn. The staff gets flustered too easily, but otherwise this is a fine choice, with the warmth of a traditional inn, with brick work, lobby planters, and elegant decorator fabrics. The breakfast room, overlooking a courtyard with a fountain and wrought-iron furniture, adds a grace note of Old Charleston. The one- or two-bedroom suites are bi-level. Thick carpeting, floral draperies, and full kitchens make them ideal for

Impressions

Charleston is ancient live oak trees, live jasmine, magnolias in sequestered gardens, the sound of horses' hoofs over cobblestone streets and the lyrical voices of flower ladies. It is the . . . cries of the colorful street vendors calling SHEEEEEE-Crab and a hundred other delights.
—Molly Heady Sillers, *Doin' the Charleston*, 1976

traveling families or business executives. Some units have fireplaces as well.

1837 Bed & Breakfast

126 Wentworth St., Charleston, SC 29401. ☎ **803/723-7166**. 8 rms. A/C TV. $69–$129 double. Rates include full breakfast and afternoon tea. AE, MC, V. Free parking off-street.

Built in 1837 by Nicholas Cobia, a cotton planter, this place was restored and decorated by two artists. It's called a "single house," because it's only a single-room wide—which makes for some interesting room arrangements. Our favorite room is number two in the Carriage House, which has authentic designs, exposed brick walls, a warm decor, a beamed ceiling, and three windows. All the rooms have refrigerators and separate entrances because of the layout, and one contains canopied poster "rice beds." (A rice bed is a four-poster in which the posts are carved with rice sheaths; rice was a principle crop in colonial Charleston.)

On one of the verandas you can sit under whirling ceiling fans and enjoy your breakfast or afternoon tea. Sausage pie, eggs Benedict, and homemade breads are served at breakfast. The parlor room has cypress wainscoting and a black marble fireplace, while the breakfast room is really part of the kitchen.

Fulton Lane Inn

202 King St. (at the corner of Market St.), Charleston, SC 29401. ☎ **800/552-2777** or 803/720-2600. Fax 803/720-2940. 21 rms, 6 suites. A/C TV TEL. $110–$180 double; $195–$235 suite. Rates include continental breakfast. MC, V.

Set amid the densest concentration of businesses in Charleston's commercial core, this hotel is composed of two contiguous houses, one built of brick in 1913, its neighbor of stucco in 1989. Inside, there's an elevator, a hearty welcome for children, an airy, summery decor with bright colors, and in some of the suites, cathedral ceilings. Some have whirlpool tubs and working, gas-fired fireplaces, and although most are larger than you might have expected, there's a conspicuous lack of antique furniture, a fact that doesn't seem to bother the clientele at all. Breakfast, which is brought to the bedrooms on silver trays, is the only meal served. No smoking.

ⓢ Hampton Inn

345 Meeting St., Charleston, SC 29401. ☎ **800/426-7866** or 803/723-4000. 168 rms, 4 suites. A/C TV TEL. $92–$102 double; $97–$112 suite. Children under 18 stay free in parents' room. Rates include continental breakfast. AE, DC, DISC, MC, V. Parking $7.

A 10-minute walk from the City Market, near the Historic District, this Hampton Inn (a motor hotel) is preferred to the other Hampton Inn (a motel) at 11 Ashley Pointe Drive. Situated opposite the visitors' center (where many tours depart), it has some of the familiar Hampton Inn designs and features along with reproduction appointments. The colonial lobby is filled with natural woods and Oriental rugs. The fireplace is a warm addition, and coffee and tea are always available. You won't find much in the way of views here, but there is a fine outdoor pool with a deck, an exercise room, and ample parking. The accommodations, although pretty standard, are attractive, with pastel florals and modern baths. Housekeeping is of a good standard.

Indigo Inn/Jasmine House

1 Maiden Lane, Charleston, SC 29401. ☎ **800/845-7639** or 803/577-5900. Fax 803/577-0378. 40 rms (Indigo Inn), 10 rms (Jasmine House). A/C TV TEL. $125–$140 double in the Indigo Inn; $140–$180 double in the Jasmine House. 10% discounts available in midwinter. Rates include continental breakfast. AE, DISC, MC, V. Parking free.

This pair of hotels is set across the street from one another. They share the same owners and the same reception area within the Indigo Inn. Originally conceived as a warehouse for indigo in the mid-19th century, and gutted and radically reconstructed in the 1980s, the larger of the two (the Indigo Inn) offers comfortable rooms with standardized, 18th-century decor and comfortable furnishings. Rooms within the Jasmine House (an 1843 Greek Revival mansion whose exterior is painted buttercup yellow) are much more individualized. Each has a ceiling of about 14 feet, a color scheme and theme markedly different from any of its neighbors, crown moldings, whirlpool tubs, and floral-patterned upholsteries. Both inns serve breakfast; parking is available only in the lot at the Indigo Inn.

⊙ John Rutledge House Inn

116 Broad St., Charleston, SC 29401. ☎ **800/476-9741** or 803/723-7999. Fax 803/720-2615. 15 rms, 4 suites. A/C MINIBAR TV TEL.

$135–$170 double; $235 suite. Rates include continental breakfast.
AE, MC, V. Free parking.

Many of the meetings that culminated in the formation of the
United States were conducted within this fine 18th-century house,
now the most prestigious inn in Charleston. We think it towers
over its major rivals in town, such as the Planters Inn and the
Ansonborough, which are also worthy contenders. Its original
builder was one of the signers of the Declaration of Independence,
and later served as Chief Justice of the U.S. Supreme Court. It was
built in 1763, with a third story added in the 1850s. Impeccably
restored to its Federalist grandeur, it is enhanced with discreetly
concealed electronic conveniences. Tea and afternoon sherry are
served in a spacious upstairs sitting room, where mementos of
the building's history and antique firearms, elaborate moldings,
and marble fireplaces help to enhance the distinguished aura.

Kings Courtyard Inn

198 King St., Charleston, SC 19401. ☎ **800/845-6119** or 803/723-7000.
Fax 803/720-2608. 44 rms. A/C TV TEL. $130–$170 double. Children
under 12 stay free in parents' room. Off-season 3-day packages available.
Rates include complimentary breakfast. AE, MC, V.

The tiny entry to this three-story 1853 inn in the Historic District
is deceiving, because it opens inside to a brick courtyard with a
fountain. The fireplace warms the small lobby, which has a brass
chandelier; our only complaint is that we didn't find the reception
staff very helpful when we stopped in. Besides the main courtyard,
two others offer fine views from the breakfast room. The owners
bought the building next door and appropriated 10 more rooms into
the existing inn. Your room might be fitted with a canopy bed, Oriental rugs over hardwood floors, armoires, and even a gas fireplace.
Some units have refrigerators. Rates include evening chocolates and
turndown service; there's also a whirlpool on site.

Lodge Alley Inn

195 East Bay St., Charleston, SC 29401. ☎ **803/722-1611** or 800/
845-1004 (outside SC), 800/821-2791 (in SC). Fax 803/722-1611, ext.
7777. 33 rms, 60 suites. A/C MINIBAR TV TEL. $125–$145 double; $135–
$300 suite. Children under 13 stay free in parents' room. AE, MC, V. Free
valet parking.

This is a sprawling historic property extending from its entrance on
the busiest commercial street of the Old Town toward a quiet brick-
floored courtyard in back. It was originally conceived as a trio of
19th-century warehouses; today, it evokes a miniature village in

Louisiana, with a central square, a fountain, landscaped shrubs basking in the sunlight in back, and easy access to the hotel's Cajun restaurant, The French Quarter. Accommodations include conventional hotel rooms, suites, and duplex units with sleeping lofts overhead. Throughout, the decor is American country, with pine floors and lots of colonial accents. Some units have fireplaces, and most have retained the massive timbers and brick walls of the original warehouses. The staff is usually polite and helpful, but because the hotel is the site of many small conventions, they might be preoccupied with the demands of whatever large group happens to be checking in or out at the time.

Mills House Hotel

115 Meeting St. (between Queen and Broad Sts.), Charleston, SC 29401. ☎ **800/874-9600** or 803/577-2400. Fax 803/722-2112. 200 rms, 14 suites. A/C TV TEL. $135–$190 double; $195–$225 suite. Children under 19 stay free in parents' room. AE, CB, DC, DISC, MC, V. Parking $12 nearby.

Staid, upscale, and conservative, this seven-story hotel is a landmark in Charleston. When it was built in 1853, it was hailed as "the finest hotel in America south of New York City" and hosted every big name of the antebellum era and, later, the Gilded Age. Regrettably, it sank into disrepair by the 1930s, became an eyesore and a hazard, and was eventually bought for $135,000 in 1967—less than the price of its original construction.

Regrettably, much to the dismay of the new owners, the core was not structurally sound enough for refurbishment. But they salvaged its architectural adornments, and after demolishing the core, a copy of the original, with lower ceilings and more bedrooms, was erected in its place. Today, the hotel prides itself on its lack of razzle-dazzle and its well-mannered professionalism. Rooms are traditionally furnished with antique reproductions and, most often, half-tester beds. Accommodations come in a wide range of shapes and sizes, although most windows tend to be small. It may not be the most prestigious large hotel in Charleston anymore, but nonetheless, it continues to attract loyal clients who still appreciate its slightly faded charms.

Dining/Entertainment: The hotel's Barbadoes Room is one of the finest in town (see section 4, "Dining," below). No breakfast is served, however.

Services: Room service, laundry, and baby-sitting.

Facilities: A small indoor pool.

✪ Two Meeting Street Inn

2 Meeting St., Charleston, SC 29401. ☎ **803/723-7322.** 9 rms. A/C TV.
$130–$225 double. Rates include continental breakfast and afternoon tea.
No children under 12. No credit cards.

Set in an enviable position near the Battery, this house was built in
1892 and offered as a wedding gift from a prosperous father to his
daughter. Inside, the proportions are as lavish and gracious as the
Gilded Age could provide. You'll see stained-glass windows, mementos, and paintings that were either part of the original architecture
or collected by the present owners, the Spell family. Most bedrooms
contain four-poster beds and ceiling fans; some units offer access to
a commodious network of balconies.

Vendue Inn

19 Vendue Range, Charleston, SC 29401. ☎ **803/577-7970** or 800/
845-7900. Fax 803/722-8381. 40 rms, 5 suites. TV TEL. $110–$140 double;
$150–$215 suite. Rates include continental breakfast. AE, DISC, MC, V. Free
parking.

Set on the site of what functioned in the 1800s as a warehouse for
French-speaking dockworkers, this is a small, charming, three-story
inn that manages to convey some of the personalized touches of a
B&B. Its public areas meander along a series of narrow, labyrinthine
spaces, and the collection of antiques and colonial decorative pieces
evokes a small, cluttered, and slightly cramped inn in Europe. Bedrooms do not necessarily mimic the European model of the lobby,
however, and in some cases appear to have been the result of the
decorative experiments of the owners, with themes based on aspects
of Florida, rococo Italy, and 18th-century Charleston, depending on
the accommodation. Marble floors and tabletops, wooden sleigh
beds, and even wrought-iron canopy beds are featured in many of
them. They're eclectic and charming, though you might get a room
that's inconsistent with your vision of colonial Charleston.

Dining/Entertainment: The inn's restaurant, The Library at
Vendue Inn, is recommended separately under "Dining," below.
One of the best aspects of the place is the rooftop bar, whose view
extends out over the waterfront of historic Charleston.

MODERATE
Ansonborough Inn

21 Hassell St., Charleston, SC 29401. ☎ **800/522-2073** or 803/723-1655.
Fax 803/577-6888. 37 suites. A/C TV TEL. Sun–Thurs $79–$99 double;
Fri–Sat $109–$139 double. Children under 12 stay free in parents' room.
Rates include continental breakfast. AE, DISC, MC, V. Free parking.

This is one of the oddest hotels in the Historic District. Once they get past the not-very-promising exterior, most visitors really like the unusual configuration of rooms. Set close to the waterfront, the Ansonborough occupies a massive and bulky building originally designed around 1900 as a warehouse for paper supplies. Despite the building's height, it contains only three floors inside, allowing bedrooms with ceilings of between 14 and 16 feet, and in many cases, sleeping lofts. The lobby features exposed timbers and a soaring atrium filled with plants. Bedrooms are outfitted with copies of 18th-century furniture and accessories, though the bathrooms are vaguely reminiscent of what you'd expect from a roadside motel (molded fiberglass shower stalls and imitation marble countertops). A panoramic terrace with a hot tub has been added to the rooftop.

Ashley Inn

201 Ashley Ave., Charleston, SC 29403. ☎ **803/723-1848.** 6 rms, 1 suite, 1 two-bedroom carriage house with kitchenette. A/C TV. $94–$137 double; $140 suite; $180 carriage house. Rates include full breakfast and afternoon tea. AE, DISC, MC, V. Free parking off-street.

Partly because of its pink clapboards and the steep staircases that visitors climb to reach the public areas, this imposing bed-and-breakfast inn might remind you of a historic house in Bermuda. Originally built in 1832 on a plot of land that sold at the time for a mere $419, it's even more appealing in its decor than the Cannonboro Inn, with which it shares the same Michigan-based owners. Breakfast and afternoon tea are served on a wide veranda overlooking a brick-floored carport whose centerpiece is a formal fountain/goldfish pond evocative of Old Charleston. The public rooms, with their high ceilings and deep colors, are attractive. If you have lots of luggage, know in advance that negotiating this inn's steep and frequent stairs might pose something of a problem.

Elliott House Inn

78 Queen St. (between King and Meeting Sts.), Charleston, SC 29401. ☎ **800/729-1855** or 803/723-1855. Fax 803/722-1567. 29 rms. A/C TV TEL. $89–$130 double. Rates include continental breakfast. AE, DISC, MC, V. Parking $11.

Historians have researched anecdotes about this place going back to the 1600s, but the core of the charming inn you'll see today was built as a private home—probably for slaves—in 1861. There's a warm welcome from a very hip staff, and lots of colonial inspiration in the decor of the comfortable and carefully maintained accommodations. But despite all the grace notes and landscaping (the flowerbeds are touched up at two-week intervals throughout the year), the place has a raffish, indoor/outdoor motel-style quality that some guests find appealing. Rooms are arranged in a style you might expect to see in Key West, on tiers of balconies surrounding a verdant open courtyard. Conversation waxes free and easy beneath the city's largest wisteria arbor, near a bubbling whirlpool that can accommodate up to 12 occupants at a time. Each guest room contains a four-poster bed (no. 36 is especially appealing) and gives you the feeling that you're living in an upscale cottage. Avoid, if at all possible, those units sporting a ground-level private outdoor terrace. The terraces are too cramped to really use, don't have attractive views, and tend to be plagued with mildew because of their location.

Hawthorn Suites Hotel

181 Church St., Charleston, SC 29401. ☎ **800/527-1133** or 803/577-2644. Fax 803/577-2697. 181 suites. A/C TV TEL. $89–$155 one-bedroom suite; $200–$285 two-bedroom suite. Rates include buffet breakfast. AE, DC, DISC, MC, V. Parking $9 in underground garage.

Fairly anonymous, the Hawthorn contains many of the amenities of a conventional hotel, including a bar/lounge, a fitness center, and a swimming pool. A somber, five-story 1991 building adjacent to the historic City Market, it offers suites instead of conventional rooms, each outfitted with some type of cooking equipment. Kitchen facilities range from a wet bar, refrigerator, and microwave oven, to more fully stocked kitchenettes with enough utensils to prepare a simple dinner. Regardless of their amenities, accommodations here tend to receive heavy use, since they appeal to families, tour groups, and business travelers. Units were renovated in 1995. Breakfast is the only meal served. There's a coin-operated laundromat on the premises.

Maison DuPré

317 East Bay St., Charleston, SC 29401. ☎ **800/844-4667** or 803/723-8691. 12 rms, 3 suites. A/C TV TEL. $89–$145 double; $145–$200 suite. Rates include continental breakfast and afternoon tea. AE, MC, V.

More than any other B&B in Charleston, this one evokes the aura of a country inn in France. Its central core dates from 1803, when it was built by a French-born tailor, but since then, enlargements and improvements have incorporated three adjacent houses (two of which were hauled in from other neighborhoods of Charleston) and two carriage houses into one coherent, well-organized whole. Each of the components is unified by a brick-paved courtyard, with fountains, cast-iron furniture, and plantings.

Inside, you'll find bold 18th-century colors and a range of good-quality reproductions of antique sleigh beds, armoires, and four-posters. Many of the paintings that adorn the interior were executed by the owner, Lucille Mulholland, who, with husband Robert, makes afternoon tea (included in the price) a very pleasant event.

Planters Inn

Market Street (at Meeting St.), Charleston, SC 29401. ☎ **800/845-7082** or 803/722-2345. Fax 803/577-2125. 36 rms, 5 suites. A/C TV TEL. $90–$145 double; $150–$185 suite. Rates include continental breakfast. AE, MC, V. Free parking.

For many years, this distinguished brick-sided inn next to the City Market languished. In 1994, it was acquired by a group of hoteliers who knew who how to maintain an uppercrust historic inn, and a massive renovation was begun. The multi-million-dollar result has transformed the place into a cozy but tasteful and opulent enclave of colonial charm. There's a lobby filled with reproductions of 18th-century furniture and engravings, a staff clad in silk vests, and a parking area with exactly the right amount of spaces for the number of rooms. The bedrooms are spacious; each unit has hardwood floors, marble-sheathed baths, and a unique 18th-century decor that was fine-tuned by a team of award-wining decorators. The suites are appealing, outfitted very much as you'd expect from an upscale

---

⚏ Family-Friendly Hotels

Best Western King Charles Inn *(see page 32)*   Children under 18 stay free here in their parents' room. The location is only a block from the Historic District's market area, and families gather for relaxation at the small pool. This is one of the best "family values" in Charleston.

Ansonborough Inn *(see page 27)*   A good choice for families who'd like to stay in one of the historic inns as opposed to a cheap motel on the outskirts. A converted warehouse, it offers rooms with ceilings so high many can accommodate sleeping lofts for the kids.

Hawthorn Suites Hotel *(see page 29)*   These suites contain full kitchens or wet bars with microwave ovens and refrigerators, and offer the extra space that families need. Some units are bi-level, giving families more privacy.

private home. Afternoon tea is served in the lobby, and a well-recommended restaurant, The Planter's Café, is described separately (see section 4, "Dining").

(The) Meeting Street Inn

173 Meeting St., Charleston, SC 29401. ☎ **800/842-8022** or 803/723-1882. Fax 803/577-0851. 56 rms. A/C TV TEL. $89–$169 double. Rates include continental breakfast. AE, DISC, MC, V.

The design of this structure, built in the 1870s, was influenced by the pink-sided buildings a Charleston merchant might have visited in Barbados a few decades earlier. Like the West Indian buildings it emulates, it might be in need of a coat of paint by the time you actually visit. That only helps to enhance a thoroughly romantic flair the place has—especially at night when moonlight filters down into the brick-paved courtyard. There's no restaurant on the premises, but many lie within walking distance. Bedrooms are furnished with four-poster beds, armoires, and wood shutters. Bathrooms are pretty standard. We prefer some of the other inns in this price range, but this is a perfectly acceptable backup choice.

Victoria House Inn

208 King St., Charleston, SC 29401. ☎ **800/933-5464** or 803/720-2944. Fax 803/720-2930. 14 rms, 4 suites. A/C MINIBAR TV TEL. $120 double; $155 suite. Rates include champagne continental breakfast. MC, V. Free parking.

Originally built in 1889, when it was conceived as the city's branch of the YMCA, this brick-sided building retains some of its institutional flavor on the outside, despite a richly textured veneer of draperies and upholsteries on the inside. Associated with the more upscale (and more expensive) John Rutledge House, it has a small but cheerful lobby with elaborate moldings, an elevator for access to the other floors (a total of three), and easy access to the shops and boutiques that line its street-level facade. Many bedrooms have wallpaper in patterns of flowers and vines, and reproductions of antique furnishings. Breakfast is the only meal served.

INEXPENSIVE

⑤ Barksdale House Inn

27 George St., Charleston, SC 29401. ☎ **803/577-4800.** Fax 803/853-0482. l4 rms. A/C TV TEL. $69–$160 double. Rates include continental breakfast. No children under 7. MC, V. Free parking.

This is a neat, tidy, and well-proportioned Italianate building, originally constructed as an inn in 1778, near the City Market. Later it was massively altered and enlarged by the Victorians. Behind the inn, guests enjoy a flagstone-covered terrace, where a fountain splashes. Bedrooms often contain four-poster beds and working fireplaces, and about a half-dozen have whirlpool tubs. Throughout, the furnishings, wallpaper, and fabrics evoke the late 19th century. Sherry and tea are served on the back porch in the evening.

Best Western King Charles Inn

237 Meeting St. (between Wentworth and Society Sts.), Charleston, SC 29401. ☎ **800/528-1234** or 803/723-7451. Fax 803/723-2041. 91 rms. $69–$159 double. Off-season discounts available. Children under 18 stay free in parents' room. A/C TV TEL. AE, DC, DISC, MC, V. Free parking.

One block from the Historic District's market area, this three-story hotel has a colonial-inspired restaurant where breakfast is served, a small pool, and a helpful staff. Rooms are better than you might expect from a motel. Some have balconies, but views are limited. Although short on style, the King Charles is reliable, a good value, and convenient to most everything.

Cannonboro Inn

184 Ashley Ave., Charleston, SC 29403. ☎ **803/723-8572.** Fax 803/723-9080. 7 rms, 1 suite. A/C TV. $79–$120 double; $150 suite. Rates include full breakfast. Free parking. No children under 11. AE, DISC, MC, V.

Originally built as a private home in 1856 by a rice planter, this buff-and beige-colored house was established as a bed-and-breakfast in 1990. The decor isn't as carefully coordinated, or as relentlessly upscale, as many of its competitors in town; instead, there's a sense of folksy, comfortable informality throughout. Although there's virtually no land around this building, a wide veranda on the side creates a "sit and talk for a while" mood. Each accommodation contains a canopy bed; old-fashioned formal, bow-fronted furniture; and cramped, somewhat old-fashioned bathrooms.

Charleston Columns Guesthouse

8 Vanderhorst St., Charleston, SC 29403. ☎/fax **803/722-7341.** 4 rms (2 with private bath), 2 suites. A/C. $75–$80 double without bath; $90 double with bath; $110–$125 suite. Rates include continental breakfast. No credit cards.

It stands in isolated grandeur, a distinguished historic house hemmed in on all sides by more modern buildings. Fronted with double verandas supported with differing orders of neoclassical columns, it was built in 1855 by a Confederate colonel and judge, and occupied after that by two of the city's elected officials since then. Today, it functions as a warm and hospitable guesthouse where owners Jim Wylie and Frank Lail welcome a mostly gay and lesbian clientele. Bedrooms are filled with 19th-century antiques and, to a greater degree, recent reproductions. Some of the units are within an antique, circa 1840 carriage house, with incredibly thick 14-inch brick walls. Continental breakfasts are served communally from a well-stocked buffet.

NEAR THE AIRPORT

Charleston Marriott

4770 Marriott Dr., Charleston SC 29418. ☎ **800/228-9290** or 803/ 747-1900. Fax 803/744-2530. 293 rms, 1 suite. A/C TV TEL. $85–$99 double, $59 double with 21-day advance reservation; $200–$315 suite. Honeymoon and golf packages available. AE, DC, MC, V. Free parking.

This place, a 15-minute drive north of the old town's center, is really an airport hotel (it's close to the junction of Montague Avenue and I-26, a short 5-minute drive from the airport). But its low rates make it an appealing choice for leisure travelers who don't mind the long haul from the Historic District. Its amenities are clean, modern, comfortable, and eminently suitable for business travelers or tourists who don't have their hearts set on quaint charm. Designed in an eight-story format, across the road from a shopping mall, it incorporates many dramatic decorative features, 24-hour room service, convention space and meeting facilities, a bar, an indoor/outdoor restaurant, and both indoor and outdoor swimming pools. Rooms, in the standard Marriott format, are comfortable and exactly what you'd expect, although views open onto the highway.

La Quinta Motor Inn

2499 La Quinta Lane, North Charleston, SC 29405. ☎ **803/797-8181.** Fax 803/569-1608. 120 rms, 2 suites. A/C TV TEL. $54 double; $64 suite. Children under 18 stay free in parents' room; cribs also free. AE, DC, DISC, MC, V. Take I-26 north to Ashley-Phosphate Rd. (Exit 209).

This is conveniently located near the Charleston International Airport. You can call the inn directly from the airport baggage-claim area for free shuttle service to the hotel. Rooms in this clean, comfortable, well-run chain motel are standard but comfortable, and beds are extra-long. No-smoking rooms are available, and pets are welcome. There's also a pool. Shoney's restaurant next door will provide room service from 6am to 11pm.

4 Dining

Foodies from all over the Carolinas flock to Charleston for some of the finest dining in the South. You get not only the most refined cookery of the Low Country but an array of French and international specialties as well. Space does not permit us to preview all the outstanding restaurants of Charleston, much less the merely good ones, but we've rounded up our very top choices below.

A culinary experience unique to Charleston is the **Market Street Food Court,** lying between South Market and Church streets. Daily from 8am to 5pm, you can patronize a dozen or so little establishments contained in the food court area of the City Market. Some begin their day by serving breakfast, but most make their money at lunch, offering their menus to both the business community and visitors. The decor is inexpensive—mostly brick with canvas flags and cheap multicolored chairs. You can buy Chinese, Japanese, Italian, pizza, Greek, or American fare, in addition to subs, sandwiches, and cookies. Swensen's Ice Cream is here too, as is A.W. Shuck's Oyster Bar.

THE HISTORIC DISTRICT
VERY EXPENSIVE
✪ Restaurant Million

2 Unity Alley. ☎ **803/577-7472**. Reservations required. Jacket and tie required for men. Main courses $22–$26; fixed-price dinner $45–$70. AE, DC, MC, V. Mon–Sat 6:30–10pm. Closed first 2 weeks of Jan. FRENCH.

This place, a member of the Relais & Châteaux organization, is as upscale as anything you're likely to find in all of South Carolina, a well-coifed gem of a setting within what was originally conceived as a tavern in 1788. George Washington is said to have lost a set of false teeth during a drunken banquet here, but today, all vestiges of colonial rowdiness have been gracefully masked with French tapestries and accessories evocative of 18th-century Williamsburg. The owner, French-born celeb Philippe Million, offers carefully groomed service and a dash of Gallic charm. Menu items include lobster salad accented with artfully carved rosettes of beets; breast of duck flavored with aged bordeaux; sophisticated preparations of foie gras and turbot; and a dessert trolley that requires a skilled pastry chef many hours to prepare. To all these dishes, the restaurant applies a classic technique with first-rate ingredients. The results are remarkable, your single finest (and probably most expensive) dining experience in Charleston.

Charleston Dining

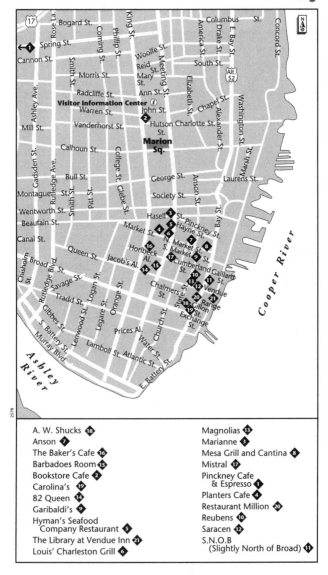

A. W. Shucks ⑱
Anson ❼
The Baker's Cafe ⑯
Barbadoes Room ⑮
Bookstore Cafe ❷
Carolina's ⑲
82 Queen ⑭
Garibaldi's ❾
Hyman's Seafood
  Company Restaurant ❺
The Library at Vendue Inn ㉑
Louis' Charleston Grill ❻

Magnolias ⑬
Marianne ❸
Mesa Grill and Cantina ❽
Mistral ⑰
Pinckney Cafe
  & Espresso ❶
Planters Cafe ❹
Restaurant Million ⑳
Reubens ❿
Saracen ⑫
S.N.O.B
  (Slightly North of Broad) ⑪

There's also the more inexpensive **McCrady's** (☎ 803/ 853-8484) downstairs, offering grills, soups, salads, and sandwiches.

EXPENSIVE
✪ Anson

12 Anson St. ☎ **803/577-0551**. Reservations recommended. Main courses $14–$20. AE, DC, DISC, MC, V. Sun–Thurs 5:30–11pm; Fri–Sat 5:30pm–midnight. LOW COUNTRY/MODERN AMERICAN.

We simply love this place. Locals know they're likely to spot Charleston's society types here; newcomers just recognize it as a hip, stylish, big-city venue with all the softly upholstered grace notes you'd demand from a top-notch restaurant in New York or Chicago, but with added touches of Low Country charm. The setting is a brick-sided warehouse built a century ago to store ice. The present owners have added ornaments of superb taste, including New Orleans–style iron balconies, Corinthian pilasters salvaged from de-molished colonial houses, and enough Victorian rococo to make diners feel pampered.

A well-trained staff in long white aprons will describe to you dishes inspired by traditions of the coastal Southeast. But this isn't exactly down-home cooking, as you'll soon see after sampling the fried cornmeal oysters with potato cakes; the lobster, corn, and black-bean quesadillas; the cashew-crusted grouper with champagne sauce, and the rack of lamb in a crispy Dijon-flavored crust with mint sauce. Our favorite specialty is the crispy flounder, which rival chefs have tried to duplicate but just can't match.

Barbadoes Room

In the Mills House Hotel, 115 Meeting St. ☎ **803/577-2400**. Reservations recommended for dinner. Main courses $14.95–$19.95. AE, DISC, DC, MC, V. Daily 11am–2pm; Mon–Sat 6:30–11pm, Sun 6:30–10:30pm. SOUTHERN/SEAFOOD.

This is the showcase dining area within one of the city's best-known and most reputable hotels. It was selected as the site of a dinner held in honor of the then-married Prince Charles and Princess Di when they were in Charleston. The decorative theme evokes the planter's life of the 18th century, when many local traders grew rich from trade with Europe, the West Indies (especially Barbados), and Africa. Plantation fans whirl air gently through a room accented with high ceilings and arches. Menu items include Charleston she-crab soup; pan-fried Low Country crabcakes; grilled breast of duck with a tarragon pear sauce; tenderloin of pork with a curried fruit compote; blackened shrimp and scallops with grit cakes; and a Low

Country gratin of oysters and crabmeat. Dessert might be a mud pie as dense and dark as the swamplands that flank the nearby coastline (but infinitely more appetizing). The chef shows precision and sensitivity in most dishes, and that's why the locals keep coming back.

✪ Louis' Charleston Grill

In the Charleston Place Hotel, 224 King St. ☎ **803/577-4522.** Reservations recommended. Main courses $14.75–$21; fixed-price Sun brunch $15–$18. AE, DC, MC, V. Daily 6–11pm; Sun brunch 11am–2pm. MODERN LOW COUNTRY/AMERICAN.

When the Omni Hotel (now the Charleston Place) was built in the mid-1980s, its architects included a marble-floored, mahogany-sheathed dining room whose opulence surpassed many of the grand and formal dining salons of Europe. After fits and stops, the space was eventually leased to Louis Osteen, a South Carolinian who turned it into one of the top 25 restaurants in America, according to the editors of *Esquire* magazine. Today, the decor makes absolutely no concessions to southern folksiness, and Louis' Charleston Grill reigns as one of the city's most luxurious and most artful dining venues.

Unlike the decor, the food does pay homage to local traditions. Putting a fresh twist on classic dishes is the rule of the day. Menu items change with the season and the inspiration of Louis and his wife, Marlene, but might include grilled lamb ribs with a shallot-flavored pepper butter; McClellanville lump crabmeat with lobster cakes and mustard sauce; panfried baby flounder with Vidalia onion marmalade; or veal chops with bourbon-flavored blue cheese.

✪ Planters Café

In the Planters Inn, 112 North Market (at Meeting Street). ☎ **803/723-0700.** Reservations recommended for dinner. Main courses $11.95–$22.95. AE, MC, V. Mon–Sat 11:30am–3pm and 5–10pm, Sun 11:30–3pm and 5–9pm. Bar open 11:30 until the last customer leaves. INTERNATIONAL.

Stylish, upscale, and amusing, and set on the street level of the previously recommended Planters Inn (with which it is not associated in any way), this is one of the Historic District's most likable and best-managed restaurants, a fit rival to Anson nearby. Outfitted with postmodern, wood-grained flair, and tucked away behind the kind of cocktail lounge where you might be tempted to linger a bit longer than you should, it's known for its ultra-hip staff, superb food, and an ambience reminiscent of an upscale, artsy European bistro.

👪 Family-Friendly Restaurants

Reubens *(see page 45)*   When given a choice, children of Charleston like to be taken here, where the menu does a virtual song and dance to please them. A wide array of Vienna beef hot dogs are served, along with all sorts of sandwiches and burgers (in many different styles). Kids have a hard time deciding between the traditional cheesecakes or the melt-in-your-mouth fudge brownies.

Magnolias *(see page 40)*   Southern hospitality and charm keep this place buzzing day and night. Lunch is the best time for families and children, with an array of soups, appetizers, salads, sandwiches, and pastas. But in-the-know local kids go easy on these, saving room for the daily array of homemade Southern desserts, perhaps a warm cream-cheese brownie with white-chocolate ice cream and chocolate sauce.

Pinckney Café & Espresso *(see page 44)*   Near the City Market, this warm and casual spot is coffeehouse in decor, but with a surprising array of food to please families with small children. Try one of the Pinckney pasta dishes. At lunch a wide array of sandwiches and omelets are featured.

The food is imaginative and "worth the detour," as Michelin might say. There is also a choice of dishes for low-cholesterol, low-calorie dining. Menu items include bronzed mahi-mahi; a lightly spiced tuna steak with a curried salsa; herb-grilled tenderloin of pork; grilled ostrich steak with a port and leek sauce; and mint-pesto loin of lamb.

MODERATE
Carolina's
10 Exchange St. ☎ **803/724-3800.** Reservations recommended. Main courses $9.85–$23. AE, DISC, DC, MC, V. Daily 5:30–11pm. AMERICAN.

Perhaps because of its name, and partly because of the skill of its designers in adapting an antique warehouse into a stylish, minimalist enclave of hip-dom, this restaurant is usually included on any local resident's short list of noteworthy local bistros. Despite its nod to yesteryear, this place sports a black, pink, and white decor you might expect to see in California. It's the brainchild of a German-born restaurateur, who tailored the menu to specifically appeal to nostalgia.

The result is a skillful and aggressively marketed compendium of old-time dishes with uptown flair. Examples include Carolina quail with goat cheese; salmon with coriander sauce; loin of lamb with jalapeño chutney; the best crab cakes in town; and an almost excessively elaborate version of local grouper cooked in an almond and black sesame-seed crust, and topped with crabmeat and lemon-butter sauce. As you dine, admire the antique French movie posters adorning the walls.

82 Queen

82 Queen St. ☎ **803/723-7591.** Reservations recommended for dinner. Main courses $9.95–$19.95. AE, MC, V. Daily 11:30am–3pm and 6–10pm. LOW COUNTRY.

This is probably the most unusual compendium of real estate in Charleston—three 18th- and 19th-century houses clustered around an ancient magnolia tree, with outdoor tables placed in its shade. If you ask, someone will list an even older set of dates connected with the property (it was part of a land grant originally issued in 1688), but few diners really pursue those histories, preferring instead to concentrate on the Low Country cuisine. The menu is filled with flavor and flair, with dishes that include an award-winning version of she-crab soup laced with sherry; fried Carolina alligator with black-bean sauce, fresh tomato salsa, and sour cream; Carolina bouillabaisse; shrimp and chicken gumbo with andouille sausage and okra; and crab cakes with a sweet pepper and basil remoulade sauce.

The Library at Vendue Inn

19 Vendue Range. ☎ **803/577-7970.** Lunch salads, sandwiches, and platters $3.75–$7.50; main dinner courses $15.95–$17.25. AE, MC, V. Mon–Sat 11:30am–2:30pm; Mon–Thurs 6–9:30pm, Fri–Sat 5:30–10pm. SOUTHERN/INTERNATIONAL.

This place lies at the end of a labyrinth of narrow corridors that interconnect with the reception area of the previously recommended Vendue Inn. Its most unusual aspect is its diminutive size, and its seemingly awkward division into a network of small-scale dining rooms, each outfitted in a decorative theme unrelated to its neighbors. The most visible of the dining areas is outfitted like a library (with an admittedly very small collection of reading material), whose scholarly atmosphere is softened with candlelight and napery.

The cuisine is innovative, even progressive, as you'll soon discover when faced with such appetizers as Miss Peggy's spicy pea cakes with salsa or sour-mashed barbecue shrimp and grits. One delectable pasta—a first for most diners—is made with blackened oysters and saffron alfredo. Shrimp Awendaw is sautéed with a julienne of country ham and fresh kiwi, all in a Chardonnay sauce. If all this sounds too much, you can still get such old-fashioned favorites as grilled filet mignon or a mixed grill.

Magnolias

185 East Bay St. ☎ **803/577-7771.** Reservations recommended. Main courses $14.50–$24.95. AE, MC, V. Sun–Thurs 11:30am–11pm; Fri–Sat 11:30am–midnight. SOUTHERN.

Charleston's hottest restaurant, at least during our most recent visit, this place manages to elevate the vernacular cuisine of the Deep South into a hip, postmodern art form suitable for big-city trendies. After the Savings and Loan debacle of the Reagan years, its owners managed to acquire the city's Customs house, a venerable but decrepit structure originally conceived in the 1820s and rebuilt in the 1890s. After awesome expenditures on renovations, the space now resembles a sprawling network of interconnected loft apartments in New York City, with heart-pine floors, faux-marble columns, and massive beams. Everybody's favorite lunch here is an open-faced veal meatloaf sandwich, though we found it rather dull. The soups and salads tend to be excellent, however, especially one made with field greens with a lemon lingonberry vinaigrette and crumbled blue cheese. Down South dinners include everything from Carolina carpetbaggers filet with parmesan-fried oysters, green beans, and Madeira and Bèarnaise sauce, to chicken and dumplings with shiitake mushrooms.

Marianne

235 Meeting St. (at Hasell St.). ☎ **803/722-7196.** Reservations recommended. Main courses $11–$25; fixed-price four-course dinner $25. AE, DC, DISC, MC, V. Mon–Thurs 6pm–midnight; Fri–Sat 6pm–1am; Sun 5–11pm. FRENCH.

This bistro is set within the much-restored premises of what was originally built in the 1800s as a warehouse. Inside, within a brick-lined dining room separated into segments by rows of brick arches, you'll imagine you're in a corner of the French countryside. The cuisine, naturally, is prepared with energy, full-bodied flavors, and verve, and if your waiter pronounces the names of the dishes with a pronounced Southern drawl, you won't care. Menu items include grouper à la Paul Bocuse (wrapped in thinly sliced potatoes, sautéed and baked, then served on a fondue of leeks); and a peppersteak in the style of the great *bistros de gare* of Paris, flambéed in peppercorns, cream, and brandy. Mushrooms stuffed with crabmeat is a worthy starter, steeped more in the traditions of the Low Country of South Carolina than France, but nonetheless distinguished.

Mistral

99 South Market St. ☎ **803/722-5708.** Reservations recommended. Main courses $13–$19; children's menu $4.95. AE, DC, DISC, MC, V. Mon–Sat 11am–5pm; Mon–Thurs 5–10pm, Fri–Sat 5pm–midnight. CONTINENTAL/ CAJUN.

Appropriately situated across a narrow street from the crowded kiosks of what was originally conceived in the 19th century as Charleston's food and vegetable markets, this is the kind of French bistro you'd find in a working-class district of Paris or New Orleans. There's a comfortably outfitted bar at one end of the room, a diffident, and sometimes skeptical, reception, and accessories which include posters of Paris movie halls and oldtime French movie stars. Daily specials are posted on blackboards. Menu items include crabcakes with fried shrimp; noisette of mahi-mahi dredged in pecan flour; talapia fish stuffed with smoked oysters and leeks; bouillabaisse; chicken with a rosemary-cream sauce; and a succulent vegetarian pasta prepared with eggplant, peppers, goat cheese, gorgonzola, and penne-style pasta. Most of these dishes are right on the mark, although the cookery is inconsistent.

Saracen

141 E. Bay St. ☎ **803/723-6242.** Reservations recommended. Main courses $10.95–$17.95. AE, DC, MC, V. Dining room Tues–Sat 6–10pm; bar Tues–Fri 6pm–2am, Sat 6pm–midnight. MODERN AMERICAN/ INTERNATIONAL.

Its name derives from the style of architecture of the 19th-century building that contains it: Saracen revival. Originally built in 1853 as the headquarters of the Farmers and Exchange Bank, this building is said to be the only authentic example of the style in the United States. Restaurateur Charlie Farrell, who learned her culinary techniques in Louisiana and Paris, ripped out the interior's second floor in the 1980s, painted the soaring ceiling blue with white stars, and created a hushed and often solemn setting that (except for the good food) has been likened to the interior of a church. Menu items are eclectic, and occasionally experimental. Sauces are light, and there is a deft touch of seasonings. Examples include breast of duck with honey-thyme sauce and cider vinegar; agnolotti pasta with goat cheese, red peppers, asparagus points, and garlic; Thai-glazed loin of lamb, pan-roasted oysters with thyme; and a delectable version of orange-flavored crème brulée.

The building's upper balcony, incidentally, is home to Charlie's Little Bar, a cozy watering hole that features live jazz and blues every Friday and Saturday night after 9:30pm. Whisky with soda costs from $3.75.

S.N.O.B. (Slightly North of Broad)

192 East Bay St. ☎ **803/723-3424.** Reservations accepted for six or more. Main courses $10.95–$16.95. AE, MC, V. Mon–Fri 11:30am–3pm; daily 5:30–11pm. SOUTHERN.

There's an exposed kitchen, a high ceiling crisscrossed with ventilation ducts, and vague references to the South of long ago—including a scattering of wrought iron—in this snazzily rehabbed warehouse. The place promotes itself as Charleston's culinary maverick, priding itself on updated versions of the vittles that kept the South alive for the first 300 years of its history, but, frankly, the menu seems tame compared with the innovations being offered at many of its upscale, Southern-ethnic competitors. Once you get past the hype, however, you might actually enjoy the place. Former diners have included Timothy ("007") Dalton, Lee Majors, Sly Stallone, and superlawyer Alan Dershowitz. Main courses can be ordered in medium and large sizes, a fact appreciated by dieters. Flounder stuffed with deviled crab, grilled dolphin glazed with pesto on a bed of tomatoes, and grilled tenderloin of beef with green peppercorn sauce are examples of the well-prepared but not particularly Southern menu. For dessert, it's the chocolate pecan torte for us.

INEXPENSIVE

Ⓢ A.W. Shucks

70 State St. ☎ **803/723-1151.** Reservations not necessary. Main courses $9–$15. AE, DC, DISC, MC, V. Sun–Thurs 11:30am–10pm; Fri–Sat 11am–11pm. SEAFOOD.

This is an honest-to-god oyster bar, a sprawling, salty tribute to the pleasures of shellfish and the memorabilia of the fishers who gather them. A short walk from the Public Market stands this solid build-ing, which has been heavily restored (it was once a warehouse for Nabisco). The setting is filled with rough timbers, a long bar where thousands of crustaceans have already been cracked open and con-sumed, and a dining room. The menu offers oysters and clams on the half shell, seafood chowder, deviled crab, shrimp Créole, and oysters prepared in at least a half-dozen different ways. Chicken and beef dishes are also listed on the menu, but they're nothing special. A wide selection of international beers is sold. Absolutely no one cares how you dress—it's hard to maintain an elegant wardrobe anywhere near the premises of an oyster roast.

The Baker's Café

214 King St. ☎ **803/577-2694.** Main courses $5.95–$10.95. Mon–Fri 8am–3pm, Sat–Sun 9am–3pm. INTERNATIONAL.

The menu selection at the Baker's Café is more complete than you'll find in a coffee shop. The rose-colored walls, ceiling fans, track lighting, local art, wood-slatted chairs, and plum/brown tables create a cozy ambience. Egg dishes are a specialty, including eggs Florentine, eggs Copenhagen, and the local favorite—two poached eggs on a bed of Canadian snowcrab, Hollandaise, and rusks. Simple selections include croissants, muffins, Danish pastries, and scones. Sandwiches are also served. Brunch is popular on weekends.

Bookstore Café

412 King St. (at Hutson St.). ☎ **803/720-8843.** Main courses $1.95–$6.95. No credit cards. Mon–Fri 8am–2:30pm; Sat–Sun 9am–2pm. AMERICAN.

There isn't a big selection of books here, but that doesn't keep Charleston's Greenwich Village set away. The wallpaper looks like bookshelves, and the baskets, ceiling fans, and wood tables and chairs all make the artsy decor work. Specials are written on a blackboard. Breakfast begins with that classic, shrimp and grits with eggs, accompanied by a Madeira wine sauce, although you can order three-egg omelets as well—even one made for vegetarians, another with poached salmon. Potato casseroles are a feature at lunch; one—called Folly—is made with country ham, fresh tomato, broccoli, onions, *pomme* sauce, mushrooms, and peppers. Soups, salads, and stir fries round out the bill of fare. The beer bread is homemade.

Garibaldi's

49 S. Market St. ☎ **803/723-7153.** Reservations recommended. Main courses $7.95–$14.50. MC, V. Sun–Thurs 6–10:30pm; Fri–Sat 6–11pm. ITALIAN.

In the center of the historic Charleston Market, Garibaldi's is a successful Italian dining choice that also has branches in Columbia and Savannah. The interior, with its bistro atmosphere, is decorated with wicker pieces, ladderback chairs, track lights, ceiling fans, and Italian memorabilia. You might start your meal with a salmon appetizer and continue with a pasta selection. The seafood specials are good, too, including the dolphin, stuffed grouper, and blackened tuna. The chef makes his own desserts and offers outdoor dining in fair weather.

Hyman's Seafood Company Restaurant

215 Meeting St. ☎ **803/723-6000.** Reservations not necessary. Seafood dinners and platters $4.95–$17.95. DISC, MC, V. Daily 7am–11pm. SEAFOOD.

It was established a century ago by a family of Russian immigrants, and has remained true to the old-fashioned traditions that thousands of clients find appealing. The building containing it sprawls over most of a city block, near Charleston Place, in the commercial heart of Charleston's business district. Inside, there's a takeaway deli loaded with salmon, lox, and smoked herring—all displayed in the style of the great kosher delis of New York City. Technically, the restaurant contains two different sit-down sections—one devoted to deli-style sandwiches, chicken soup, and salads; the other to a delectably messy choice of fish, shellfish, lobsters, and oysters. We can ignore the endorsement of old-time Senator Strom Thurmond, but take more seriously the praise of such big-time foodies as Barbra, Oprah, and Baryshnikov.

Mesa Grill & Cantina

311/2 N. Market St. ☎ **803/723-3770.** Main courses $3.95–$13.95. AE, CB, DC, DISC, MC, V. Sun–Thurs 11am–midnight, Fri–Sat 11am–2am. SOUTHWESTERN.

Who'd have thought that this seaman's chapel with pastel-colored stained glass would ever become a Southwest restaurant? But it seems like a perfect blending. The owners have pulled the same colors used in the stained glass into the body of the restaurant, added a cactus here and there, some terra-cotta pots, and voilà—a dining spot with a loyal following. Besides the main church, there is a courtyard for al fresco dining. The menu includes burgers, sandwiches, fajitas, or baby-back ribs. Although the fare is nothing to rave about, patrons flock here for the fun and convivial atmosphere.

Pinckney Café & Espresso

18 Pinckney St. (at Motley Lane). ☎ **803/577-0961.** Reservations required only for parties of 6 or more. Main courses $6.95–$14.95. No credit cards. Tues–Thurs 11:30am–3pm, Fri–Sat 11:30am–2:30pm, Tues–Sat 6–10pm. AMERICAN.

Lying just two blocks north of the City Market, this fun spot is casual, warm, and inviting. Picture a yellow-frame, 19th-century home turned coffeehouse and restaurant. You'll find wide hardwood floors, comfortable slatted chairs, a fireplace, and a porch with ceiling fans for outdoor dining. The crowd is rather yuppie-ish. On the menu (written on a blackboard brought to your table) will be a creamy lemon broccoli soup with rosemary and thyme, sandwiches, omelets, and main courses. Specials may include a spinach quesadilla with seasoned spinach and jack and feta cheese, all stuffed in a crisp flour tortilla and served with sour cream and salsa; turkey marsala; salmon cakes with a shallot and dill cream sauce and stone-ground grits; or Pinckney's pasta made with homemade cheese tortellini with shrimp and scallops in a tomato and scallion cream sauce. On the lighter side are specialty coffees, including the Café Market Street, which is espresso with cocoa, sugar, cinnamon, nutmeg cream, and whipped cream; and the cappucino float. Wine and beer are available.

Reubens

251 Meeting St. (at Wentworth). ☎ **803/722-6883.** Breakfast $1.99–$3.25; soups, sandwiches, salads, and platters $1–$5.25. No credit cards. Mon–Sat 8am–4pm. DELI.

It's the best-marketed deli in Charleston, plastered with the photographs of virtually every newscaster and sportscaster in the state, as well as memorabilia of the owner's favorite football team, the Washington Redskins. If you don't see what you want, be sure to ask for it. (Clients are bolstered at the entrance by the sight of large signs exhorting, "Don't be shy!") Everything is served cafeteria style, amid a pine-trimmed decor that's almost aggressively cheerful. The menu includes soups, salads, sandwiches, and Vienna-style hot dogs and sausages, all inspired by New York delis. The staff is polite and genuinely helpful in instructing you in how to navigate through the self-service line-ups. Although breakfast is popular, everything is locked up tight in time for the late afternoon closing, so don't expect anyone to serve you dinner.

AT THE MUNICIPAL MARINA

Marina Variety Store

17 Lockwood Blvd. ☎ **803/723-6325.** Main courses $4–$8. AE, MC, V. Daily 6am–9:30pm. SEAFOOD/LOW COUNTRY.

For more than a quarter of a century, this spot has been serving locals and boat owners who put in to the adjacent dock along the Ashley River next to the municipal marina. You can feed the entire family here without doing serious injury to your pocketbook. The restaurant occupies one side of a store that sells fishing supplies and souvenirs and overlooks the yacht basin. You can enjoy such downhome Low Country specialties as okra soup or chili, a variety of sandwiches, or fried-fish dinners, all at budget prices. Breakfast is served till 11am. Picture windows frame the comings and goings of all sorts of boats—maybe you'll even see a Chinese junk sail past. Orders are placed at the counter, and waitresses bring the food to comfortable booths.

IN MOUNT PLEASANT

Supper at Stack's

In the Captain Guild's Inn, 101 Pitt St., Mount Pleasant. ☎ **803/884-7009.** Reservations required. Fixed-price four-course supper $29. AE, MC, V. Tues–Sat 6–10pm. LOW COUNTRY.

Housed within a historic B&B (with which it is not associated in any managerial way) in the 19th-century suburb of Mount Pleasant, 7 miles from the heart of historic Charleston, this is the culinary equivalent of a folksy, family-oriented inn. Menus are without a shred of European pretense, and are listed, down-home style, on a chalkboard at one end of the old-fashioned dining room. Within the shadow of a 19th-century icebox, which the owners have converted into a modern refrigerator, you can order such specialties as catfish, salmon, duck, leg of lamb, and wholesome desserts like you wished your grandmother used to make. Beer and wine are served.

Village Café

415 Mill Street, Mount Pleasant. ☎ **803/884-8095.** Reservations recommended. Lunch salads, sandwiches, and platters $4–$8; dinner main courses $8–$21. AE, DC, DISC, MC, V. Mon–Sat 11am–3pm; Mon–Thurs 5:30–10pm, Fri–Sat 5:30–10pm. Sun brunch 10:30am–2:30pm. INTERNATIONAL.

We think this place is more appealing than any of its competitors within the Charleston suburb of Mount Pleasant, a 10-minute drive southeast of the city's historic core. It occupies a clapboard-sided building which, although built in the 1980s, was deliberately designed to resemble a much older structure, perhaps a private house. A massive brick fireplace greets you near the entrance, and a quartet of dining rooms stress a theme of early Americana. Lunchtime features lasagna, sandwiches (including a succulent version of portabello mushrooms with crabmeat), and salads. Dinners are more elaborate, with goat cheesecake served on a bed of mesclun greens, pecan-crusted loin of lamb, grilled tenderloin of pork, and filet of grouper seared in black pepper.

5   Seeing the Sights

SUGGESTED ITINERARIES

If You Have 1 Day

Far too short, but make the best of it by taking an early morning carriage tour of the Historic District. The driver (who's also a guide) will fill you full of the legend and lore of Charleston. After patting the horse goodbye, explore the Old Market area in the very heart of the city. After lunch at the market, wander through the old streets, looking into a garden here, a church there. In the evening dine at one of Charleston's great restaurants, such as Anson. Don't leave town without sampling she-crab soup, the local favorite.

If You Have 2 Days

Spend Day 1 as recommended above. On your second day, visit one or two of the memorable mansions of Charleston, especially the Heyward-Washington House, the Nathaniel Russell House, or the Edmonston-Alston House. For lunch, drop in at Reubens for the best sandwiches in Charleston. In the afternoon take a boat tour to Fort Sumter, where the Civil War began. In the late afternoon, take a guided walking tour of Old Charleston and then dine in a typical colonial tavern that night.

If You Have 3 Days

Spend Days 1 and 2 as recommended above. On the third day, leave Charleston behind and plan a full-day visit to Magnolia Plantation and the Audubon Swamp Gardens. It's one of the major attractions of South Carolina. If you finish early enough, you can return to explore Charles Towne Landing, a 663-acre park, site of the first colonial settlement in South Carolina.

HISTORIC HOMES

✪ Edmondston-Alston House

21 East Battery. ☎ **803/722-7171.** General admission $6; combination ticket with Nathaniel Russell House (see below) $10 (see below). Guided tours Tues–Sat 10am–4:30pm, Sun–Mon 1:30–4:30pm.

On High Battery, an elegant section of Charleston, this house (built in 1825 by Charles Edmondston, a merchant and wharf owner) was one of the earliest constructed in the city in the late Federalist style. After economic reverses, he sold it to Charles Alston, a Low

Country rice planter, who modified the style, changing it more to Greek Revival (popular at the time). The house has remained in the Alston family, who now open the first two floors to visitors. Their heirloom furnishings, silver, and painting collection can be viewed. It was here in 1861 that General Beauregard joined the Alston family to watch the bombardment of Fort Sumter. Robert E. Lee once found refuge here when his hotel uptown caught on fire.

Nathaniel Russell House

51 Meeting St. ☎ **803/722-3405.** Admission $5 general, $10 combination ticket with Edmonston-Alston House (see above). Guided tours Mon–Sat 10am–4:30pm, Sun and holidays 2–4:30pm.

One of America's finest examples of Federal architecture, this 1808 house was completed by Nathaniel Russell, one of Charleston's rich merchants. Over the years it's been put to many uses, including stints as a girls' school and a convent. It's celebrated architecturally for its "free-flying" staircase, spiraling unsupported for three floors. The staircase's elliptical shape is repeated throughout the house. The interiors are ornate and still decorated with period furnishings; check out the elegant music room with its golden harp and neoclassical-style sofa.

Heyward-Washington House

87 Church St. (between Tradd and Elliott Sts.). ☎ **803/722-0354.** Admission $6 adults, $3 children 3–12, free for children 2 and under. Combination ticket including Charleston Museum and Joseph Manigault House $15. Mon–Sat 10am–5pm, Sun 1–5pm. Tours every 1/2 hour; last tour at 4:30pm.

In a district of Charleston called "Cabbage Row" stands this 1772 house. It was built by Daniel Heyward, "the rice king," and was the setting for Dubose Heyward's *Porgy*. President Washington, who liked to sleep around, bedded down here in 1791. It was also the home of Thomas Heyward Jr., a signer of the Declaration of Independence. Many of the fine period pieces in the house were the work of Thomas Elfe, one of America's most famous cabinetmakers. The restored kitchen from the 1700s is the only historic kitchen in the city open to the public. It stands behind the main house, as do the servants' quarters and a garden.

Calhoun Mansion

16 Meeting St. (between Battery and Lamboll Streets.). ☎ **803/772-8205.** Admission $10 adults, $5 children 6–14, free for children 5 and under. Thurs–Sun 10am–4pm. Closed holidays.

Charleston Attractions

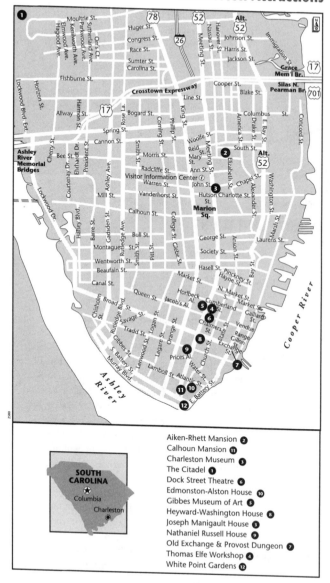

Aiken-Rhett Mansion ❷
Calhoun Mansion ⓫
Charleston Museum ❸
The Citadel ❶
Dock Street Theatre ❻
Edmonston-Alston House ❿
Gibbes Museum of Art ❺
Heyward-Washington House ❽
Joseph Manigault House ❸
Nathaniel Russell House ❾
Old Exchange & Provost Dungeon ❼
Thomas Elfe Workshop ❹
White Point Gardens ⓬

This 1876 Victorian showplace is complete with period furnishings (including a few original pieces), porcelain and etched-glass gas chandeliers, ornate plastering, and woodwork of cherry, oak, and walnut. The ballroom's 45-foot-high ceiling has a skylight.

Joseph Manigault House

350 Meeting St. (diagonally across from the visitors' center on the corner of John Street.). ☎ **803/722-2996.** Admission $6 adults, $3 children 3–12, free for children 2 and under. Combination ticket including Heyward-Washington House and Charleston Museum $15. Mon–Sat 10am–5pm, Sun 1–5pm.

This 1803 Adams-style residence on the register of National Historic Landmarks was the home of a wealthy rice planter. The house features a curving central staircase and an outstanding collection of Charleston, American, English, and French period furnishings.

NEARBY PLANTATIONS

✪ Middleton Place

Ashley River Rd. (14 miles NW of Charleston on Hwy. 61). ☎ **803/556-6020.** Admission $12 adults, $6 children 6–12, free for children 5 and under to tour gardens and stableyard; $6 extra to tour house. Gardens and stableyard daily 9am–5pm; house Tues–Sun 10am–4:30pm, Mon 1:30–4:30pm.

This was the home of Henry Middleton, president of the First Continental Congress, whose son Arthur was a signer of the Declaration of Independence. Today the National Historic Landmark includes this country's oldest landscaped gardens, the Middleton Place House, and the Plantation Stableyards. The gardens, begun in 1741, reflect the elegant symmetry of European gardens of that period. Ornamental lakes, terraces, and plantings of camellias, azaleas, magnolias, and crape myrtle accent the grand design.

The Middleton Place House itself was built in 1755, and in 1865 all but the south flank was ransacked and burned by Union troops. It was restored in the 1870s as a family residence and today houses collections of fine silver, furniture, rare first editions by Catesby and Audubon, and portraits by Benjamin West and Thomas Sully. In the stableyards, craftspeople demonstrate life on a plantation of yesteryear. There are also horses, mules, hogs, cows, sheep, and goats.

A plantation lunch is served at the Middleton Place Restaurant—a replica of an original rice mill. *American Way* magazine cited this restaurant as one of the top ten representing American cuisine at its best. Specialties include she-crab soup, hoppin' John (a traditional Southern dish of rice and black-eyed peas, flavored with salt pork), and ham biscuits, along with okra gumbo, Sea Island shrimp, and corn pudding. Service is daily from 11am to 3pm. Dinner is served only on Friday and Saturday from 5 to 9pm, and is likely to include panned quail with ham, sea scallops, or broiled oysters. For dinner reservations, call **803/556-6020.**

Drayton Hall

Old Ashley River Rd. ☎ **803/766-0188.** Admission $7 adults, $4 children. Mar–Oct, daily 10am–4pm, with tours on the hour; Nov–Feb, daily 10am–3pm. Closed Thanksgiving Day and Christmas. On Hwy. 61, 9 miles northwest of Charleston.

This is one of the oldest surviving plantations, built in 1738 and owned by the Drayton family until 1974. Framed by majestic live oaks, the Georgian-Palladian house is a property of the National Trust for Historic Preservation. Its handcarved woodwork and plasterwork represent New World craftsmanship at its finest. Since such modern elements as electricity, plumbing, and central heating have never put in an appearance, the house is much as it was in its early years.

✪ Magnolia Plantation

Hwy. 61. ☎ **803/571-1266.** Admission to garden, $9 adults, $7 senior citizens, $7 children 13 to 19, $4 children 6–12, free for children 5 and under; plantation house tour $5 additional extra. Add $1 Mar–May. Audubon Swamp Garden $5 adults, $3 senior citizens, $2 children 6–12, free for children 5 and under. Combination ticket in conjunction with Magnolia Plantation makes the Audubon Swamp Garden admission $3 adults, $2 senior citizens, $1 children 6–12, free for children 5 and under. Plantation and gardens daily 8am–5pm.

Ten generations of the Drayton family have lived here continuously since the 1670s. They haven't had much luck keeping a roof over their heads: The first mansion burned just after the Revolution, and the second was set afire by General Sherman. But you can't call its replacement "modern." A simple, pre-Revolutionary house was barged down from Summerville and set on the basement foundations of its unfortunate predecessors.

The flowery gardens of camellias and azaleas—among the most beautiful in America—reach their peak bloom in March and April but are colorful year-round. You can tour the house, the gardens (including an herb garden, horticultural maze, topiary garden, and biblical garden), and a petting zoo; visit a waterfowl refuge; and walk or bike through wildlife trails. Other sights include an antebellum cabin that was restored and furnished, a plantation rice barge on display beside the Ashley River, and a Nature Train that carries guests on a 45-minute ride around the plantation's perimeter.

Low Country wildlife is visible in marsh, woodland, and swamp settings. The **Audubon Swamp Garden**, also on the grounds, is an independently operated 60-acre cypress swamp offering a close look at egrets, alligators, wood ducks, otters, turtles, and herons.

Boone Hall Plantation

Long Point Rd., Mount Pleasant (on U.S. 17, 9 miles north of Charleston). ☎ **803/884-4371**. Admission $7.50 adults, $6 seniors 55 and over, $3 children 6–12, free for children 5 and under. Apr–Labor Day Mon–Sat 8:30am–6:30pm, Sun 1–5pm; day after Labor Day–Mar Mon–Sat 9am–5pm, Sun 1–4pm.

This unique plantation is approached by a famous avenue of oaks, huge old moss-draped trees planted in 1743 by Capt. Thomas Boone. The first floor of the plantation house is elegantly furnished and open to the public. Outbuildings include the circular smoke-house and slave cabins constructed of bricks made on the plantation.

SPECTACULAR GARDENS

See also the listing for Magnolia Plantation, above under "Nearby Plantations."

✪ Cypress Gardens

U.S. 52, Moncks Corner (24 miles north). ☎ **803/553-0515**. Admission mid-Feb–Apr (not including boat rides) $6 adults, $5 seniors, $2 children 6–16, free for children 5 and under. Off-season $5 adults, $4 seniors, $1 children 6–16, free for children 5 and under. Daily 9am–5pm.

This 163-acre swamp garden was used as a freshwater reserve for Dean Hall, a huge Cooper River rice plantation, and was given to the city in 1963. Today, its giant cypress trees, draped with Spanish moss, provide an unforgettable setting for flat-bottom boats that glide among their knobby roots. Footpaths in the garden wind through a profusion of azaleas, camellias, daffodils, and other colorful blooms. Visitors share the swamp with alligators, pileated woodpeckers, wood ducks, otter, barred owls, and other abundant species that inhabit the swamp year-round. The gardens are worth a visit at any time of year, but they're at their most colorful from March through April.

MUSEUMS

✪ Charleston Museum

360 Meeting St. ☎ **803/722-2996**. Admission $5 adults, $3 children 3–12, free for children 2 and under. Combination ticket including Joseph

Manigault House and Heyward-Washington House $15. Mon–Sat 9am–
4:30pm; Sun 1–5pm.

The Charleston Museum, founded in 1773, is the first and oldest
museum in America. The museum's collections preserve and inter-
pret the social and natural history of Charleston and the South
Carolina coastal region. The full-scale replica of the famed Confederate submarine *Hunley* standing outside the museum is one of the
most photographed subjects in the city. The museum also exhibits
the largest Charleston silver collection, early crafts, historic relics,
and the state's only children's "Discover Me" room, with hands-on
exhibits for children.

American Military Museum

40 Pinckney St. (near Church and Market Streets). ☎ **803/723-9620.**
Admission $5 adults; $1 children 12 and under; free for military personnel
in uniform. Mon–Sat 10am–6pm, Sun 1–6pm.

Dedicated to the men and women who have served in the U.S.
armed forces, this museum displays uniforms and artifacts from all
branches of the military. There are relics of virtually every armed
conflict in which this country has been involved. Civil War buffs
come here to look at that collection, but there are exhibits from the
Spanish-American War, the War of 1812, Indian Wars, World War
I and II, and even the Korean and Vietnam wars.

Gibbes Museum of Art

135 Meeting St. ☎ **803/722-2706.** Admission $5 adults, $4 seniors and
students 6–17, free for children 5 and under. Tues–Sat 10am–5pm, Sun–
Mon 1–5pm. Closed holidays.

Established in 1905 by the Carolina Art Association, the Gibbes
Museum contains an intriguing collection of prints and drawings

Impressions

*Just as one generation of Charlestonians had recovered from the
Revolution, the next generation was indiscreet enough to start the
Civil War—the "War of Northern Aggression" you can still hear it
called here—and the Yankees and carpetbaggers plundered the city all
over again. For decades, the the old Charlestonians were left huddled
in their crumbling mansions "too poor to paint and too proud to
whitewash." I can remember visiting Charleston with my parents in
the Depression years, and looking upon its Georgian houses and Greek
temples as a vast classical ruin.*
    —Charles Kuralt, *Charles Kuralt's America* (1995)

from the 18th century to the present. Landscapes, genre scenes, panoramic views of Charleston harbor, and portraits of South Carolinians are displayed. See especially *Thomas Middleton* by Benjamin West, *Charles Izard Manigault* by Thomas Sully, or *John C. Calhoun* by Rembrandt Peale. The museum's collection of some 400 miniature portraits ranks as one of the more comprehensive in the country. The Wallace Exhibit includes 10 rooms, 8 replicated from historic American buildings and 2 from classic French styles. Styles range from a plain dining room in the house of a sea captain on Martha's Vineyard to the elegant drawing room of Charleston's historic Nathaniel Russell House (see above).

CHURCHES & SYNAGOGUES

✪ St. Michael's Episcopal Church

14 St. Michael's Alley (at Meeting and Broad Streets). ☎ **803/723-0603.** Free admission. Mon–Fri 8:45am–4:45pm.

This is the oldest church in the city, dating from 1761. Its eight bells (imported in 1764) are well traveled: They were sent back to England as a British prize of war during the Revolution; back in the United States, they were burned during the Civil War, and had to cross the Atlantic again to be recast. The chandelier, installed in 1803, has been lighted by candles, gas, and electricity. Washington worshiped here during his 1791 Southern tour.

Congregation Beth Elohim

90 Hasell St. (between King and Meeting Streets). ☎ **803/723-1090.** Free admission. Mon–Fri 10am–noon.

Dating from 1840, this is the oldest synagogue in continuous use in the United States, and the second oldest in the country. The original, built in 1794, burned in 1838; its Greek Revival replacement is considered one of America's finest examples of that style. The synagogue was the birthplace of Reform Judaism in 1824. Attracted by the civil and religious freedom of South Carolina, Jews first arrived after 1670. By 1749 there were enough members to organize a congregation and to consecrate a small house of worship.

French Huguenot Church

136 Church St. (between Queen and Chalmers Streets). ☎ **803/722-4385.** Free admission. Services Sun at 10:30am.

This church (built 1844–45) is the fourth on this site; the first was built in 1687. In the early days, much of the congregation came downriver by boat, so services were planned so they could arrive on the ebb tide and go home on the flood. It's the only French Hugue-not church in the United States that still uses the French liturgy.

St. Mary's Roman Catholic Church

89 Hasell St. (between Meeting and King Streets). ☎ **803/722-7696.** Free admission. Daily 8am–4pm.

This is the mother church (built in 1839) of the Roman Catholic dioceses of South Carolina, North Carolina, and Georgia. An earlier church (1789) burned on this site in 1838.

PARKS & GARDENS

Old Santee Canal State Park (☎ **803/899-5200**) is one of the city's newest and finest parks. It was landscaped along the banks of the old Santee Canal, reached by taking I-26 west from the center, exiting at Hwy. 52. Drive through Goose Creek to Moncks Corner to reach it. Miles of boardwalks and trails await visitors, who can explore the natural beauty of the region at their leisure, any time daily from 9am to 5pm. Canoes can be rented for rides along Biggin Swamp (yes, Virginia, there are alligators). Less frightening are the ospreys and blue herons who also inhabit this wild and untamed area. An **Interpretive Center** provides information about the area dating from 4000 B.C.

Family fun is promised at the **Palmetto Islands County Park** (☎ **803/884-0832**) in Mount Pleasant, near Boone Hall. Instead of the wild nature of Old Santee (see above), it offers more organized fun in the form of a big toy playground, mile-long canoe trails, picnic sites, an observation tower, a water playground, toddler slides, marsh boardwalks, and plenty of jogging trails and bicycle paths. Bordering Boone Hall Creek are public fishing and boating docks. The park is open daily. Hours are 10am to 5pm November through March; 9am to 7pm May through August; and 9am to 6pm April, September, and October. Admission is $1.

Folly Beach County Park (☎ **803/588-2426**) is a beach park with some 4,000 feet of ocean frontage along the Atlantic, plus some 2,000 feet of riverfront frontage. Lifeguards protect swimmers along a 600-foot beachfront. Group picnics and Low Country oyster roasts seem a perennial feature around here at the **Pelican Watch Shelter.** There's a 300-vehicle parking lot, along with such amenities as dressing rooms, toilets, and outdoor showers. Equipment to rent includes beach umbrellas, beach chairs, and rafts. Cost is $8 per vehicle. In April, September, and October, hours are daily 10am to 6pm; May through August daily 9am to 7pm; and November through March daily 10am to 5pm.

If you don't have a car and still want to enjoy a park, make it the **Charleston Waterfront Park,** lying along 1,280 feet of waterfront property bordering Concord Street in the center of the city. City officials, by landscaping and cleaning up this park area, revitalized a section of Charleston. Numerous benches for Forrest Gump types and picnic tables are available, as are a grassy public green and a pier. Admission is free. The park is open daily from 6am to midnight (but we don't advise hanging out there too late at night because of the danger of muggings).

VIEWS

We always head for the **Battery** (if you want to be official about it, the **White Point Gardens**) to get back into the feel of this city. It's right on the end of the peninsula, facing the Cooper River and the harbor. There's a landscaped park, shaded by palmettos and live oaks and filled with walkways lined with old monuments and other war relics. The view toward the harbor looks out to Fort Sumter. We like to walk along the sea wall on East Battery and Murray Boulevard and sink slowly into the history of Charleston. You might then venture into the neighborhood to see the architecture.

MORE ATTRACTIONS

The Citadel

Moultrie Street and Elmwood Avenue. ☎ **803/953-5006.** Free admission. Daily 24 hours for drive-through visits; museum Sun–Fri 2–5pm, Sat noon–5pm. Closed religious and school holidays.

The all-male Citadel was established in 1842 as an arsenal, and to serve as a refuge for whites in case of a slave uprising. In 1922, it was moved to its present location, where it received worldwide notoriety in 1995 during the failed attempt of Shannon Faulkner to join the ranks.

After winning a legal battle to be admitted, Faulkner dropped out. Her ordeal at the Citadel drew fiercely divided opinions. News of her resignation was greeted with whooping and dancing at the female-free campus. However, best-selling author Pat Conroy, a Faulkner supporter, said, "They made sure that everyone in America saw that that college hates women. They've made a blood sport of hating in South Carolina." Conroy's novel *The Lords of Discipline* is based on his four years at the school.

The campus of this military college, with its buildings of Moorish design, featuring crenellated battlements and sentry towers, is

★ Frommer's Favorite Charleston Experiences

Playing Scarlett & Rhett at Boone Hall. Over in Mount Pleasant, you can pretend you're one of the romantic figures in Margaret Mitchell's *Gone with the Wind* by paying a visit to this 738-acre estate, a cotton plantation settled by Major John Boone in 1681. It was used for background shots in the films *Gone with the Wind* and *North and South*.

Going Back to Colonial Days. At Charles Towne Landing you get the best insight into how colonists lived 300 years ago when they established the first English settlement in South Carolina. A visit here features hands-on activities. Even the animals the settlers encountered—from bears to bison—roam about. You can also enjoy 80 acres of gardens by walking along the marsh or bicycling past lagoons that reflect blossoming camellias and azaleas.

A Cuppa at the Charleston Tea Plantation. Lying only 15 miles south of Charleston on Wadmalaw Island, this plantation boasts the only tea grown in America. Called American Classic, it is the tea served at the White House. But in case Bill and Hillary don't invite you for a cup, you can sample it here. A cup of this tea is the freshest on the shelves, as imported teas can take 9 to 12 months for delivery—making this visit a unique experience possible nowhere else in America.

especially interesting on Fridays when the college is in session and the public is invited to a precision drill parade on the quadrangle at 3:45pm. For a history of the Citadel, stop at the **Citadel Memorial Archives Museum** (☎ 803/953-6846).

Old Exchange & Provost Dungeon

122 East Bay St. ☎ **803/727-2165.** Admission $4 adults, $3.50 seniors, $2 children 7–12, free for children 6 and under. Daily 9am–5pm. Closed Jan 1, Thanksgiving Day, Dec 24–25 and 31.

This is a stop many tourists overlook; in fact, most local sightseeing companies only stop here if requested. However, it's considered to be one of the three most important colonial buildings in the United States, because of the role it played as a prison during the American Revolution. In 1873, the building became City Hall. You'll also find here one of the largest collections of antique chairs in the nation—each of the Daughters of the American Revolution brought a chair here from home in 1921.

✪ Charles Towne Landing

1500 Old Towne Rd. (S.C. 171, between U.S. 17 and I-126). ☎ **803/852-4200.** Admission $5 adults, $2.50 seniors and children 6–14, free for children 5 and under and for the disabled. Daily 9am–6pm.

This 663-acre park is located on the site of the first 1670 settlement. Underground exhibits show the colony's history, and there's a re-creation of a small village, a full-scale replica of a 17th-century trading ship, and a tram tour for $1 (or you can rent a bike). Because trade was such an important part of colonial life, a full-scale reproduction of the 17th-century trading vessel *Adventure* is an excellent addition to the site. After touring the ship, you can step into the Settler's Life Area and view a 17th-century crop garden where rice, indigo, and cotton were grown. There's no flashy theme park atmosphere: What you see as you walk under huge old oaks, past freshwater lagoons, and through the Animal Forest (which has animals of the same species that lived here in 1670) is what those early settlers saw.

Fort Moultrie

Sullivan's Island, West Middle Street (10 miles east of Charleston; watch for signs). ☎ **803/883-3123.** Free admission. Apr–Sept daily 9am–6pm; winter daily 9am–5pm.

Only a palmetto log fortification at the time of the American Revolution, the fort was only half completed when it was attacked by a British fleet in 1776, the year on which construction was launched. Colonel William Moultrie's troops repelled the invasion in one of the first decisive American victories of the Revolution. The fort was subsequently enlarged into a five-sided structure with earth and timber walls 17 feet high. The British didn't do it in, but an 1804 hurricane ripped it apart. By the War of 1812 it was back and ready for action.

Osceola, the fabled leader of the Seminoles in Florida, was incarcerated and eventually died here. In the 1830s, Edgar Allen Poe served as a soldier at the fort; he set his short story *The Gold Bug* on Sullivan's Island. The fort also played roles in the Civil War, the Mexican War, and the Spanish-American War—even World Wars I and II. But by 1947 it had retired from action.

ESPECIALLY FOR KIDS

For more than 300 years Charleston has been the home of pirates, patriots, and presidents. Your child can see firsthand the **Great Hall at the Old Exchange,** where President Washington danced, and the **Provost Dungeons,** where South Carolina Patriots spent their last days; and touch the last remaining structural evidence of the **Charleston Sea Wall**. Among the attractions listed above, children will take special delight in **Charles Towne Landing** and **Middleton Place**.

Kids and Navy vets will also love the aircraft carrier **U.S.S. Yorktown** at Patriots Point (two miles east of the Cooper River Bridge). Its World War II, Korea, and Vietnam exploits are documented in exhibits, and general naval history is illustrated through models of ships, planes, and weapons. You can wander through the bridge wheelhouse, flight and hangar decks, chapel, sick bay, and several other areas, and view the film *The Fighting Lady,* depicting life aboard the carrier. The *Yorktown* is the nucleus of the world's largest naval and maritime museum. Also at Patriots Point, and welcoming visitors aboard, are the nuclear ship *Savannah,* the world's first nuclear-powered merchant ship; the World War II destroyer *Laffey;* the World War II submarine *Clamagore;* and the cutter *Ingham.* Patriots Point is open from 9am to 6pm daily April through October, 9am to 5pm November through March. Admission is $9 for adults, $8 for seniors over 62 and military personnel in uniform, $4 for kids 6 to 11, and free for kids 5 and under. (Adjoining is the fine 18-hole public Patriots Point golf course for moms and dads.) For further information, call **803/884-2727.**

Another kid pleaser, **Best Friend,** lying adjacent to the Visitor Center on Ann Street (☎ **803/973-7269**), combines a museum and an antique train that features a full-size replica of the 1830 locomotive that was the first steam engine in the U.S. to establish regularly scheduled passenger service. The present train was constructed from the original plans in 1928 and donated to Charleston in 1993. Hours are Monday through Saturday from 9am to 5pm and Sunday from 1 to 5pm; admission is free.

WALKING TOUR
Old Charleston

The following is really a two-in-one tour, since we've made a distinction (as do Charlestonians) between "south of Broad Street" and "north of Broad Street." If you have the luxury of 2 days to devote to this charming city, we strongly recommend that you explore each area in depth on successive days.

Start: White Point Gardens at the Battery.
Finish: Aiken-Rhett Mansion, Elizabeth Street between Mary and Judith streets.

Time: Six hours without touring historic attractions; add from
$^1/_2$ to 1 hour for each tour.
Best Times: Any time except midday, when the heat can be quite
steamy, especially in summer months. Early evening is pleasant if
you don't plan to tour attractions.
Worst Times: Rush hours Monday through Friday, when there is
just too much traffic.

We'll start south of Broad Street. Turning your back to the
water, you'll face a row of large, graceful houses that line South
Battery. When you walk away from the park, it's as if you're
going through a sort of gateway into the rest of town.

Once off South Battery, almost every home is of historic or
architectural interest. You'll find detailed information on the tour
in the sections above. After a stroll through White Point Gardens,
walk up Meeting Street to the:

1. **Calhoun Mansion,** at 16 Meeting St., then return to South
   Battery Street and walk east two blocks alongside one gracious
   mansion after the other. Loiter a moment or two at East Battery
   Street to savor the harbor view, then turn north to the:

2. **Edmonston-Alston House,** at 21 East Battery. Take a few minutes to cross the street to the waterfront park. Continue north to
   the next intersection and turn left on Water Street for one block,
   then right on Church Street and continue north to the:

3. **Heyward-Washington House,** at 87 Church St. Continuing
   north, you'll pass:

4. **Catfish Row.** Its real name is Cabbage Row (after the vegetables
   that used to be sold on the sidewalk). It's a row of connected
   buildings from 89 to 91 Church Street. Duboise Heyward
   changed its name in his novel *Porgy,* and when he and George
   Gershwin collaborated on the opera *Porgy and Bess,* its fame
   spread all over the world.

   At Church and Elliott streets, turn left to reach:

5. **St. Michael's Church,** at Meeting and Broad streets. Look inside,
   then stroll through the adjoining graveyard, with headstones
   dating back over the centuries.

   ☕ **TAKE A BREAK**   By now you may be ready for a bite
   to eat. **Reubens Downtown Delicatessen,** at Broad and Meeting streets, is a good place for snacks, or if that doesn't suit
   your mood, you're in the perfect spot to choose any number of

restaurants and coffeehouses. Check our favorites in the dining section for a few tips.

Now we'll head north of Broad Street. While you're in the vicinity, you may want to stop in at:

6. **City Hall,** at Broad and Meeting streets, to have a look at the portrait gallery in the Council Chamber. The famous John Trumbull portrait of George washington is there, along with Samuel F.B. Morse's painting of James Monroe.

The adjacent park at:

7. **Washington Square** holds monuments to a whole slew of prominent South Carolinians, as well as the Fireproof Building, this country's first.

Walk two blocks north to Queen Street and turn right to reach the:

8. **Dock Street Theatre,** on the corner of Queen and Church streets. Continue east toward the waterfront and turn south at Church Street to visit the:

9. **Huguenot Church,** Church Street between Queen and Chalmers.

Now turn north on Church Street and walk the few blocks to the:

10. **Old City Market,** at East Bay and Market streets. It's a fascinating collection of open stalls under brick sheds with tile roofs that stretch for roughly three blocks. On either side of the open sheds, old market buildings have been leased to small boutiques filled with craft items, linens, cookware, clothing, gifts, and such.

Back at the corner of Meeting and North Market, you'll find a stand for:

11. **The Charleston Carriage Company.** This may be an ideal time to treat yourself to a horse-drawn carriage ride through many of the streets you've just been walking, as well as a few more (see "Organized Tours," below).

Our course is now along Market Street several blocks north to the:

12. **Joseph Manigault Mansion,** Meeting Street between John and Hutson. At this intersection, plan a leisurely interval at the:

13. **Charleston Museum,** this country's oldest, with several fine collections of 18th-century silver and other interesting exhibits.

When you can tear yourself away, walk north on Meeting to Wragg Street and turn right for the:

14. **Aiken-Rhett Mansion,** 48 Elizabeth St., which was Civil War headquarters for General P.G.T. Beauregard and his Confederate troops. It is now closed to the public.

6 Organized Tours

The Charleston Carriage Co., 96 N. Market St. (☎ 803/577-0042), offers narrated horse-drawn carriage tours through the Historic District daily from 9am to dusk. There is free shuttle service from the visitor center and downtown hotels. The cost is $13 for adults, $12 for seniors, and $8 for children.

Palmetto Carriage Tours, 40 N. Market St., at Guignard (☎ 803/723-8145), uses mule teams instead of the usual horse and carriage for its guided tours of Old Charleston. Tours originate at the Rainbow Market. There is free shuttle van service from the visitor center. The cost is $15 for adults, $14 for senior citizens, and $5 for children.

The Civil War era comes alive again on a unique walking tour conducted by **Jack Thomson** (☎ 803/722-7033), a guide well versed in the lore of "The War of Northern Aggression." You can stroll down cobblestone streets and listen to firsthand accounts and anecdotes that recount the embattled city of Charleston during its years of siege by Union troops. Tours depart at 9am Wednesday through Sunday (March through December) from the Mills House Hotel Courtyard at 115 Meeting St. Adults pay $12 and children under 12 go free; reservations are appreciated.

One of the best offbeat walking tours of Charleston is the **Charleston Tea Party Walking Tour** (☎ 803/577-5896), lasting 2 hours and costing $13 for adults or $6 for children up to 12. Departing year-round Monday through Saturday at 9:30am to 2pm, tours originate at Kings Courtyard Inn, 198 Kings St. The tour goes into a lot of nooks and crannies of Charleston, including secret courtyards and gardens. (And of course, there's tea at the end.)

Architectural tours of Charleston's 18th-century structures within the original "walled city" begin at 10am, and tours of 19th-century architecture along Meeting Street and the Battery begin at 2pm. Departures are in front of the Meeting Street Inn, 173 Meeting St. Tours last 2 hours and are daily except Sunday and Tuesday. The cost is $13 (free for children 12 and under). For reservations, call **803/893-2327.**

Fort Sumter Tours, 205 Kings St., Suite 204 (☎ 803/722-1691), offers a "Harbor and Fort Sumter Tour" by boat, departing daily from the City Marina and from Patriots Point Maritime Museum. This is the only tour to stop at Fort Sumter, target of the opening shots of the Civil War. The cost is $9.50 for adults, $4.75 for children 6 to 11, free for children 5 and under. They also have an interesting "Charleston Harbor Tour," with daily departures from Patriots Point. The 2-hour cruise passes the Battery, Charleston Port, Castle Pinckney, Drum Island, Fort Sumter, and the aircraft carrier *Yorktown*, and sails under the Cooper River Bridge and on to other sights. The cost is $9.50 for adults, $4.75 for ages 6 to 11, free for children 5 and under.

7 Beaches & Outdoor Pursuits

BEACHES

Three great beaches are within a 25-minute drive of the center of Charleston. If you're lucky enough to stumble onto a traditional Carolina beach party, you might be introduced to the Shag, South Carolina's state dance, as well as beach music—sounds made famous in the state's beach communities by such bands as The Tams and The Drifters.

In the West Islands, **Folly Beach,** which had degenerated into a tawdry Coney Island–type amusement park, is making a comeback following a multi-million dollar cleanup (though even after the effort, it remains the least pristine of the area's beaches). The best bathroom and changing facilities west of the Holiday Inn are found here. At the western end of the island is the **Folly Beach County Park,** including bathrooms, parking, and shelter from the rain.

In the East Cooper area, both **Isle of Palms** and **Sullivan's Island** offer miles of beaches, most bordered by beachfront homes. Windsurfing and jet skiing are popular here, but you shouldn't engage in these activities in front of the islands' commercial districts.

Kiawah Island has the area's most pristine beach, far preferable than Folly. See chapter 3 for details.

BIKING

Charleston is basically flat and relatively free of traffic except on its main arteries at rush hour, so biking is a popular local pastime and relatively safe. Many of the city parks also have trails set aside for bikers.

Your best bet for bike rentals is **The Bicycle Shoppe,** 280 Meeting St. (☎ **803/722-8168**), which rents bikes for $3 per hour or $15 for a full day. A credit card imprint is required as a deposit.

BOATING & SAILING

A true Charlestonian is at home on the sea as much as on land. Many local families spend their Sunday afternoons sailing. One of the best places for rentals is **Wild Dunes Yacht Harbor,** Isle of Palms (☎ **803/886-5100**), where 15-foot boats—big enough for four sailors—rent for $75 for 4 hours. A larger pontoon boat—big enough for 10 passengers—goes for $150 for 4 hours.

DIVING

Several outfitters are available in the Charleston area, providing rentals and ocean charters but also instruction for neophytes. Local divers favor **Aqua Ventures,** 426 W. Coleman Blvd., Mt. Pleasant (☎ **803/884-1500**), which offers diving trips off the local shoreline costing $50 to $70 per person. You can rent both diving and snorkeling equipment from them. Diving equipment costs $6 for a tank and $10 for a regulator. Hours are Monday through Saturday from 10am to 6pm.

Another possibility is **The Wet Shop,** 5121 Rivers Ave. (☎ **803/744-5641**), which rents scuba equipment for $35 a day, including two tanks, a regulator, wet suit, diving knife, and weight belt. From May through October hours are Monday through Saturday from 10am to 7pm (closes at 6pm off-season).

FISHING

The Low Country's numerous creeks and inlets are filled with flounder, trout, and spot-tail or channel bass, among other freshwater catches. Offshore fishing charters are also available, and reef fishing is an option, where you'll find a variety of fish such as cobia, black sea bass, or king mackerel. Anglers also venture to the Gulf Stream for sailfish, marlin, wahoo, dolphin, or tuna. Some of the best striped bass fishing available in America can be found at nearby **Lake Moultrie.** For those who'd like a true Low Country experience, a crabbing excursion can also be arranged.

The **Folly Beach Fishing Pier** at Folly Beach opened in 1995. The wooden pier, 25 feet in width, extends 1,045 feet into the Atlantic Ocean. Facilities include restrooms, a tackle shop, and a restaurant. It is accessible for the disabled.

Deep-sea fishing or inshore fishing is best arranged at the previously recommended **Wild Dunes Yacht Harbor,** Isle of Palms (☎ **803/886-5100**). A fishing craft holding up to six persons rents for $600 for 6 hours, including everything but food and drink. Reservations must be made 24 hours in advance.

GOLF

Charleston is said to be the home of golf in America. Charlestonians have been playing the game here since the 1700s, when the first golf clubs arrived from Scotland. (Back then, golfers wore red jackets for greater visibility.) With 17 public and private courses, there is a golf game waiting for every buff.

Wild Dunes Resort, Isle of Palms (☎ **803/886-6000**), offers two championship golf courses designed by Tom Fazio. **The Links** is a 6,722-yard, par-72 layout taking the player through marshlands, over or into huge sand dunes, through a wooded alley, and ending with a pair of oceanfront finishing holes once called "the greatest east of Pebble Beach, California." The course opened in 1980 and has been ranked in the top 100 greatest courses in the U.S. by *Golf Digest* and the top 100 in the world by *Golf Magazine. Golf Digest* also ranks the Links as the 13th greatest resort course in America. The **Harbor Course** offers 6,402 yards of Low Country marsh and Intracoastal Waterway views. This par-70 layout is considered target golf, challenging players with two holes that play from one island to another across Morgan Creek. Greens fees at these courses can range from $35 to $100, depending on the season. Clubs can be rented at either course for $25 for 18 holes, and professional instruction costs $30 for a 45-minute session. Both courses are open daily from 7am to 7pm year-round.

Your best deal if you'd like to play at any of the other Charleston area golf courses is to contact **Charleston Golf Partners** at **708/549-9770,** or 800/247-5786. They represent 15 golf courses, with packages starting at $79 per person from May through June and September 1 through December 1. In off-season, packages start at $69 per person. Prices include greens fees on one course, a hotel room based on double occupancy, and taxes. Call Monday through Friday from 10am to 6pm. Travel professionals here will customize your vacation with golf course selections and tee times. They can also arrange rental cars and airfares.

HIKING

There are several possibilities in the Charleston area. The most interesting hiking trails begin around Buck Hall in the **Francis Marion National Forest,** McClellanville (☎ **803/887-3257**). The area also has 15 camping sites costing $10 per night, plus a boat ramp and fishing. The park lies some 40 miles north of the center of Charleston via U.S. 52. The site consists of some 250,000 acres of swamps, with towering oaks and pines.

Other hiking trails are at the **Edisto Beach State Park,** State Cabin Rd., on Edisto Island (☎ **803/869-2156**).

HORSEBACK RIDING

Our pick is **Seabrook Island Resort,** 1002 Landfall Way, Seabrook Island (☎ **803/768-1000**), although reservations for these guided rides are needed 3 to 4 days in advance. It has not only an equestrian center but offers both trail rides and beach rides. The beach ride for advanced riders only leaves at 8am daily, costing $60 per person, and the trail ride also for advanced riders leaves at 10:30am daily, going for $45 per person. Rides for beginners are also offered, lasting one hour and costing $35.

PARASAILING

Island Water Sports, South Beach Marina (☎ **803/671-7007**), allows you to soar up to 700 feet over the waves. The cost ranges from $35 to $45, depending on the number of feet of line used. Open year-round, hours are daily from 9am to 7:30pm.

TENNIS

As with golf, Charlestonians have been playing tennis since the early 1800s. The **Charleston Tennis Center,** Farmfield Avenue (west of Charleston on Hwy. 17), is your best bet, with 15 well-maintained outdoor courts, lit for night play. The cost is only $2.50 to reserve court time. Hours are Monday through Thursday from 8:30am to 10pm, Friday from 8:30am to 7pm, Saturday from 9am to 6pm, and Sunday from 10am to 6pm.

Another possibility is the **Shadowmoss Plantation Golf & Country Club,** 20 Dunvegan Dr. (☎ **803/556-8251**), where tennis can be played free daily from 7am to 8pm.

WINDSURFING

Long a favorite of windsurfers, the Low Country coast is known for its temperate waters and wide open spaces. Windsurfing can be arranged through **Sailsports Sailboards,** 1419 Ben Sawyer Blvd., Mt. Pleasant (☎ **803/884-1508**), renting surfboards for $5 per 24 hours. It is open Monday through Saturday from 10am to 6pm and Sunday from 11am to 4pm.

Another possibility is **McKevlin's Surf Shop,** 1101 Ocean Blvd., Isle of Palms (☎ **803/886-8912**), renting surfboards for $5 per day. Hours are 10am to 6pm daily in summer (call for off-season hours, which are subject to change).

...and silk florals, paintings, toiletries, lace, and cut crystal. ...ay through Saturday from 10am to 6pm.

226 King St. ☎ **803/722-5951.**

...d jewelry is sold here, along with the finest collection ...14K-gold slide bracelets in town. Some of the jewelry ...a quality. The staff will also help you create jewelry of ...sonal design, including a choice of stones. Open Mon-...Friday from 10am to 6pm, Saturday from 9:30am to ...Sunday from noon to 5pm.

...welers

☎ **803/577-4497.**

...custom designed by "old world"–trained craftspeople. ...ct offshoot of a store opened by the Geiss family in ...9. It is an official watch dealer for names such as ...ucci, and Raymond Weil. Repair jobs are given spe-...here. Open Monday through Friday from 10am to ...rday from 10am to 2pm.

☎ **803/853-1938.**

...r more than a quarter of a century, Muller is one of ...ading jewelers. Some of its timepieces are unique, and ...e crystal and china, along with silver and other items ...The store also designs custom-made pieces. Open ...gh Saturday from 10am to 5:30pm.

...ARDS

...oggling Board Co.

...03/723-4331.

...1830s joggling boards have been a Charleston tradi-...ion of Mrs. Benjamin Kinloch Huger, a native who ...form of exercise for her rheumatism. Mrs. Huger's ...s sent her a model of a joggling board, suggesting that ...tly bounce on the board for exercise. Its fame soon ...e board soon turned up in gardens, patios, and on ...hout the Charleston area. After World War II, jog-...ecame rare because of the scarcity of timber and the ...or. However, the tradition was revived in 1970. The ...produces a joggle bench, a duplicate of the joggling

8 Shopping

King Street is lined with many special shops and boutiques. The **Shops at Charleston Place,** 130 Market St., is an upscale complex of top designer clothing shops (Gucci, Jaeger, Ralph Lauren, and more), and the **State Street Market,** just down from the City Market, is another cluster of shops and restaurants.

ANTIQUES
Laura's Closet
18 Anson St. ☎ **803/577-5722.**

Five rooms full of just about every collectible are found in this old Charleston house. Antiques and reproductions form part of the inventory, along with hand-smocked and hand-sewn dresses, unique needlework, and dozens of accessories. Laura Jenkins Thompson, a known designer, offers original dresses as well. There is also a collection of jewelry and sterling silver. Open Monday through Saturday from 10am to 5pm, Sunday from 1 to 5pm.

Livingston Antiques
163 King St. ☎ **803/723-9697.**

For nearly a quarter of a century, the discriminating antique hound has patronized the showroom of this dealer. Both authentic antiques and reproductions good enough to fool most eyes are sold. If you're interested, the staff will direct you to their 30,000-square-foot warehouse on West Ashley. Open Monday through Saturday from 9am to 6pm.

ART
African-American Art Gallery
43 John St. ☎ **803/722-8224.**

With some 2,900 square feet of exhibition space, this is the largest African-American art gallery in the South. The original artwork is changed every 2 months. On permanent display are the works of name African artists, including Dr. Leo Twiggs and historical artist Joe Pinckney. Open Monday through Saturday from 10am to 6pm.

Lowcountry Artists
87 Hasell St. ☎ **803/577-9295.**

In a former bookbindery, this gallery is operated by eight local artists, who work in oil, watercolor, drawings, collage, woodcuts, and other media. Open Monday through Saturday from 10am to 5pm.

Waterfront Gallery
167 East Bay St. (at Queen Street). ☎ **803/722-1155.**

Facing Waterfront Park, this gallery is the premier choice for viewing the work of South Carolina artists, with the largest assemblage of such art in town. Some 21 local artists are presented, with original works beginning at $95. For sale are pieces ranging from sculpture to oils. Open Sunday through Thursday from 11am to 6pm, Friday and Saturday from 11am to 10pm.

AUDUBON PRINTS
The Audubon Shop & Gallery
245 King St. ☎ **800/453-BIRD** or 803/723-6171.

The finest gallery of its kind in South Carolina, this outlet attracts birders and others to view its collection of not only Audubon prints but botanical and wildlife prints as well, both original and reproduction. Wildlife posters are also sold. There is also a collection of telescopes and binoculars for Low Country birdwatching expeditions. A framing service is available. Open Monday through Saturday from 10am to 7pm, Sunday from noon to 5pm.

BOOKS
Atlantic Books
310 King St. ☎ **803/723-4751.**

Amelia and Gene Woolf offer thousands of good used books at moderate prices, along with a collection of rare books. Their specialties are books on South Carolina and the Civil War. They also have a good collection of the works of Southern authors, along with modern first editions as well as books on Americana, children's literature, and nautical subjects. Open Monday through Saturday from 10am to 6pm, Sunday from 1 to 6pm.

CIVIL WAR MEMORIBILIA
Sumter Military Antiques & Museum
54 Broad St. ☎ **803/577-7766.**

Relics from that "War of Northern Aggression" are sold here. You'll find a collection of authentic artifacts that range from firearms and bullets to Confederate uniforms and artillery shells and bullets. There are some interesting prints along with a collection of books on the Civil War. Open Tuesday through Saturday 10:30am to 5:30pm.

CRAFTS
Charleston Crafts
38 Queen St. ☎ **803/723-2938.**

This is a permanent showcase for work in basically all known material clay, wood, and fiber. Handmade basketry, leather works, traditional c Gifts range from traditional to m Saturday from 10am to 5pm, Sund

FASHION
Carol J's of Charleston
40 North Market St. in the Rainbow Ma

Embroidered and appliqued appa sories and gifts, are sold here at th ton. Leisure wear with matching Various collectibles are also sol design for you. Open Monday 5:30pm.

Nancy's
342 King St. ☎ **803/722-1272.**

On the main street, Nancy's sp who wants to be both active and silk, and cotton are sold along jewelry. Nancy's aims for a "t Saturday from 10am to 5:30pm

GIFTS
Charleston Collections
233 King St. ☎ **803/722-7267.**

The best-stocked gift shop i prints by local artists, Charlest lamps, and fine linen. There's pins, earrings, sterling silver barrettes. Sweetgrass baskets to 6:30pm.

Hamilton House
102 Broad St. ☎ **800/688-969(**

In this 1844 antebellum Ch dise will appeal to the tradit Antiques and accessories fo

lamp
Ope

JEWEL
Dazzles
Charlest

One-c
of han
is of h
your o
day th
7:30pr

Geiss & S
116 East B

Jewelry
This is
Brazil i
Rolex, l
cial atte
5:30pm,

Muller Jew
129B Marke

In busine
Charlesto
it also sel
for the h
Monday t

JOGGLING
Old Charles
652 King St.

Since the e
tion, the c
sought a n
Scottish co
she sit and
spread, and
porches thr
gling board
high cost of
company al

board but only 10 feet long (as opposed to the original 16 feet) and 20 inches from the ground. Open Monday through Friday 8am to 5pm.

LEATHER
LAND—The Leather Collection
281A King St. ☎ 803/723-7300.

This is the leading specialist in Charleston for leather goods crafted from Colombian leather. Come here for fine luggage as well as attaché cases, along with leather belts and handbags. It's also a place at which to shop for that special wallet. Each piece is stylish and well made—designed to last. Open Monday through Saturday from 10am to 5:30pm.

LINENS
Stoll's Alley Shop
10 Stoll's Alley (off Church Street). ☎ 803/722-8585.

Charleston's best linen shop is found here in an 18th-century Charleston "single house." Merchandise includes monogrammed towels and shower curtains, bathroom accessories, blanket covers and shams, all-cotton sheets, along with some unusual gifts. Open Monday through Saturday from 9:30am to 5:30pm.

NEEDLEWORK
Claire Murray
295 King St. ☎ 803/722-0900.

Claire Murray, a well-known artist, specializes in beautifully crafted hooked-rug designs. Locally, she is credited with having revived this almost disappearing craft. Designs are available in not only hooked rug but counted-cross stitch and needlepoint. Her kits are complete with all the materials needed to create such work yourself. Open Monday through Saturday 10am to 5pm.

PERFUME
Scents Unlimited
92 North Market St. ☎ 803/853-8837.

Favorite fragrances are found here, and prices for the most part are relatively reasonable. The shop evokes a perfumery in Europe. Scents creates its own exclusive brands, and also features classic and popular fragrances. Open Monday through Thursday from 10am to 9pm, Friday and Saturday 10am to 10pm, and Sunday 10am to 6pm.

9 Charleston After Dark

THE PERFORMING ARTS

Charleston's major cultural venue is the **Dock Street Theatre,** 133 Church St. (☎ **803/965-4032**), a 463-seat theater first built in 1736. The original burned down in the early 19th century, and the Planters Hotel was constructed around its ruins. Since 1936 the theater has come back and is home to the **Charleston State Company,** a local nonprofit theater group offering classes and education in both the technical and dramatic aspects of theater. The company's season is from mid-September through May. Dock Street hosts various companies throughout the year, with performances ranging from Shakespeare to *My Fair Lady*. It is most active at the annual Spoleto Festival USA in May and June. Admission prices are generally $15.50 for adults, $13.50 for senior citizens, and $10.50 for students with I.D. The box office is open Monday through Thursday from noon to 5pm, Friday and Saturday 10am to 8pm, and Sunday 10am to 3pm.

Robert Ivey Ballet, 1910 Savannah Hwy. (☎ **803/556-1343**), offers both classical and contemporary as well as children's ballet programs. This 40-member troupe performs four to six major shows annually, with two of those geared toward children. The group performs at various venues throughout the Charleston area, with general admission prices costing $12.50 for adults or $8 for children.

The **Charleston Symphony Orchestra,** 14 George St. (☎ **803/723-7528**), performs through the state but its main venue is the Gaillard Auditorium at Charleston Southern University. This troupe of 40 permanent members, which can reach out to embrace another 80 local musicians if needed, has a season from September through May. Small chamber concerts to full orchestral programs are performed. A local distributor of tickets is **SCAT** (call **803/577-4500** for tickets or information about performances).

Footlight Players, Inc., 20 Queen St. (☎ **803/722-7521**), is a small players group that's the best-known local community theater, with a season extending from October through May. Call for tickets or information Monday through Friday from noon to 5pm or from noon to curtain time on days of actual performance.

Low Country Legends Music Hall, 30 Cumberland St. (☎ **803/722-1829**), offers entertainment Old Charleston style. Shows range from ghost stories to contemporary folk rock to

African spirituals. Trying to re-create the style of entertainment
once legendary in the Low Country, a cast of songwriters and
performers mix music, legends, and folk stories into one. Box office
hours are Monday through Friday from 8am to 10pm, Saturday
10am to 10:30pm, and Sunday noon to 5pm. Tickets sell for $14
adults, $10 students with identification, or $7 for children, with a
10% discount offered to senior citizens.

   Charleston Ballet Theatre, 280 Meeting St. (☎ 803/723-
7334), is one of South Carolina's finest professional ballet companies. The season begins in late October with productions such as
Dracula continuing into the early spring. Ticket prices vary with the
show.

THE CLUB & MUSIC SCENE
Acme Bar & Grill
5 Faber St. ☎ **803/577-7383.** No cover.

   Acme proved to be such a popular bar in Mt. Pleasant (see listing
below) that it has extended its operation here. In spite of its name,
no food is served. This is strictly a dance club with a DJ playing
alternative rock, and the occasional live band appears. Open daily
8pm to 4am.

Chef & Chef
102 North Market St. ☎ **803/722-0732.** Cover $3 to jazz club Fri–Sat.

   This dinner and jazz club is the place to go in the City Market area
in the heart of Charleston. The kitchen prepares a complete American menu ranging from appetizers to desserts. The jazz club is called
the Blues Room; it's located on the third floor and is open only on
Friday and Saturday from 9:30pm to 2am. The restaurant serves
daily from 6 to 11pm, and live jazz (with no cover charge) is usually featured here as well, nightly from 8pm on. There's also a
special Sunday jazz brunch from 11am to 2:30pm.

Henry's
54 North Market St. ☎ **803/723-4363.**

   One of the best places for jazz in Charleston, this club features a live
band on Friday and Saturday. Otherwise, you get taped top 40
music for listening and dancing. Happy hour, with drink discounts
and free appetizers, is Monday through Friday from 4 to 7pm.

Jukebox
4 Vendue Range (across from the Waterfront Park). ☎ **803/723-3431.**
Cover $3 men, $2 women Fri–Sat 9pm–1am.

One of the most popular clubs in town, Jukebox offers a DJ playing not only current top 40 music but hits from the 1950s and '60s. At various times throughout the evening bartenders and staffers will perform skits, dance, or lip sync to their favorite songs. There's a buffet for grazing from 5 to 8pm Wednesday through Saturday. The club is open Monday through Friday from 5pm to 2am, Saturday from 7:30pm to 2am.

The Market St. Mill

99 South Market St. ☎ **803/722-6100.**

A live band performs each Tuesday, Friday, and Saturday evening from 11pm until closing, and on every evening there's a band playing in the patio from 5:30 to 10:30pm. A limited menu features pizza, pasta, steak, sandwiches, and a variety of salads. Happy hour with reduced prices is from 4 to 7pm daily. The club is open Sunday and Monday from noon to 2am and Tuesday through Saturday from 11am to 2am. After 10pm only those 21 years of age or older are admitted.

Tommy Condon's Irish Pub

160 Church St. ☎ **803/577-3818.** No cover.

In a restored warehouse in the City Market area, this Irish pub—also a family restaurant—is filled with memorabilia of Old Ireland. The bartender turns out such drinks as a Leprechaun punch or a glass of real Irish ale, and most definitely Irish coffee. The menu offers not only Irish food but Low Country specials such as shrimp and grits or jambalaya. The pub hosts a full bar with happy hours, featuring reduced drink prices from 5 to 7pm Monday through Friday. Live Irish entertainment is on tap Wednesday through Sunday from 8:30pm until closing. Regular hours are daily from 11:30am to midnight, with no food served after 10pm.

THE BAR SCENE

Acme Bar & Grill

413 Coleman Blvd., Mt. Pleasant. ☎ **803/884-1949.**

This is one of the most popular after-dark venues in Mt. Pleasant for professional twenty- and thirtysomethings to mix and mingle. There's a nightly happy hour from 4 to 7pm with half-price drinks.

Arizona's Inside

14 Chapter St. ☎ **803/577-5090.**

Arizona's is a great place to people-watch. The chef serves seafood but specializes in Southwestern cuisine and "cowboy steaks." There's a large bar with a Friday night happy hour from 4 to 7pm, when the place is packed.

Charleston Sports Pub & Grill

4 Linguard Alley. ☎ **803/577-8887.**

This popular sports bar is located smack in the center of activity at South Market Street. Inside, you'll find two dozen TV monitors so you won't miss a split second of any sports action, and the decor consists of lots of sports memorabilia. There are also tables outside, with some under cover.

First Shot Bar

In the Mills House Hotel, 115 Meeting St. ☎ **803/577-2400.**

Our preferred watering hole is this old standby where we've seen such visiting celebrities as Gerald Ford and Elizabeth Taylor (not together) over the years. The bar is one of the most elegant in Charleston—a comfortable place to sink back and enjoy a relaxed cocktail. If you get hungry, the kitchen will whip you up some shrimp and grits.

The Griffon

18 Vendue Range. ☎ **803/723-1700.**

A lot of Scotch and beer is consumed at this ever-popular Irish pub. A full array of home-cooked specials from the old country are served as well, including such pub grub favorites as steak pies, bangers and mash, and the inevitable fish and chips. On Friday and Saturday night, seafood is available.

Mike Calder's Pub

288 King St. ☎ **803/577-0123.**

Mike Calder's place is a local favorite, with 15 imported beers on tap from England, Scotland, and Ireland. The bartender's special is a Bloody Mary. A menu offers soups, salads, sandwiches, and steaks, and on Friday and Saturday nights seafood is featured. All the food is homemade.

Vicery's Bar & Grill

15 Beaufain. ☎ **803/577-5300.**

This is one of the most popular gathering places in Charleston for young people, especially students. It's also a good dining choice, with an international menu, including jerk chicken and gazpacho. What makes it popular is its 16-ounce frosted mug of beer for $1, and the convivial atmosphere.

Wild Wing Café

36 North Market St. ☎ **803/722-WING.**

This is the hot spot in the market district. The bar is busy, really busy, most nights. The atmosphere is casual, as is the dress of the mostly young clientele, and the food is your typical chicken-wings-and-quesadillas type fare. After all those hot, spiced wings, the cold beer keeps flowing. Napkins—big terrycloth numbers—help you wipe up all the grease on those sticky fingers.

A DINNER CRUISE

The most memorable evening in Charleston might be aboard the luxury yacht *Spirit of Charleston,* enjoying a 3-hour cruise that feature a four-course dinner and live entertainment and dancing, as the vessel glides through Charleston harbor. The cost is $32.95, not including drinks or service. Departures are from City Marina on Lockwood Boulevard. For schedules and bookings, contact **Fort Sumter Tours,** 205 King St. (☎ **803/722-1691**).

LATE-NIGHT BITES

Café Rainbow

282 King St. ☎ **803/853-9777.**

If you want a place to hang out and people-watch or perhaps meet someone in the evening, head for this café, with its casual, cheery ambience. Patrons are always playing chess on the large board in the front window, while others sit on sacks of coffee beans and watch. The menu is light, with items priced from $1.50 to $3.95. Try a quiche, croissants with jam, homemade Belgian waffles with berries and nuts, muffins, or cookies; or you can visit just for coffee, caffe mocha, hot cocoa, or iced mochaccino.

Frannie's Diner

137 Market St. ☎ **803/723-7121.**

Step back to the 1950s where even at 3am you can order some of your favorite foods, the kind that Elvis used to fill up with. Breakfast is served around the clock. The decor is right out of the old diner days—red, white, and black with chrome-trimmed red booths, pink and blue neon, '50s photos, and a jukebox playing *Happy Days* favorites. On the menu is French toast, blueberry pancakes, sausage and gravy with biscuits, and a number of sandwich standards. The brownie with ice cream is the perennial Girl Scout dessert choice; wine and beer are also served.

Fulford-Egan Coffee & Tea House
231 Meeting St. ☎ **803/723-4374.**

Featured once in *National Geographic,* this house has been acknowledged as having the largest coffee accessory and teapot collection in the United States. The first floor is decorated with European memorabilia, and there are outdoor tables. More than 100 selections of tea and 70 different kinds of coffee are offered. The menu also offers pasta salads, soups both hot and cold, croissants, soft ice cream, and various breads, including Texas-style muffins. There's a retail shop upstairs, selling limited-edition teapots from Europe, among other items.

Kaminsky's Most Excellent Café
78 N. Market St. ☎ **803/853-8270.**

Following a night of jazz or blues, this is a good spot for resting your feet and ordering just the power boost you need to make it through the rest of the evening. The handsome bar offers a wide selection of wines and, out of the traffic flow, is ideal for people-watching. The desserts are sinful, especially the Italian cream cake and the mountain chocolate cake.

GAY & LESBIAN BARS

The Arcade
5 Liberty St. ☎ **803/722-5656.** Cover $2–$5.

Set in the heart of historic Charleston, on the premises of what was originally a 1930s movie theater, this is the largest and most high-energy dance bar in Charleston. Catering with equal ease to gay men and women, it features between two and four bars (depending on the night of the week). The atmosphere ranges from quiet and conversational to dance-a-holic and manic. Open Thursday through Sunday from 9:30pm to 3am.

Déja Vu II
445 Savannah Highway, West Ashley. ☎ **803/556-5588.** Cover $3–$5.

Opened in 1995, this is the newest, and some say, coziest and warmest "ladies' bar" in the Southeast. Rita Taylor, your host, transformed what was originally a supper club into a cozy enclave with two bars and live entertainment on weekends (usually from "all-girl" bands). The clientele is almost exclusively gay and 75% female. Gay men are welcome—the ambience is unpretentious and charming, and definitely not exclusionary to sympathetic patrons of any ilk. Platters of simple country food are offered if you're hungry. Open daily from 5pm to 2am.

Dudley's

346 King St. ☎ **803/723-2784.** Cover $1.

This is the coziest, clubbiest, and—in its low-key way—the most welcoming gay bar in Charleston. Some regulars compare it to a gay man's version of "Cheers," because of its wood paneling and brick interior, and its amused and bemused sense of blasé permissiveness. Most of the dialogue occurs on the street level where an advance call from nonmembers is considered necessary to guarantee admittance. Upstairs is a "game room" with pool tables and very few places to sit. Open daily from 4pm to 2am. (The cover is charged as a means of ensuring the establishment's status as a private club.)

3

Side Trips from Charleston

*F*rom historic small towns to the intriguing landscapes of South Carolina's barrier islands, Charleston is surrounded by wonderful places to explore. All of the following destinations can be seen as quick day trips, but we've recommended a few lodgings in case you decide to linger.

1 Isle of Palms

A residential community bordered by the Atlantic Ocean and lying 10 miles north of Charleston, this island, with its salt marshes and wildlife, has been turned into a vacation retreat. The attractions of Charleston are close at hand, but the Isle of Palms is also a self-contained destination, with shops, dining, an array of accommodations, plus two championship golf courses.

Charlestonians have been flocking to the island for holidays since 1898; the first hotel opened here in 1911. And what's the attraction? How about 7 miles of wide, white sandy beach? Sailing and windsurfing are popular, and you can even go crabbing and shrimping in the creeks.

I-26 intersects with I-526 heading directly to the island via the Isle of Palms Connector (S.C. 517).

WHERE TO STAY
✪ Wild Dunes Resort

Isle of Palms (P.O. Box 20575), Charleston, SC 29413. ☎ **800/845-8880** or 803/886-6000. Fax 803/886-2916. 280 villas, 24 cottages. A/C TV TEL. $129–$375 villa or cottage. Golf packages available. AE, MC, V. Free parking.

A bit livelier than Kiawah Island, its major competitor, this 1,600-acre resort has not only two widely acclaimed golf courses, but an array of other outdoor activities. The resort's own private beach stretches over $2^1/2$ miles. Set on landscaped grounds, this complex of villas lies on the north shore. Many families settle in here for a long stay, almost never venturing into Charleston. Guests are housed in condos, a series of cottages and villas, each individually decorated. Many have only one bedroom, but others as many as six. Villas and cottages are built along the shore, close to golf and tennis. Furnishings are done in a tasteful resort style, and units have kitchens, washer/dryers, and spacious bathrooms with dressing areas. Some of the best units have screened-in balconies.

Dining/Entertainment: T.G.I. Friday's is just one of the options for dining, along with a deli offering sandwiches and pizzas.

Facilities: Activities include surfcasting and an array of water sports. There's a racquet club, a yacht harbor on the Intracoastal Waterway, nature trails, and bicycling, plus children's programs. Tennis buffs find 19 hard-surface courts, and there are 20 pools in all.

2   Kiawah Island

This private residential and resort community, sprawling across 10,000 acres, lies 21 miles south of Charleston. Named for the Kiawah Indians who inhabited the islands in the 17th century, it today consists of two resort villages, East Beach and West Beach.

The community fronts a 10-mile stretch of Atlantic beach; magnolias, live oaks, pine forests, and acres of marsh blanket the island. The best beach is found at **Beachwalker County Park** on the southern end of the island. Go before noon on Saturday and Sunday, however, as the limited parking is usually gone by then. Canoe rentals are available for use on the Kiawah River, and the park offers not only a boardwalk, but bathrooms, showers, and a changing area.

Kiawah boasts many challenging golf courses, including one designed by Jack Nicklaus at Turtle Point (*Golf Digest* rates this one among the top 10 courses in South Carolina). Golf architect Pete Dye designed a $2^{1}/_{2}$-mile oceanfront course to host the 1991 PGA Ryder Cup Match. *Tennis* magazine rates Kiawah as one of the nation's top tennis resorts, with its 28 hard-surface or Har-tru clay courts. Anglers are also attracted to the island, especially in spring and fall.

WHERE TO STAY
Kiawah Island Resort

Kiawah Island (P.O. Box 12357), Charleston, SC 29412. ☎ **800/654-2924** or 803/768-2122. Fax 803/768-9386. 150 inn rms, 48 suites, 300 villas. A/C TV TEL. $145–$185 double; $145–$245 suite or villa. AE, DC, MC, V. Free parking.

The resort offers a wide range of accommodations, everything from rooms at the inn to villas with as many as four bedrooms. A self-contained community, the complex opened in 1976 at West Beach village. Since then East Beach village has joined the community, although West Beach is the only one with shops. Regular hotel-like rooms are available in four buildings, opening onto either the lagoon or the Atlantic. King-size or two double beds are available, along with private balconies and combination baths. Villas are casually furnished, with complete kitchens and such amenities as washers and dryers.

Dining/Entertainment: Several dining options await guests, at such rooms as the Jasmine Porch and Veranda, or perhaps Indigo House. Diners have tables facing the lagoon at the Park Café. Low Country and international dishes are featured.

3 Edisto Island

Isolated, and enveloped with a kind of melancholy beauty, Edisto lies some 45 miles south of Charleston. Named after its early Native American inhabitants, the island saw the arrival of the first Europeans—the Spanish—in the 1500s. In the century that followed, the English arrived, forming permanent settlements and cultivating indigo and rice. But by the late 18th century, sea island cotton was the crop that would bring wealth to the islanders. Some plantations from that era are still standing.

Edisto Island today attracts families from Charleston and the Low Country intent on a beach holiday, as the island is known for its profusion of white sandy beaches. Water sports include surfcasting, deep-sea fishing, shrimping, and sailing.

To get there, take U.S. 17 west from Charleston for 21 miles, then head south along Hwy. 174 the rest of the way.

Edisto Beach State Park, State Cabin Road, sprawls across 1,255 acres, opening onto 2 miles of beach. There's also a well-signposted nature trail. You can bring a picnic lunch to be enjoyed under one of the shelters. In addition, the park has 75 camping sites with full hookups, and 28 with no hookups. Camp sites cost $17.28 per night (the same price for RV hookups). Five cabins are available for rent as well, ranging from $52 to $57 daily. There are two restaurants within walking distance of the camp, plus a general store nearby.

WHERE TO STAY

Cassina Point Plantation Bed & Breakfast

1642 Clark Rd. (P.O. Box 535), Edisto Island, SC 29438. ☎ **803/ 869-2535.** 4 rms (each with half bath, 2 full hall baths outside rooms). A/C. $105–$125 double. Rates include full breakfast. No credit cards.

Overlooking fields where sea cotton once flourished, this former antebellum plantation was built in the late 1840s as a wedding gift. But by the 1860s, it was occupied by Federal troops during the Civil War. Recently restored, it offers four well-furnished guest rooms, without phones or TV (those items are found in the lounge). Antiques fill the rooms, which offer double beds except one with two singles. This is a nonsmoking environment, and young children aren't encouraged. On the tidal creek about 8 miles from the beach, the B&B rents canoes ($10 per day) and kayaks ($15 to $25 per day).

Fairfield Ocean Ridge

King Cotton Rd., Edisto Island, SC 29438. ☎ **800/845-8500** or 803/869-2561. 40 units. A/C MINIBAR TV TEL. One-bedroom villa $190; Two-bedroom villa $240; Two-bedroom deluxe villa $270. AE, DISC, DC, MC, V.

At the south end of Edisto Beach, this 300-acre resort is a favorite summer rendezvous for the Charleston family trade. Birders also flock to the area, as do beachcombers, and there is plenty of good fishing along with summer picnics. Golf, jet skiing, parasailing, and tennis are among the other recreational activities. A time-share resort, Fairfield rents villas and condos ranging from a one-bedroom villa up to a two-bedroom duplex villa with sleeping lofts. Each villa is complete with kitchen and is individually furnished according to the owner's taste. Most rooms have VCRs, and fax service is available at the rental office. There is a restaurant on the premises, serving a free continental breakfast only on Mondays.

WHERE TO DINE

The Old Post Office

Hwy. 174 at Store Creek. ☎ **803/869-2339.** Main courses $17–$20. MC, V. Tues–Sat 6–10pm. SOUTHERN.

This is the most prominent building you're likely to see as you drive across Edisto Island, about 5 miles from the beach. As its weathered clapboards and old-time appearance imply, this structure was originally conceived as a combined post office and general store. Partners David Gressette and Philip Bardin, who transformed the premises in 1988, prepare a worthwhile compendium of Low Country southern cuisine, and serve it in copious portions. Try Island corn-and-crabmeat chowder; Orangeburg onion sausage with black-bean sauce; scallops and grits with mousseline sauce; fried quail with duck-stock gravy; and "fussed-over" pork chops with hickory-smoked tomato sauce and mousseline. All main courses are accompanied by salads, vegetables, and bread.

Summerville **83**

4 Summerville

This historic town, where Charlestonians used to go to escape summer heat and malaria, is listed on the National Register of Historic Places. Located 25 miles north of Charleston via I-26 (Exit 199), it's a treasure trove of buildings from the 19th century—mainly 1850 to the early 1900s—many built by Low Country rice planters. Gardens of azaleas, wisteria, and camellias bloom in town.

Today, Summerville is known for its old country stores and antique shops—most on East Richardson Avenue, Main Street, and Old Trolley Road. Names of stores range from Antiques 'n Stuff to Granny's Attic—corny but appropriate. The town maintains two lighted recreational fields, three parks, and four playgrounds with six tennis courts within the town limits. Picnics are possible at **Givhans Ferry State Park** nearby and at **Francis Beidler Forest.**

WHERE TO STAY

Woodlands Resort & Inn

125 Parsons Rd., Summerville, SC 29483. ☎ **800/774-9999** or 803/875-2600. Fax 803/875-2603. 20 rms, 8 suites. A/C TV TEL. Sun–Thurs $175–$225 double, $200–$275 suite; Fri–Sat $225–$275 double, $250–$325 suite. Rates include full breakfast. No children under 12. AE, DISC, DC, MC, V.

Only a 30-minute drive from Charleston, this Classical Revival building was constructed in 1906. With white pillars out front, it's one of the finest places to stay in the Low Country outside of town. Woodlands, now restored and turned into a hotel, stands on 42 landscaped acres. Regular bedrooms are furnished in traditional style with king- or queen-size beds, a sitting area, cable TV with VCR, and large baths. The inn also offers eight more luxurious suites, roomy and tasteful, with large Jacuzzi tubs.

Dining/Entertainment: A full Southern breakfast—including grits, if you want them—arrives every morning, and, later in the day, you can sample Low Country cooking in the full-service, 85-seat restaurant that attracts many locals.

Services: Room service, laundry.

Facilities: Croquet, tennis, swimming, and biking are free; golf is available nearby.

WHERE TO DINE

Alexander's Station

116 South Main St. ☎ **803/875-1100.** Main courses $10.95–$16.95. Daily 11:30am–2:30pm; Sun–Thurs 5:30–10pm, Fri–Sat 5:30–10:30pm. MC, V. LOW COUNTRY.

In the heart of things, opening onto the town square, this restaurant evokes the era when rice planters and their families came to Summerville by train to escape the heat at home. Opened by the same owners who made a name for themselves at 82 Queen Street in Charleston, Alexander's specializes in the area's best Southern cookery, including barbecued shrimp and grits, she-crab soup, or (to get you going) Southern black-bean soup. At night, the chef showcases his fried seafood (in low-cholesterol oil), McClellanville crabcakes, and Low Country pork loin.

5 Beaufort

Below Charleston and 30 miles north of Hilton Head, Beaufort (that's "BEW-fort") is an old seaport with narrow streets shaded by huge live oaks and lined with 18th-century homes (the oldest was built in 1717 and is at Port Republic and New Streets). This was the second area in North America discovered by the Spanish (1520), the site of the first fort (1525) on the continent, and of the first attempted settlement (1562).

And if you find that Beaufort looks familiar, that's probably because this town has been used as a setting for several films, including *The Big Chill, Forrest Gump,* and *The Prince of Tides.*

ESSENTIALS

Getting There   If you're traveling from the north, take I-95 to Exit 33, then follow the signs to the center of Beaufort. From the south, including Hilton Head, take I-95 to Exit 8 and follow the signs.

Visitor Information   The **Beaufort Chamber of Commerce,** 1006 Bay St. (P.O. Box 910), Beaufort, SC 29901 (☎ 803/524-3163), has self-guided tours and lots of other information about this historic town. Visitor center hours are Monday through Saturday from 9:30am to 5:30pm, and Sunday from 10am to 5pm.

If you plan to come in early to mid-October, write the **Historic Beaufort Foundation,** P.O. Box 11, Beaufort, SC 29901, for specific dates and detailed information on their 3 days of antebellum house-and-garden tours.

EXPLORING THE TOWN

The Spirit of Old Beaufort, 210 Scott's St. (☎ 803/525-0459), takes you on a journey through the old town, exploring local history, architecture, horticulture, and Low Country life. You'll see houses not accessible on other tours. Your host, clad in period costume, will guide you for 2 hours Tuesday through Saturday from 10am to noon and 1:30 to 3:30pm. The cost is adults $10, teens $7.50 (children 12 and under free). Tours depart from just behind the John Market Verdier House Museum.

The **John Market Verdier House Museum,** 801 Bay St. (☎ **803/524-6334**), is a restored 1790 house that's been partially furnished to depict the life of a merchant planter from 1790–1825. It's one of the best examples of the Federal period and was once known as the Lafayette building, since the Marquis de Lafayette is said to have spoken from here in 1825. It is open Tuesday through Saturday from 11am to 3pm, charging adults $4; children $2.

St. Helen's Episcopal Church, 501 Church St. (☎ **803/524-3163**), traces its origin back to 1712. Visitors, admitted free Monday through Saturday from 10am to 4pm, can see its classic interior and visit its graveyard, where tombstones served as operating tables during the Civil War.

In the surrounding area, the most interesting excursion is to **Parris Island** (☎ **803/525-3650**), 10 miles south of the center of Beaufort. This is the famous U.S. Marine Corps Recruit Depot, with a visitor center (go to Building 283). Hours are daily 10am to 4:30pm. There you can learn about driving and bus tours (free) around the grounds, where you see an Iwo Jima monument, a monument to the Spanish settlement of Santa Elena (1521), and a memorial to Jean Ribaut, the French Huguenot and founder of Charlesfort in 1562. Begun in 1891, the depot grew to become the main recruit training center in the U.S. Swords drills and parade marches are interesting to watch, and even better is the music of the Marine Corps Band.

The **Parris Island Museum** (☎ **803/525-2951**) tells the history of the island from 1521. Admission is free; open daily from 10am to 4:30pm.

Impressions

Beaufort, June 6, 1863

Dear Mother,

This is an odd sort of place. All the original inhabitants are gone—and the houses are occupied by Northerners.

Your loving son,
Robert Gould Shaw

WHERE TO STAY

Bay Street Inn

601 Bay St., Beaufort, SC 29902. ☎ **803/522-0050.** 8 rms. $95–$165 double. Rates include continental breakfast. AE, DISC, MC, V.

One of the most elegant historic homes in town, the Bay Street Inn looks across a quiet road toward a view of a saltwater estuary. Originally built in 1852 by owners of a plantation on nearby Dataw Island, and later used by Union troops during the Civil War as an officers' club, it was sold for back taxes, fell into disrepair, and hobbled along as a private home until someone transformed the place into a B&B in the 1980s. Our favorite room is no. 7, a cellar accommodation outfitted incongruously (but charmingly) in a Southwestern theme. Seven of the rooms have working fireplaces, and many have hookups for TV sets.

✪ The Beaufort Inn

809 Port Republic St., Beaufort, SC 29902. ☎ **803/521-9000.** Fax 803/521-9500. 15 rms. A/C MINIBAR TV TEL. $120–$185 double. Rates include continental breakfast. AE, MC, V.

This is the most appealing hotel in Beaufort, the preferred lodging for whatever movie star happens to be shooting a film in town at the time. Originally built in 1907 by a prosperous lawyer, it became the town's most respectable inn just after the stock market crash of 1929. Today, the woodwork and moldings inside are among the finest in Beaufort, and its circular, four-story staircase is the subject of numerous photographs and architectural awards. Bedrooms, each decorated in a brightly colored style different from its neighbors, are conversation pieces, each carefully crafted and comfortable.

Rhett House Inn

1009 Craven St., Beaufort, SC 29902. ☎ **803/524-9030.** Fax 803/524-1310. 10 rms. A/C TV TEL. $125–$175 double. Rates include continental breakfast. AE, MC, V.

Spacious and graceful, this inn places more emphasis on nostalgia and glamour than any other bed-and-breakfast in town. It has more style and better furnishings than many other B&Bs in this part of the state. None of this occurred effortlessly, as a dialogue with the owners will quickly reveal. Breakfast and afternoon tea are included in the price, and there's an in-house restaurant open to the public Wednesday through Saturday from 6:30 to 9pm, although advance reservations are required.

Sea Island Inn

1015 Bay St., Beaufort, SC 29902. ☎ **800/528-1234** or 803/522-2090. Fax 803/521-4858. 43 rms. A/C TV TEL. $69–$89 double. Rates include continental breakfast. AE, DC, MC, V.

This place was built in 1959 on the site of one of Beaufort's most historic and venerable hotels. Nary a shred of the original building still exists. What you'll find is a basic two-story motel, fairly unremarkable in appearance except for the touches of cast iron in the facade facing the street, and elegant brown bricks that despite their newness manage to look antique. Very few of the rooms have sea views: Most overlook a small swimming pool separated from the rest of the motel within a brick-sided courtyard. Though the rooms are nothing special, they're comfortable and clean.

Two Suns Inn

1705 Bay St., Beaufort, SC 29902. ☎ **800/532-1244** or 803/522-1122. Fax 803/522-1122. 5 rms. TEL. $110–$122 double. Rates include full breakfast. AE, MC, V.

It was built in 1917 as one of the grandest homes in its prosperous neighborhood, with views over the coastal road and the tidal flatlands beyond. Every imaginable modern convenience was added, including a baseboard vacuum-cleaning system, an electric callbox, steam heat, and—most shocking of all—a conspicuous lack of any entrance vestibule. In 1943, the colonial revival building was sold to the Beaufort Board of Education as housing for unmarried female teachers, and allowed to run down. In 1990, a retired music teacher and band leader, Ron Kay, with his wife Carroll, bought the place as part of "an accidental stop along the way to North Carolina" and transformed it into a cozy and warmly decorated B&B. Part of its appeal stems from its lack of pretension, as a quick glance at the homey bedrooms and uncomplicated furnishings will quickly show.

A NEARBY RESORT

Flat and marshy, with raised outcroppings of ancient trees and sand dunes, the 3,000 acres which comprise Fripp Island, 19 miles south of Beaufort on U.S. 21, were never inhabited by European settlers, partly because of its waterlogged soil, mangrove swamps, and bugs. Mapmakers define it as the sea island most distant from the South Carolina mainland, and botanists and ecologists revel in the way it has to be reached via U.S. 21, which meanders through the marshes and creeks of three other islands. A refuge of waterfowl and reptiles, it slumbered throughout the era when Hilton Head and its neighbors nearby were burgeoning. But in 1990, an earlier (failed) attempt at development was renewed when a new group of investors bought the entire island for $8 million, poured another $10 million into its development, and began the long and difficult task of pulling the complex into the 20th century.

Fripp Island Resort

One Tarpon Blvd., Fripp Island, SC 29920. ☎ **800/845-4100** or 803/838-3535. Fax 803/828-2733. 220 units. A/C TV TEL. $85 suite with kitchenette; villas and cottages with kitchen, $170–$180 for one bedroom; $180–$225 for two and three bedrooms; $220–$270 for four bedrooms. Discounts for stays of one week, 15% reductions for stays from Nov–Apr. AE, MC, V.

This sprawling resort takes up the whole island, and access is limited to guests. After you check into a Cape Cod–inspired main building, site of a restaurant, you're shown to your villa, ranging from one to four bedrooms. The style of the villas—perhaps not as controlled as they should be—range from Key West–style clapboard to California marina modern. The decor depends on the taste of the individual villa owner and may not agree with yours. The resort doesn't achieve the level of some of its major competitors on Hilton Head such as Palmetto Dunes or the Westin. But natural beauty abounds on the island, and there are extensive bicycle paths, 10 tennis courts, sandy beaches and dunes, scattered swimming pools, and an 18-hole golf course. At least four different restaurants are scattered about. Getting away from it all in a rugged Low Country setting remains Fripp's greatest appeal.

WHERE TO DINE

The Anchorage

1103 Bay St. ☎ **803/524-9392.** Reservations needed. Main courses $17.50–$21. AE, DC, DISC, MC, V. Mon–Sat 11am–2:30pm and 5:30–8:30pm. AMERICAN/SEAFOOD.

In a mansion dating from 1770, this is the most atmospheric choice in town, located in a landmark house overlooking Beaufort River. The place looks as if it was ripped directly from the pages of Pat Conroy's *The Great Santini*. Once the home of a rich Port Royal plantation owner, the stately residence today offers a well-prepared and elegantly served cuisine, including a Low Country seafood platter and perhaps the best seafood gumbo in town.

✪ Beaufort Inn Restaurant

In the Beaufort Inn, 809 Port Republic St. ☎ **803/621-9000.** Reservations recommended. Main courses $13.95–$26.95. AE, MC, V. Daily 6–10pm; Sun 8am–1pm as well. INTERNATIONAL.

Stylish and urbane, and awash with colonial lowland references, this is a carefully decorated restaurant where many locals like to come for special celebrations or important business dinners. Set within the previously recommended inn, it features candlelit dinners with such vegetarian main courses as a roasted pepper a nd eggplant torte. Meat courses include chicken piccata with artichokes and sundried tomatoes, and grilled filet mignon with herbal gorgonzola butter and shiitake mushrooms. And check out the traditional crispy whole flounder with a strawberry/watermelon chutney.

Emily's

906 Port Republic St. ☎ **803/522-1866.** Reservations recommended. Tapas $2.50–$8; main courses $17–$21. AE, MC, V. Drinks and tapas Mon–Sat 4:30–11pm; main courses Mon–Sat 6–10pm. INTERNATIONAL.

This is our favorite restaurant in Beaufort, a warm spot whose ambience and attitude almost remind us of a restaurant in Scandinavia. That's hardly surprising, since its bearded owner is an emigré from Sweden who happened to feel comfortable in the South Carolina lowlands after years of life at sea. Some folks just go to the bar for tapa-sampling. Tapas include miniature portions of tempura shrimp, fried scallops, stuffed peppers, and at least 20 others. At table, menu items might include a cream of mussel and shrimp soup rich enough for a main course; filet "black and white" (filets of beef and pork served with Jarnaise sauce); duck with orange sauce; Weiner schnitzel; and a changing assortment of catch of the day, all served in stomach-stretching portions.

ⓢ New Gadsby Tavern

822 Bay St. ☎ **803/525-1800.** Reservations not necessary. Main courses $4.95–$18.95. AE, DC, DISC, MC, V. Mon–Sat 11:30am–10pm, Sun 11am–9pm. LOW COUNTRY/INTERNATIONAL.

It's the longest and narrowest dining room in town, an oak trimmed, nautically inspired tavern that runs, much like a railroad car, between the town's main street and the Henry Chambers Waterfront Park. You'll have a different perspective on this place depending on which of the two entrances you enter, but don't overlook the possibility of having a drink in the 1890s-style pub near the seafront entrance of this place. The food is hearty, tavern-style fare: she-crab soup, barley bean shrimp salad, peel-and-eat shrimp, jambalaya, Daufuskie crabcakes, and house-style oyster pie. Children's menus are offered (simple dishes like spaghetti or burgers), as well as 10 kinds of sandwiches.

4

Hilton Head

*T*he largest sea island between New Jersey and Florida, and one of America's great resort meccas, Hilton Head is surrounded by the Low Country, where all the romance, beauty, and graciousness of the Old South survive. The coastline is among the most scenic in the Southeast. Broad, white sandy beaches are warmed by the Gulf Stream, and their rolling dunes are lined by towering pines and wind-sculpted live oaks and palmettos, all draped in Spanish moss. Graceful sea oats wave in the wind, their presence anchoring the beaches.

The subtropical climate here makes all this beauty the ideal setting for golf and fishing. Spring arrives early and summer lingers until late October. Far more sophisticated and upscale than Myrtle Beach and the Grand Strand, Hilton Head depends on 12 miles of beautiful, uncrowded beach to draw visitors. Some of the finest saltwater fishing on the East Coast is found in the surrounding waters and in the Gulf Stream some 60 miles offshore. Today the island's "plantations" (as most resort areas here call themselves) still preserve something of the leisurely lifestyle that's always held sway here, and offer it to all comers.

Although it covers only 42 square miles (it's 12 miles long, and 5 miles wide at its widest point), Hilton Head feels spacious, thanks to judicious planning from the start of its development in 1952. And that's a blessing, since about half a million resort guests visit annually (the permanent population is about 25,000). The broad beaches on its ocean side, sea marshes on the sound, and natural wooded areas of live and water oak, pine, bay, and palmetto trees in between have all been carefully preserved amid the commercial explosion. This lovely setting attracts artists, writers, musicians, theater groups, and craftspeople. The only "city" (of sorts) is Harbour Town, at Sea Pines Plantation, a Mediterranean-style cluster of shops and restaurants.

1 Essentials

GETTING THERE

It's easy to fly into Charleston and drive to Hilton Head. See chapter 1 for complete details on all the airlines, and chapter 2 for details on car rentals at the airport. (Hilton Head is only about 65 miles south of Charleston.) If you're driving from other points south or north, it's easy to exit off I-95 to reach the island. It's also just 52 miles northeast of Savannah and located directly on the Intracoastal Waterway.

VISITOR INFORMATION

The **Island Visitors' Information Center,** Hwy. 248 at Hwy. 46 (☎ **803/757-4472**), is found just before you cross over from the mainland. It offers a free "Where to Go" booklet, including a visitors' map and guide. Hours are 9am to 6pm daily.

The **Hilton Head Visitors' and Convention Bureau** (Chamber of Commerce), 1 Chamber Dr. (☎ **803/785-3673**), offers free maps of the area and will assist you in finding places of interest and outdoor activities. It will not, however, make hotel reservations. Hours are Monday through Friday from 8:30am to 5:30pm, Saturday 10am to 4pm, and Sunday noon to 4pm.

GETTING AROUND

U.S. 278 is the divided highway that runs the length of the island. If you'd like to leave the driving to someone else, **Yellow Cab** (☎ **803/686-6666**) has flat two-passenger rates determined by zone; an additional person is charged $2 extra.

SPECIAL EVENTS

Springfest is a March festival featuring seafood, live music, stage shows, and tennis and golf tournaments. In early or mid-April, top tennis players congregate for the *Family Circle* **Magazine Cup Tennis Tournament**, held at the Sea Pines Racquet Club. Outstanding PGA golfers also descend on the island in mid-April for the **MCI Heritage Classic** at Harbour Town Golf Links. To herald fall, the **Hilton Head Celebrity Golf Tournament** is held on Labor Day weekend at Palmetto Dunes and Sea Pines Plantation.

2   Beaches, Golf, Tennis & Other Outdoor Pursuits

You can have an active vacation here any time of year; Hilton Head's subtropical climate ranges in temperature from the 50s to the mid-80s in summer. And if you've had your fill of historic sights in Savannah or Charleston, don't worry—the "attractions" on Hilton Head mainly consist of nature preserves, beaches, and other places to play.

Though it was not officially open when we last visited, the **Environmental Museum of Hilton Head** (☎ 803/689-6767) is slated to host seven separate walks and guided tours of the island. Tours will go along island beaches and explore the salt marshes, stopping at Native American sites and the ruins of old forts or long-gone plantations. Most of the emphasis will be on the ecology of local plants and animals. Fees are scheduled at $5 for adults and $3 for children ages 5–12 (4 and under free). For reservations, contact the museum Monday through Saturday from 10am to 5pm, or Sunday from noon to 4pm.

BEACHES

Travel and Leisure ranked Hilton Head's beaches as "among the most beautiful in the world," and we concur. The island offers some 12 miles of white sandy beaches, plus others fronting Calobogue and Port Royal sounds, all set against a backdrop of natural dunes, live oaks, palmettos, and tall Carolina pines. The sands are extremely firm, providing a good surface for biking, hiking, jogging, and beach games. In summer, watch for the endangered loggerhead turtles that lumber ashore at night to bury their eggs there.

At high tide, many of the beaches still remain wide for most activities, except biking, of course. At low tide, the width of the island's beaches is often enormous.

All beaches on Hilton Head are public. Land bordering the beaches, however, is private property. Most beaches are safe, although there's sometimes an undertow at the northern end of the island. Lifeguards are posted at only the major beaches, and concessions are available to rent you beach chairs, umbrellas, and water-sports equipment.

There are four public entrances to Hilton Head's beaches. The main parking and changing areas are found on Folly Field Road, off U.S. 278 (the main highway) and at Coligny Circle, close to the

Hilton Head Island

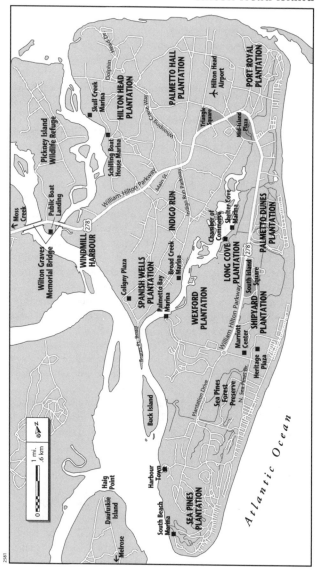

Holiday Inn. Other entrances (signposted) from U.S. 278 lead to Singleton and Bradley beaches.

The most frequently used is adjacent to Coligny Circle: the North and South Forest Beach (enter from Pope Avenue across from Lagoon Road). You'll have to use the parking lot opposite the Holiday Inn, paying a $4 daily fee until after 4pm. The adjacent Beach Park has toilets and a changing area, as well as showers, vending machines, and phones. It's a family favorite.

Of the beaches on the island's north, we prefer Folly Field Beach. Toilets, changing facilities, and parking are available.

GOLF

With 22 challenging golf courses on the island, and an additional nine within a 30-minute drive, this is heaven for professional and novice golfers. Some of golf's most celebrated architects, including George and Tom Fazio, Robert Trent Jones, Pete Dye, and Jack Nicklaus, have designed championship courses on the island. Wide, scenic fairways and rolling greens have earned Hilton Head the reputation of being the resort with the most courses on the "World's Best List."

Many of Hilton Head's championship golf courses are open to the public, including the **George Fazio Course** at Palmetto Dunes Resort (☎ **803/785-1138**), an 18-hole, 6,534-yard, par-70 course, named in the top 50 of *Golf Digest*'s "75 Best American Resort Courses." The course has been cited for its combined length and keen accuracy. The cost is $74.50 for 18 holes, and hours are daily from 7am to 6pm.

Old South Golf Links, 50 Buckingham Plantation Dr., Bluffton (☎ **800/257-8997** or 803/785-5353), is an 18-hole, 6,772-yard, par-72 course, open daily from 7:30am to 7pm. It's recognized as one of the "Top 10 New Public Courses" by *Golf Digest,* which cites its panoramic views and setting ranging from an oak forest to tidal salt marshes. Greens fees range from $48 to $55. The course lies on Hwy. 278, one mile before the bridge leading to Hilton Head.

Hilton Head National, Hwy. 278 (☎ **803/842-5900**), is a Gary Player Signature Golf Course, including a full-service pro shop and a grill and driving range. It's an 18-hole, 6,779-yard, par-72 course with gorgeous scenery that evokes Scotland. Greens fees range from $40 to $75, and hours are daily from 7am to 7pm.

Island West Golf Club, Hwy. 278 (☎ **803/689-6660**), was nominated by *Golf Digest* as "best new course of the year." With its backdrop of oaks, elevated tees, and rolling fairways, it's a challenging but playable 18-hole, 6,803-yard, par-72 course. Greens fees range from $33.60 to $49.50, and hours are from 7am to 6pm daily.

Harbour Town Golf Links, Sea Pines Resort (☎ 803/ 363-4485), home of the annual MCI Golf Course, is also outstanding. The panoramic views alone are worth the visit to this 18-hole, 6,916-yard, par-71 course. Its finishing hole fronts the waters of Calibogue Sound. Greens fees range from $88 to $172.20, and hours are daily from 7:20am to 6pm.

Ocean Course, Sea Pines Resort (☎ 803/842-1894), the island's first, is still favored by golfers as a resort classic. Its dramatic beachfront 15th hole is one of the most photographed on Hilton Head, with its views of the ocean. Renovated in 1995, the course is open daily from 7am to 6pm. It is an 18-hole, 6,933-yard, par-72 course. Greens fees are $64 for 18 holes.

The **Robert Trent Jones Course** at the Palmetto Dunes Resort (☎ 803/785-1138) is an 18-hole, 6,710-yard, par-72 course with a winding lagoon system that comes into play on 11 holes. The cost is $74.50 for greens fees for 18 holes, and hours are daily from 6:30am to 6pm.

TENNIS

Tennis magazine rated Hilton Head as one of its "50 Greatest U.S. Tennis Resorts." No other domestic destination can boast of a greater concentration of tennis facilities, with more than 300 courts ideal for beginners and intermediate and advanced players. The island has 19 tennis clubs, seven of which are open to the public. A wide variety of tennis clinics and daily lessons are also found here.

Sea Pines Racquet Club, Sea Pines Plantation (☎ 803/ 671-2494), has been ranked by *Tennis* magazine as a top-50 resort and was selected by the *Robb Report* as the best tennis resort in the U.S. The club has been the site of more nationally televised tennis events than any other location, and is the home of the *Family Circle* Magazine Cup Women's Tennis Championships. Tennis is free to guests of the hotel; otherwise, there's an $18 per-hour charge. There are 25 clay and 5 hard courts (hard courts are lit for night play).

Other leading tennis courts are found at **Port Royal Racquet Club,** Port Royal Plantation (☎ 803/686-8803), which offers 10 clay and 4 hard courts, plus 2 natural-grass courts with night games possible. Charges range from $18 to $20 per hour, and a one-day reservation is recommended.

Hilton Head Island Beach and Tennis Resort, 40 Folly Field Rd. (☎ 803/842-4402), features a dozen hard, lighted courts, costing only $8 per hour. Palmetto Dunes Tennis Center, **Palmetto Dunes Resort** (☎ **803/785-1152**), has 19 clay, 2 hard, and 4 artificial-grass courts (some lighted for night play). Hotel guests get a discount; otherwise, the charge is $18 per hour.

BIKING

Some beaches are firm enough to support wheels, and every year cyclists seem to delight in dodging the waves. Children on bicycles often appear to be racing the fast-swimming dolphins in the nearby water.

Enjoy Hilton Head's 25 miles of bicycle paths, but stay off U.S. 278, the main artery, which has far too much traffic.

Most hotels and resorts rent bikes to guests. If yours doesn't, try **Hilton Head Bicycle Co.,** off Sea Pines Circle at 11B Archer Dr. (☎ **803/686-6888**). Cost is $10 per day, but only $15 for 3 days. Baskets, child carriers, locks, and head gear are supplied, and the inventory includes cruisers, BMXs, mountain bikes, and tandems. Hours are Monday through Friday from 9am to 5pm, and Saturday and Sunday from 8am to 5pm.

Another rental possibility is **South Beach Cycles,** South Beach Marina Village in Sea Pines (☎ **803/671-2453**), offering beach cruisers, tandems, child carriers, and bikes for kids. There's free delivery island wide. Cost is $8 per half day, $10 for a full day, or $19 for 3 days. Hours are 9am to 6pm daily.

CRUISES & TOURS

To explore Hilton Head's waters, contact **Adventure Cruises, Inc.,** Shelter Cove Harbour, Suite G, Harbourside III (☎ **803/785-4558**). Outings include a nature cruise to Daufuskie Island (made famous by Pat Conroy's *The Water is Wide* and the film *Conrack*), with a guided safari on a jungle bus, costing adults $13 and children $7 round-trip. Departures are daily at 12:15pm, with a return to Hilton Head at 4:30pm.

Other popular cruises include a dolphin-watch cruise, 2 hours long, costing adults $10 and children $5. A sunset dinner cruise aboard the vessel *Adventure* costs adults $29 and children $15, including a 3-hour look at the Carolina Low Country and an all-you-can-eat buffet. Another offbeat cruise is the Murder Mystery Theatre aboard the vessel *Holiday,* costing $25 for adults and $12.50 for children. Passengers mingle with professional actors as the drama unfolds. It's presented in July and August on Thursdays at 9:30pm.

FISHING

No license is needed for saltwater fishing, although freshwater licenses are required for the island's lakes and ponds. The general season for fishing offshore is from April through October. Inland fishing is good between September and December. Crabbing is also popular; crabs are easy to catch in low water from docks, boats, or right off a bank.

Off Hilton Head you can go deep-sea fishing for amberjack, barracuda, sharks, and king mackerel. Many vessels are available for rent. We've recommended only those with the best track record. Foremost is **A Fishin' Mission,** 145 Squire Pope Rd. (☎ 803/ 785-9177), captained by Charles Getsinger aboard his 34-foot *Sportsfish.* Ice, bait, and tackle are included. Reservations are needed 1 to 2 days in advance. The craft carries up to six people, costing $300 for a half day, $450 for ³/₄ day, or $600 for a full day.

Top Shot, Harbour Town Marina (☎ 803/384-1314), also takes sports fishers out on its 33-foot vessel. Since 1991, this has been perhaps the most chartered boat on Hilton Head, requiring reservations at least 2 days in advance. The craft holds up to six fishers, costing $270 for 4 hours, $395 for 6 hours, and $520 for 8 hours.

A cheaper way to go deep-sea fishing—for only $32 per person—is aboard *The Drifter* (☎ 803/671-3060), a party boat that departs from the South Beach Marina Village. Ocean-bottom fishing is possible at an artificial reef 12 miles offshore.

KAYAK TOURS

Eco-Kayak Tours, Palmetto Bay Marina (☎ 803/785-7131), operates guided tours in Broad Creek. Four or five trips are offered each day; most cost $35 per person, and anyone from ages 7 to 82 is welcome to participate. The Eco-Explorer outing begins at 8am; the excursion lasts 2 hours and costs $17 for adults and $12 for children under 12. The tour explores the South Carolina Low Country environment, and you'll see local wildlife along the way.

Outside Hilton Head, the **Plaza at Shelter Cove** (☎ 803/ 686-6996) and **South Beach Marina Village** (☎ 803/671-2643) allow you to tour Low Country waterways by kayak. A 2-hour Dolphin Nature Tour, costing $35, takes you through the salt-marsh creeks of the Calibogue Sound or Pinckney Island Wildlife Refuge. Their Off-Island Day Excursion at $60 per person takes you

Hilton Head's Wonderful Wildlife

Hilton Head has preserved more of its wildlife than most other East Coast resort destinations. Birds and alligators roam freely beside lagoons and streams.

Hilton Head Island alligators are a prosperous lot and, in fact, the S.C. Department of Wildlife and Marine Resources uses the island as a resource to repopulate state parks and preserves where alligator numbers have greatly diminished. These creatures represent no danger if given a respectful distance. However, as strange as it may seem, some unsuspecting tourists, thinking the dead-still alligators are some sort of Disney props, often approach the reptiles and hit them or kick at them. This, obviously, isn't a wise thing to do.

Many of the large waterbirds that regularly grace the pages of nature magazines are natives of the island as well. More than 350 species of native American birds have been sighted on the island in the past decade, including the snowy egret, the large blue heron, and the osprey.

Here, too, is the white ibis with its strange curving beak, plus the smaller cattle egrets, which first arrived on Hilton Head Island in 1954 from a previous South American habitat. They follow the island cows, horses, and tractors to snatch grasshoppers and other insects.

The island's Audubon Society reports around 200 species every year in its annual bird count, but beyond the birdlife, Hilton Head also counts deer, bobcat, loggerhead turtles, otter, mink, and even a few wild boar among its residents. The bobcats are difficult to see, lurking in the deepest recesses of the forest preserves and in the undeveloped parts of the island. The deer, however, are

along the Carolina barrier islands and the surrounding marshlands. These trips are 6 to 8 hours long, and include lunch.

HORSEBACK RIDING

Riding through beautiful maritime forests and nature preserves is reason enough to visit Hilton Head. We like **Lawton Fields Stables,** 190 Greenwood Dr., Sea Pines (☎ **803/671-2586**), offering rides for both adults and kids through the Sea Pines Forest Preserve. (Kids ride ponies.) The cost is $30 per person for a ride lasting about one hour and 15 minutes. Reservations are necessary.

easier to encounter. One of the best places to watch these timid creatures is Sea Pines Plantation on the southern end of the island. With foresight, the planners of this plantation set aside areas for deer habitat back in the 1950s when the island master plan was conceived.

The loggerhead turtle, an endangered species, nests extensively along Hilton Head's 12 miles of wide, sandy beaches. Because the turtles choose the darkest hours of the night to crawl ashore and bury eggs in the soft sand, few visitors meet these 200-pound giants. To see them, you have to make a late-night visit to the beach in the summer.

Ever-present is the bottle-nosed dolphin, usually called a "porpoise" by those not familiar with the island's sea life. Hilton Head Plantation and Port Royal Plantation adjacent to Port Royal Sound are good places to meet up with the playful dolphin, as are Palmetto Dunes, Forest Beach, or any other oceanfront locations. In the summer, dolphins are inclined to feed on small fish and sea creatures very close to shore. Island beaches are popular with bikers, and this often offers a real point of interest for these curious fellows, who sometimes seem to swim along with the riders. Several excursion boats offer tours from the island and provide an opportunity for fellowship with dolphins. Shrimp boats are guaranteed to attract hungry dolphins.

The Sea Pines Forest Preserve, the Newhall Audubon Preserve, and the Pinckney Island Wildlife Preserve, just off the island between the bridges, are of interest to nature lovers. **The Museum of Hilton Head** hosts several guided nature tours and historical walks. For information, call the museum at **803/689-6767.**

Another possibility is the Waterside Ride offered by **Sandy Creek Stables,** Jonesville Road, off Spanish Wells Road (☎ **803/ 689-3423**). This stable offers six rides daily from 9am to 4:30pm, costing $25 per person for a guided tour stretching from 2 to 3 miles. Horses wet their feet (and yours too) in the tidal pools of the Intracoastal Waterway.

JOGGING

Our favorite place for jogging is a run through Harbour Town at Sea Pines just as the sun is going down. Later you can explore the marina and have a refreshing drink at one of the many outdoor cafés. In addition, the island offers lots of paved paths and trails that cut through scenic areas. Jogging along U.S. 278, the main artery, can be dangerous because of heavy traffic.

NATURE PRESERVES

The **Audubon-Newhall Preserve,** Palmetto Bay Road (☎ 803/ 671-2008), is a 50-acre preserve on the south end of the island. Here you can walk along marked trails to observe the wildlife in its native habitat. Guided tours are available when plant life is blooming. Except for public toilets, there are no amenities. Open from sunrise to sunset; free admission.

The second leading preserve is also in the south of the island. Sea Pines Forest Preserve, **Sea Pines Plantation** (☎ 803/671-6486), a 605-acre public wilderness with marked walking trails. Nearly all the birds and animals known to live on Hilton Head can be seen here (yes, there are alligators, but there are also less fearsome creatures, such as egrets, herons, osprey, and white-tailed deer). All trails lead to public picnic areas in the center of the forest. Maps and toilets available. Open from sunrise to sunset year round, except during the Heritage Golf Classic in early April. There's a $3 fee to enter for guests not staying at Sea Pines Resort.

PARASAILING

Para-Sail Hilton Head, Harbour Town (☎ 803/363-2628), takes you in a Sea Rocket powerboat for parasailing daily from 9am to 7pm. The cost is $35 per person for 400 feet of line, or $45 for 700 feet of line, and reservations are necessary. Catamaran rides for up to six passengers are also a feature, and sailing lessons are offered.

SAILING

Ascatsgrin Sailing Charters, Palmetto Bay Marina (☎ 803/ 785-7131), is the largest charter sailboat on Hilton Head. You can pack a picnic lunch and bring your cooler aboard for a 2-hour trip— in the morning or afternoon, or at sunset. The cost ranges from $15 to $17 for adults, with children charged from $10 to $12.

The *Spray,* based in Harbour Town (☎ 803/689-BOAT), is a replica of the boat in which Captain John Slocum solo circumnavigated the globe in 1895, making history as the first to accomplish this feat. It offers dolphin, sunset, and moonlight cruises daily. Cost is $17 for adults and $15 for children for day cruises, going up to $20 for adults and $18 for children at night. Reservations are suggested.

WINDSURFING

Just outside Hilton Head, **South Beach Marina Village** (☎ 803/
671-2643) offers board rentals available by the hour for $15.
Windsurfing lessons are also available costing $45 to $75 for 3- to
6-hour courses.

OTHER WATER SPORTS

H₂0, Harbour Town (☎ 803/671-4386), features Yamaha wave-
runner rentals costing $45 single or $55 double by the hour.
Parasailing is also a feature here, costing $45 per person for either
a 400-foot or 700-foot line. Waterskiing is a major summer
activity. Two hours cost $130 for up to 4 passengers, and surfing,
kneeboarding, and hydrosliding for one hour costs $70 for up to 2
participants. The center is located next to the lighthouse, and hours
are daily from 9am to 7pm.

3 Shopping

Hilton Head is a browsing heaven, with more than 30 shopping centers spread around the island, stocked with everything from designer
clothing to island and Low Country crafts.

The major shopping areas include **Pinelawn Mall** (at Matthews
Drive and U.S. 278), with more than 30 shops and half a dozen
restaurants; and **Coligny Plaza** (at Coligny Circle), with more than
60 shops, a movie theater, foodstands, and several good restaurants.

We've found some of the best bargains in the South at **Low
Country Factory Outlet Village** (☎ 803/837-4339), on Hwy.
278 at the gateway to Hilton Head. Here are more than 45 factory
stores, including Laura Ashley, Brooks Brothers, and J. Crew. Hours
of most shops in complexes are Monday through Saturday from
10am to 9pm and Sunday noon to 6pm.

ART

Altermann & Morris Galleries
38 New Orleans Rd. ☎ 803/842-4433.

A wide collection of 19th- and 20th-century American paintings and
sculpture is offered here. The gallery is strong on Western masters
and cowboy art, with still lifes, frontier landscapes, and genre scenes.
Open Monday through Friday from 10am to 5pm, and Saturday
from 10am to 6pm.

Moonshell Gallery & Studios
At Sea Pines Plantation, 224 South Sea Pines Dr. ☎ 803/671-2262.

This is one of the island's leading art galleries, displaying the work of more than two dozen painters, craftspeople, and sculptors in a 2,400-square-foot gallery. Exhibitions change frequently. Open Tuesday through Friday from 11am to 5pm, and Saturday from 1 to 5pm.

BOOKS

Book Warehouse

Festival Centre, next to Publix. ☎ **803/689-9419.**

This outlet offers new books sometimes at discounts of 50% to 90% off publisher's retail. Bestsellers, history books, children's books, cookbooks, and computer books are sold, with profits given to the Cancer Research Department at Emory University Hospital. Open Monday through Saturday from 10am to 9pm, and Sunday from noon to 6pm.

GIFTS & CRAFTS

Harbour Town Crafts

Harbour Town. ☎ **803/671-3643.**

In the most scenic spot on the island, this store offers dozens of gifts and decorative items along with handcrafted jewelry. The famed Low Country sweetgrass baskets are also for sale here, but be warned that prices are high. Open daily from 10am to 10pm (closes at 6pm in winter).

GOLD & JEWELRY

The Goldsmith Shop

3 Lagoon Rd. (off Pope Avenue). ☎ **803/785-2538.**

Here you'll find the exquisite work of Gary Fronczak, who crafts many of the items sold here. The shop is known for its signature island charms; Gary can create a piece just for you. Open Monday through Saturday from 9:30am to 5:30pm.

Forsythe Jewelers

311 Sea Pines Center. ☎ **803/671-7070.**

Three generations of the Forsythe family have been selling one-of-a-kind pieces of jewelry, along with fine watches and unusual gifts, since 1927. Open Monday through Friday from 10am to 6pm, and Saturday 10am to 5:30pm.

PORCELAIN & CHINA

Villeroy & Boch

Low Country Factory Village, Hwy. 278. ☎ **803/837-2566.**

This is the best center for bone china, quality porcelain, and crystal. Gift items and even heirloom pieces are for sale. Open Monday through Saturday from 10am to 9pm, and Sunday from noon to 6pm.

SPORTS EQUIPMENT
Players World
The Market Place. ☎ **803/842-5100.**

The island's best-equipped sports store is a 10,000-square-foot emporium, with all sorts of tennis gear, along with beachwear and plenty of athletic footwear. Open Monday through Saturday from 10am to 9pm (earlier closings off-season) and Sunday from 1 to 6pm.

WILDLIFE PRINTS
The Hammock Company
20 Jefferson St., City Market. ☎ **800/344-4264** or 803/686-3636.

This outlet specializes in limited edition and original wildlife prints. Each print is numbered and signed. There's also a catalogue of prints available. Open Monday through Saturday from 9am to 9pm, and Sunday from 10am to 7pm in summer. The rest of the year's hours are Monday through Saturday from 9am to 8pm, and Sunday from 10am to 6pm.

4 Accommodations

There are more than 3,000 hotel and motel rooms on the island, plus 6,000 villas. Hilton Head has some of the finest hotel properties in the Deep South, and prices are high—unless you book into one of the motels run by national chains. Most places will discount rates from November through March, and golf and tennis packages are offered almost everywhere. Instead of paying the typical rack rates (off-the-street bookings), always ask about special discounts when booking, or else get your travel agent to search for a deal.

The big news in the near future will be the opening of Disney's 102-unit **Hilton Head Island Resort,** themed in classic Carolina island-style architecture; it's currently under construction on Longview Island at Shelter Cove Harbour. Vacation homes on the 15-acre island will accommodate 4, 8, or 12 guests, ranging from deluxe bedrooms to three-bedroom, four-bath grand villas. For information about its opening, call **800/800-9100.**

The oldest and most comprehensive central reservation service on the island, **Hilton Head Central Reservation Service,** P.O. Box

5312, Hilton Head Island, SC 29938 (☎ **800/845-7018** in the U.S. and Canada), can book you into any hotel room or villa on the island, and there's no fee. Hours are Monday through Saturday 9am to 5pm.

Another option is renting a private home, villa, or condo—a great choice for families if it fits into their budget. For up-to-date availability, rates, and bookings, contact **Island Rentals and Real Estate,** P.O. Box 5915, Hilton Head Island, SC 29938 (☎ **800/845-6134** or 803/785-3813). The toll-free number is in operation 24 hours, but office hours are Monday through Saturday from 8:30am to 6pm (earlier closing on some Saturdays, especially in winter).

VERY EXPENSIVE
Hyatt Regency Hilton Head

In Palmetto Dunes Plantation (P.O. Box 6167), Hilton Head, SC 29938.
☎ **800/233-1234** or 803/785-1234. Fax 803/842-4695. 476 rms, 29 suites. A/C TV TEL. $125–$280 double; $160–$975 suite. AE, DC, DISC, MC, V.

Lacking the pizzazz of the Westin, this is the largest hotel on the island, set on two landscaped acres surrounded by the much more massive acreage of Palmetto Dunes Plantation. Owned by General Electric and managed by Hyatt, it was designed in 1976 in the then-popular format of a 10-story high-rise tower virtually dominating everything around it. (Later, a five-story annex was added beside the original tower.) Although you might find it odd to keep riding an elevator to travel between your room, the beach, and the various hotel facilities, you'll quickly grow used to it. Bedrooms are smaller and less opulent than you might expect from such a well-rated hotel, but you'll be compensated for their otherwise unremarkable interiors by balconies looking out over either gardens or the water.

Dining/Entertainment: Hemingway's is one of the island's best (see "Dining," below). A cabaret-style dining and drinking club offers more diversion. Sunday brunch is an island event.

Services: Room service, baby-sitting, laundry.

Facilities: Camp Hyatt for children, outdoor pool and whirlpool, three 18-hole golf courses, 25 tennis courts, sailboats, and health club with saunas, whirlpool, indoor pool, and exercise room.

✪ Westin Resort

2 Grass Lawn Ave., Hilton Head, SC 29928. ☎ **800/228-3000** or 803/681-4000. Fax 803/681-1087. 415 rms, 38 suites. $115–$330 double; $225–$355 suite. Children under 18 stay free in parents' room. Children 4 and under eat free. AE, DC, DISC, MC, V.

Set near the isolated northern end of Hilton Head Island, on 24 acres of landscaping, this is the most opulent European-style hotel in town. Its design, including cupolas and postmodern ornamentation that looks vaguely Moorish, is Disneyesque and evokes fanciful Palm Beach hotels. If there's a drawback, it's the stiff formality. Adults accompanied by a gaggle of children and bathers in swimsuits will not necessarily feel comfortable in the reverently hushed corridors.

Bedrooms, most with ocean views, are outfitted in Low Country plantation–style furnishings, with touches of Asian art thrown in for an additional upscale flourish.

Dining/Entertainment: The Barony (see "Dining," below) is the best place for food. There's also a seafood buffet restaurant.

Services: Room service, baby-sitting, laundry.

Facilities: Health club, three top-notch golf courses, a Palm Beach–style racquet club with 16 tennis courts, and a palm-flanked swimming pool, with immediate access to a white sandy beach.

EXPENSIVE

Crystal Sands Crowne Plaza Resort

130 Shipyard Dr., Shipyard Plantation, Hilton Head Island, SC 29928. ☎ **800/465-4329** or 803/842-2400. Fax 803/842-9975. 315 rms, 25 suites. A/C MINIBAR TV TEL. $115–$260 double; $250–$550 suite. AE, DC, DISC, MC, V.

The centerpiece of 800 landscaped acres, this glorified Holiday Inn now gives its major competitor, the Westin Resort, stiff competition. Originally built in a five-story design in 1981 as a Marriott Hotel, it was renovated in 1993 to the tune of $10 million, and today maintains the most dignified lobby (a mahogany-sheathed postmodern interpretation of Chippendale decor) of any hotel on the island.

The bedrooms are nothing special, outfitted in your basic patterned fabrics and accessories. But the sheer beauty of the landscaping, the attentive service, and the well-trained staff (each of whom dress in nautically inspired uniforms) can go a long way toward making your stay memorable.

Dining/Entertainment: On the premises are three restaurants, the most glamorous of which is Portz, off the main lobby.

Facilities: The golf course was praised by the National Audubon Society for its respect of local wildlife.

✪ Hilton Head Island Hilton Resort

23 Ocean Lane (P.O. Box 6165), Hilton Head, SC 29938. ☎ **800/ 221-2222** or 803/842-8000. Fax 803/842-4988. 295 rms (all with kitchenette), 28 suites. A/C TV TEL. $70–$250 double; $160–$350 suite. AE, DC, DISC, MC, V.

This award-winning property was built in 1984 and benefitted from a $3.5 million renovation 10 years later. Many visitors choose the Hilton because of its expansive sandy beach and its hideaway position, tucked at the end of the main road through Palmetto Dunes. Notable in its low-rise design are the hallways that open to sea breezes at either end. Designed with some of the largest bedrooms on the island, this hotel also has balconies angling out toward the beach that allow sea views from every unit.

Dining/Entertainment: Mostly Seafood is the resort's premier restaurant, although cafés and bars—even a franchise of Pizza Hut on the grounds—serve less expensive fare.

Services: Room service, baby-sitting, laundry.

Facilities: The children's vacation program is run like a summer camp, and is the best on the island. There's also a modest health club, a whirlpool, a sauna, and two outdoor pools.

MODERATE

Holiday Inn Oceanfront

(P.O. Box 5728), 1 South Forest Beach Dr., Hilton Head, SC 29938. ☎ **800/465-4329** or 803/785-5126. Fax 803/785-6678. 249 rms. A/C TV TEL. $69–$179 double. AE, CB, DISC, DC, MC, V.

The island's leading motor hotel, across from Colligny Plaza, this five-story high-rise opens onto a quiet stretch of beach. Although it's outclassed by the other Holiday Inn affiliate, the Crystal Sands Crowne Plaza Resort, it is a far better bargain. Better than ever following 1995 renovations, the hotel lies on the southern side of the island, near Shipyard Plantation. Don't judge the inn by its small lobby. Just follow it to the oceanfront restaurant, or head straight for your spacious and well-furnished guest room, which is done in tropical pastels. Rooms have king or double beds, but the balconies are generally too small for use. The upper floors have the views, so you should try for one of those. In summer, children's activities are planned, and refrigerators are available for another $5 per day. Non-smoking and handicapped-accessible rooms are available.

Radisson Suite Resort

12 Park Lane (in Central Park), Hilton Head, SC. ☎ **800/333-3333** or 803/ 686-5700. Fax 803/686-3952. 156 suites. A/C TV TEL. Apr–Sept $140–$185

one-bedroom suite; off-season $100–$145 one-bedroom suite. Rates
include continental breakfast. AE, DC, DISC, MC, V.

Set on the eastern edge of Hilton Head's main traffic artery, mid-
way between the Palmetto Dunes and Shipyard Plantations, this is
a three-story complex of functionally furnished but comfortable
suites. Don't expect the amenities you might find in larger (and
more expensive) hideaways such as the Hilton and Hyatt Regency.
Limited resort facilities are on site, including a swimming pool, a hot
tub, and a cluster of lighted tennis courts. The setting is wooded
and parklike. Both families and business travelers on extended
stays appreciate the simple cooking facilities available within each
accommodation. Each unit has an icemaker, microwave, and
coffeemaker.

⑤ South Beach Marina Inn

In the Sea Pines Plantation, 232 South Sea Pines Dr., Hilton Head, SC
29928. ☎ **803/671-6498.** 17 rms (each with kitchenette). A/C TV TEL.
$55–$145 one-bedroom apt; $75–$165 two-bedroom apt. AE, MC, V.

Of the dozens of available accommodations within Sea Pines Plantation, this clapboard-sided complex of marina-front buildings is the
only place offering traditional hotel-style rooms by the night. The
compound was inspired by New England saltbox cottages, with
exteriors painted red and blue. With lots of charm, despite its aggres-
sive "theme," it meanders over a labyrinth of catwalks and stairways
above a complex of shops, souvenir kiosks, and restaurants. Each
unit inside is cozily outfitted, including a kitchenette, country-style
braided rugs, pinewood floors, and a homespun decor celebrating
rural 19th-century America.

INEXPENSIVE

⑤ Fairfield Inn by Marriott

9 Marina Side Dr., Hilton Head, SC 29928. ☎ **800/228-2800** or 803/
842-4800. Fax 803/842-4800. 120 rms, 14 suites. A/C TV TEL. $64.95–
$74.95 double; $99.95–$109.95 suite. Senior discounts and golf packages
available. Children under 18 stay free in parents' room. Rates include continental breakfast. AE, DISC, DC, MC, V.

Set in Shelter Cove, this three-story motel has all the special features
of Marriott's budget chain, including complimentary coffee always
available in the lobby, non-smoking rooms, and same-day dry cleaning. There is also easy access to the beach, golf, tennis, marinas, and
shopping. Rooms are wheelchair-accessible, and, although they sport
your average unremarkable modern decor, are a good value for
expensive Hilton Head. Families save extra money by using one

a week. Accommodations vary, incorporating everything from one-to four-bedroom villas, as well as sometimes opulent private homes when the owners are away. The clientele here includes hordes of golfers since Sea Pines is the home of the MCI Classic, a major stop on the PGA tour. If you're not a Sea Pines guest, you can eat, shop, or enjoy some of its nightlife, but there's a $3 entrance fee. For full details on this varied resort/residential complex, write for a free "Sea Pines Vacation Brochure."

CAMPING

Outdoor Resorts RV Resort & Yacht Club, 43 Jenkins Rd., Hilton Head, SC 29926 (☎ **800/845-9560** or 803/681-3256), has some 200 RV sites situated on the Intracoastal Waterway. Amenities on the premises include two pools, saunas and whirlpools, lighted tennis courts, charter-fishing arrangements, marina and ramp, grocery shop, coin laundry, and restaurant. Rates for up to four people range from $24 to $30, depending on the season.

5 Dining

All the specialties of the Low Country, along with fine European, Asian, and Mexican cuisine, are served at Hilton Head's some 150 restaurants. If you're a first-time visitor, opt for some of the local specialties, including Frogmore stew, a combination of shrimp, hot sausage, potatoes, corn, and green beans. Other specialties are oysters roasted over an open fire until they can be easily opened with a knife, and Daufuskie crab. Settings range from waterfront restaurants to hidden dives—in fact, Hilton Head has more good restaurants than any competitive resort between New York and Florida.

VERY EXPENSIVE

The Barony

In the Westin Resort, 2 Grass Lawn Ave. ☎ **803/681-4000.** Reservations recommended. Main courses $20.50–$29.50. AE, DC, DISC, MC, V. Tues–Sun 6–10pm. INTERNATIONAL.

The Barony, quick to promote itself as the only four-star AAA restaurant on Hilton Head Island, didn't shy away from installing decor that's a cross between a stage-set version of old Vienna and a brick-lined, two-fisted steakhouse. The lighting is suitably dim, the drinks appropriately stiff, and as you dine in your plushly upholstered alcove, you can check out what might be the largest wrought-iron chandelier in the state. Contrary to what you'd expect from a place like this, it caters to a resort-going crowd of casual diners, defining itself as "an upscale restaurant with a down-home feel." Everything arrives well-prepared and in copious portions, though the kitchen is obviously not willing to experiment with more creative dishes to supplement the limited selection of steak and lobster fare. But if you're not that adventurous, you'll be perfectly happy with solid versions of dishes such as New York strip steak; tenderloin of pork with purée of mangoes; grilled Long Island duck with wild-berry sauce; lobster Thermidor; or fresh Atlantic swordfish with pistachios.

✪ Hemingway's

In the Hyatt Regency Hilton Head, Palmetto Dunes Resort. ☎ **803/ 785-1234.** Reservations recommended. Main courses $21–$26. AE, DC, DISC, MC, V. Daily 5–11pm. SEAFOOD/AMERICAN.

This is the most upscale, and the most charming, hotel restaurant on the island. Though the theme of a glamorous "Papa Hemingway-as-bon-vivant" is hardly accurate, the dining experience here is fine, offering competent and unpretentious service. Decor, which includes a view of an exposed kitchen, is appropriately nautical, and the sounds of a live pianist might drift in from the late-night cocktail lounge next door. The most successful part of the menu includes your choice of fresh fish—cooked to perfection and never allowed to dry out. Other solid choices include filet mignon, bullfighter's-style paella, and chargrilled poultry with lemon-thyme sauce. Your meal might begin, incidentally, with any of a round of upscale rums, or a frothy, rum-based tropical concoction flavored with coconut, banana, pineapple, and grenadine.

EXPENSIVE

Cattails

302 Moss Creek Village. ☎ **803/837-7000.** Reservations recommended for dinner, not necessary at lunch. Lunch main courses $6.95–$9.50; dinner main courses $16.50–$21.95. AE, DC, DISC, MC, V. Mon–Sat 11:30am–2pm and 6–10pm. INTERNATIONAL/MODERN AMERICAN.

Its only drawback lies in its location within a shopping center inconveniently 17 miles north of the southern tip of the resort. Many locals, however, search this place out for its food and international zest. With high ceilings and big windows, this airy place is decorated with lace curtains, mauve walls, and lots of hanging plants. Many of the dishes are inspired by Low Country traditions; others are more international or California in feeling and flair. Examples include a roasted eggplant, red pepper, and mushroom focaccia; roasted corn and crabmeat chowder; pan-seared flounder with South Carolina pecans and white-wine butter sauce; and tempting pastas, many of them made with seafood. The owners are Iranian-born chef Mehdi Varedi and his American wife Corinne, who directs a charming staff in the dining room.

✪ Charlie's L'Itoile Verte

1000 Plantation Center. ☎ **803/785-9277.** Reservations required. Main courses $18–$25. AE, DISC, MC, V. Tues–Sat 11:30am–2pm and 6:30–9:30pm. INTERNATIONAL.

Outfitted like a tongue-in-cheek version of a Parisian bistro, with lots of amusing Gallic and Low Country memorabilia scattered over the walls, this is our favorite restaurant in Hilton Head, an opinion shared by President Clinton when it was chosen for him and a large entourage during one of his island conferences. The atmosphere is unpretentious but elegant—it's a cauldron of energy set within an otherwise sleepy shopping center. Service is attentive, polite, and infused with an appealingly hip mixture of the Old and New Worlds. The kitchen has a narrow opening allowing guests to peep inside at the controlled hysteria. Begin with shrimp-stuffed ravioli, and move on to grilled tuna with a jalapeno beurre blanc sauce, grilled quail with shiitake mushrooms and a merlot sauce, or veal chops in peppercorn sauce. End this rare experience with a biscotti or a "sailor's trifle." The wine list is impressive.

MODERATE

ⓢ Café Europa

Harbour Town, Sea Pines Plantation. ☎ **803/671-3399.** Reservations recommended for dinner. Main courses $11.95–$18.95. AE, DC, MC, V. Daily 10am–2:30pm and 5:30–10pm. CONTINENTAL/SEAFOOD.

This European eatery, one of the finest on Hilton Head, is at the base of the much-photographed Harbour Town Lighthouse, opening onto a panoramic view of Calibogue Sound and Daufuskie Island. In an informal cheerful atmosphere, you can order fish that's poached, grilled or baked, not always fried. Baked shrimp Daufuskie was inspired by local catches, stuffed with crab, green peppers, and onions. Grilled grouper is offered with a sauté of tomato, cucumber, dill, and white wine. Specialty dishes include a country-style chicken recipe from Charleston, with honey, fresh cream, and pecans. Tournedos au poivre is flambéed with brandy and simmered in a robust green peppercorn sauce. The omelets, 14 in all, are served at breakfast (beginning at 10am), and are the island's finest. And the bartender's Bloody Mary won an award as "island best" from a *Hilton Head News* contest.

The Chart House

Palmetto Bay Marina (at the end of Palmetto Bay Rd.). ☎ **803/785-9666.** Reservations recommended. Early-bird dinner (5:30–6:30pm only) $14.95; main courses $15.50–$23.95. Sun–Thurs 5:30–10pm; Fri–Sat 5:30–11pm. AMERICAN.

Opening onto Broad Creek, the Chart House (a chain) has again found a panoramic location. And once again, it has succeeded in outdistancing its competitors in the succulent flavor and tenderness of its specialty: prime rib. But seafood lovers will also find a full-service oyster bar available for appetizers, and can order the catch of the day (often grouper) as a main dish. The salad bar is the finest on the island. The staff is well trained, and dress is casual. Amazingly, the chef continues to serve you unlimited servings of fresh hot bread so delicious that it usually prevents diners from ordering any extra dishes. Mud pie, known to all Chart House fans, is the classic dessert.

Hudson's Seafood House on the Docks

1 Hudson Rd. ☎ **803/681-22772.** Reservations not accepted. Main courses $12.95–$15.95. AE, MC, V. Daily 11am–2:30pm and 6–10pm. Go to Skull Creek just off Square Pope Road (signposted from U.S. 278).

Built as a seafood processing factory in 1912, this restaurant still processes fish, clams, and oysters for local distribution—so you know everything is fresh. If you're seated in the north dining room, you'll be eating in the original oyster factory. A few "drydock" courses show up on the menu, but we strongly recommend the seafood, such as crab cakes, steamed shrimp, or blackened catch of the day. Local oysters (seasonal) are also a specialty, breaded and deep fried. Before and after dinner, stroll on the docks past shrimp boats and enjoy the view of the mainland and nearby Parris Island. Sunsets here are panoramic. Lunch is served in the Oyster Bar.

Mostly Seafood

In the Hilton Head Island Hilton Resort, in Palmetto Dunes Plantation. ☎ **803/785-1234.** Reservations recommended. Main courses $15.50–$19. AE, DC, DISC, MC, V. Daily 5:30–10pm. SEAFOOD/AMERICAN.

The most elegant and innovative restaurant within the Hilton is noted for the way its chefs combine fresh seafood into imaginative dishes. Something about the decor—backlighting and glass-backed murals painted in designs of sea-green and blue—creates the illusion that you're floating in a boat. Menu items include a worthwhile fresh grouper, plus snapper, swordfish, flounder, salmon, trout, halibut, and pompano, prepared in any of seven different ways. Dishes consistently drawing applause are corn-crusted filet of salmon with essence of hickory-smoked veal bacon and peach relish; and "fish in the bag," prepared with fresh grouper, scallops, and shrimp, laced with a dill-flavored cream sauce and baked in a brown paper bag.

Santa Fe Café

700 Plantation Center. ☎ **803/785-3838.** Reservations recommended. Lunch main courses $5.95–$7.95; dinner main courses $12.95–$21.25. AE, DISC, MC, V. Mon–Fri noon–2pm; daily 5–10pm. MEXICAN.

This is the best, most stylish Mexican restaurant in Hilton Head, with a decor inspired by Taos or Santa Fe, and a cuisine managing to infuse traditional recipes into dishes with a nouvelle flair. The setting is as rustic as Mexico's arid highlands. Menu items are fun and imaginative, often presented with colors as bright as the painted desert. Meals might include tequila shrimp; herb-roasted chicken with jalapeno cornbread stuffing and mashed potatoes laced with red chiles; grilled tenderloin of pork with smoked habanero sauce and sweet potato fries; and recommendable burritos and chimichangas. The chiles rellenos (stuffed sweet chiles) are exceptional, stuffed with California goat cheese and sundried tomatoes; and the quesadilla is one of the most beautifully presented dishes you'll find at any restaurant in town.

INEXPENSIVE

⊙ The Crazy Crab North

Hwy. 278 at Jarvis Creek. ☎ **803/681-5021.** Reservations not accepted. Main courses $9.95–$17.95. AE, DC, DISC, MC, V. Daily 5–10pm. SEAFOOD.

This is the more desirable of a pair of seafood eateries. Set within a modern, low-slung building near the bridge that connects the island with the South Carolina mainland, it serves baked, broiled, or fried versions of stuffed flounder, seafood kebabs, oysters, catch of the day, or any combination thereof. She-crab soup and New England clam chowder are prepared fresh daily; children's menus are available; and desserts are considered a high point by chocoholics. This is the chain's branch most likely to be patronized year-round by local residents.

Hofbrauhaus

Pope Avenue Mall. ☎ **803/785-3663.** Reservations recommended. Early-bird dinner (5–6:30pm only) $11.95; main courses $12.50–$14.95. AE, MC, V. Daily 5–10pm. GERMAN.

A sanitized version of a Munich beer hall, this family favorite is the only German restaurant at Hilton Head. Since 1973, it's served locals and visitors specialties such as grilled bratwurst and smoked Westphalian ham, along with Wiener schnitzel and Sauerbraten. One specialty we like to order is roast duckling with Spaetzle, red cabbage, and orange sauce. Note the stein and mug collection as you're deciding which of the large variety of German beers to order. A children's menu is also available.

6 Hilton Head After Dark

Hilton Head doesn't have the nightlife of Myrtle Beach, and, as a result, doesn't attract the serious partygoers that the Grand Strand does. But there's still a lot here, centered mainly at hotels and resorts. Casual dress (but not bathing suits) is acceptable in most clubs.

Cultural interest focuses on the Hilton Head Playhouse, **Dunnagan's Alley,** at Arrow Road (☎ **803/785-4878**), which enjoys one of the best theatrical reputations in the Southeast. Shows seat 225 persons at 8pm Tuesday through Saturday, with a Sunday matinee at 3pm. Begun almost three decades ago, the theater today presents a wide range of musicals, contemporary comedies, and classic dramas in a renovated warehouse. A new 350-seat, state-of-the-art theater may be completed sometime in 1996. Adult ticket prices range from $15 for a play to $20 for a musical. Children 12 and under pay $10.

Other island hot spots include the following:

Big Rocco's
Central Park. ☎ **803/785-9000.**

This large, bustling place is known for importing some of the best bands (often jazz) on the island. Call to find out what's happening during your visit. A deli at one side serves a bar menu until midnight. Open Monday through Saturday from 6 to 10:30pm for dinner, and Sunday from 5:30 to 10pm.

Club Indigo
In the Hyatt Regency, Palmetto Dunes Plantation. ☎ **803/785-1234.** Cover $5.

At this deluxe hotel, a fun-loving crowd in their thirties and forties listens to music or dances to pop. The setting is upscale. Beach music of the 1950s and '60s seems to get the most response from this crowd. Open Monday through Saturday from 8pm to 1:30am.

Coconuts Comedy Club

Heritage Plaza. ☎ **803/686-6887.** Cover $10.

Some of the nation's best comedians on the club circuit—not Atlantic City or Las Vegas rejects—perform here. Four to eight shows a week are presented. Light food, such as subs, pizzas, and salads, is served along with drinks. Shows are Tuesday through Saturday at 10pm in summer, at 9:30pm in the off-season.

Quarterdeck

Harbour Town, Sea Pines Plantation. ☎ **803/671-2222.**

Our favorite waterfront lounge is the best place on the island to watch sunsets, but you can visit at any time during the day after noon, and in the evening until 2am. Bar food is available. Try to go early and grab one of the outdoor rocking chairs to prepare yourself for nature's light show. There's dancing every night to beach music and the top 40 hits.

Remy's

28 Arrow Rd. ☎ **803/842-3800.**

This bar is ideal late at night, when many other places on Hilton Head have closed. The setting is rustic and raffish, and live music is often on tap. Got the munchies? You can devour buckets of oysters or shrimp served with the inevitable fries. Open Monday through Friday 11am to 4pm, Saturday 11am to 1:30pm, Sunday noon to 1:30am.

Salty Dog

South Beach Marina. ☎ **803/671-2233.**

Locals used to keep this laid-back place near the beach to themselves, but now more and more visitors are showing up. Soft guitar music or tunes like Jimmy Buffett's "Margaritaville" usually provide the background. Dress is casual. Sit under one of the sycamores, enjoying your choice of food from an outdoor grill or buffet.

Signals

In the Crystal Sands Crowne Plaza Resort, 130 Shipyard Dr. ☎ **803/ 842-2400.**

In this upscale resort you can enjoy live bands, often performing 1940s golden oldies, along with R&B, blues, and jazz. The dance floor is generally crowded. Bands perform Tuesday through Sunday from 9pm to 1am, and live jazz is heard on Monday from 6 to 9:30pm. A Sunday jazz brunch is presented from 11am to 1:30pm.

5

Savannah

*I*f you have time to visit only one city in the Southeast, make it Savannah. It's that special. And it's fast becoming a hit with tourists, now that it's familiar to millions who saw Tom Hanks in *Forrest Gump* or readers of the best-selling novel *Midnight in the Garden of Good and Evil.*

"What's special about Savannah?" we asked an old-timer. "Why, here we even have water fountains for dogs," he said.

The free spirit, the passion, and even the decadence of Savannah resembles Key West or New Orleans more than the Bible Belt down-home interior of Georgia. In that sense, it's as different from Georgia as New York City is from Upper New York State.

Savannah—pronounce it with a drawl—conjures up the cliché images of the Deep South: live oaks dripping with Spanish moss, stately antebellum mansions, mint juleps on the veranda, magnolia trees, peaceful marshes, horse-drawn carriages, and even memories of General Sherman, no one's favorite military hero here.

Today the economy and much of the city's day-to-day life still revolve around port activity. For the visitor, however, it's Old Savannah, a beautifully restored and maintained historic area, that draws the most attention. For this we can thank seven Savannah ladies who, after watching mansion after mansion be demolished in the name of "progress," managed in 1954 to raise funds to buy the dilapidated Isaiah Davenport house—just hours before it was slated for demolition to make way for a parking lot. The women banded together as the Historic Savannah Foundation, then went to work buying up architecturally valuable buildings and reselling them to private owners who would promise to restore them. As a result, more than 800 of the 1,100 historic buildings of Old Savannah have been restored, using original paint colors—pinks and reds and blues and greens. This living museum is now the largest urban National Historic Landmark District in the country—some 2¹/₂ square miles, including 20 one-acre squares that still survive from Oglethorpe's dream of a gracious city.

A LOOK AT THE PAST

Spanish missions gained a brief foothold on St. Simons and Jekyll islands as early as 1566, but "civilization" came to stay on this part of the Atlantic coast on February 12, 1733, when Gen. James Oglethorpe arrived at Yamacraw Bluff with 114 English settlers—nonconformist Protestants and former inmates of England's debtor prisons who were looking at the New World for a new beginning. Oglethorpe's idealism encompassed a new future for the unfortunates he'd brought with him. He planned a town that would provide space, beauty, and comfort for every resident of the colony: a settlement of houses, each with its own garden plot, laid out around town squares (there were 24 in the original plan) and with an orderly mercantile section. Thus Savannah was America's very first "planned city."

The natural deep-water harbor soon attracted Spanish, Portuguese, German, Scots, and Irish immigrants, and a lively sea trade brought seafarers from all over the world—along with hordes of pirates who put into the port from time to time. In 1775, when Savannah got word that war had broken out at Lexington, Massachusetts, a patriot battalion was hastily formed. Savannah changed hands frequently during the Revolution. The city was named the state capital following the 1776 Declaration of Independence, and remained so until 1807, when proslavers managed to have the government moved to Milledgeville.

The years between the Revolutionary and Civil wars were a period of great prosperity for Savannah; many of the classic revival, Regency, and Georgian colonial homes you'll see restored today were built at that time. It was the era of King Cotton and great tobacco farms. Cotton "factors" (brokers) kept track of huge fortunes along River Street on what came to be known as Factors Walk. Through it all, builders, merchants, and shippers kept to Oglethorpe's master plan for the city, preserving the parks and squares in the midst of all the commercial hubbub.

When secession rumblings reached fever pitch in 1861, Georgia's governor ordered state troops to seize Fort Pulaski, 15 miles east of Savannah, even though the state did not withdraw from the Union until 16 days later. The war brought devastation to the area, since Sherman ended his march to the sea here in December 1864. Sherman entered into Savannah more quietly than was his usual custom, since Confederate General Hardee had evacuated his troops to spare this city the destruction Sherman had left in his wake all across the state.

1 Orientation

ARRIVING

Savannah International Airport is 8 miles west of downtown just off I-16. **American** (☎ 800/433-7300), **Delta** (☎ 800/221-1212), **United** (☎ 800/241/6522), and **USAir** (☎ 800/428-4322) have flights from Atlanta and Charlotte, which are both served by many other carriers. Limousine service from the airport to downtown locations (☎ **912/966-5364**) costs $15. Taxi fare is $15 for one person, $3 for each additional passenger.

From north or south, I-95 passes 10 miles west of Savannah, with several exits to the city, and U.S. 17 runs through the city; from the west, I-16 ends in downtown Savannah and U.S. 80 also runs through the city from east to west. AAA services in Savannah are available through **AAA Auto Club South,** 712 Mall Blvd. (☎ **912/352-8222**).

The train station is at 2611 Seaboard Coastline Dr. (☎ **912/234-2611**), some 4 miles southwest of downtown. For **Amtrak** schedule and fare information, call **800/USA-RAIL.** Cab fare into the city is around $4.

VISITOR INFORMATION

The Savannah Visitor Center at 301 Martin Luther King Jr. Blvd., Savannah, GA 31401 (☎ **912/944-0456**), is open Monday through Friday from 8:30am to 5pm, Saturday and Sunday from 9am to 5pm. The staff is friendly and efficient. There's an audiovisual presentation for a small fee ($1 adults, 50¢ children); organized tours; and self-guided walking, driving, or bike tours with excellent maps, cassette tapes, and brochures.

Tourist information is also available from the **Savannah Area Convention & Visitors Bureau,** 222 W. Oglethorpe Ave., Savannah, GA 31401 (☎ **800/444-2427** or 912/944-0456). For information on current happenings, call **912/233-ARTS.**

CITY LAYOUT

Every other street—north, south, west, and east—is punctuated by a "green lung." The grid of 21 scenic squares was laid out by General James Oglethorpe, the founder of Georgia, in 1733. The design—still in use—has been called "one of the world's most revered city plans." It is said that if Savannah didn't have its history and its architecture, it would be worth a visit just to see the city layout.

Bull Street is the dividing line between east and west. On the south side is odd numeration of street numbers, with even street numbers falling on the north side.

NEIGHBORHOODS IN BRIEF

The Historic District   The real reason to visit Savannah, the Historic District takes in both the Riverfront and the City Market, described below. It is bordered by the Savannah River and Forsyth Park at Gaston Street, and Montgomery and Price Streets. Within its borders are more than 2,350 architecturally and historically significant buildings in a $2^1/_2$-square mile area. About 75% of these buildings have been restored.

Riverfront   The most popular tourist district of Savannah, Riverfront borders the Savannah River. In 1818 about one-half of Savannah fell under a quarantine during a yellow-fever epidemic. River Street, once lined with warehouses holding "King Cotton," never fully recovered and fell into disrepair, until its rediscovery in the mid-1970s. A massive urban-renewal project turned this strip into a row of restaurants, art galleries, shops, and bars.

City Market   The market lies at Jefferson and West Julian Streets, bounded by Franklin Square on its western flank and Ellis Square on its eastern frontier. Two blocks from River Street and bordering the Savannah River, City Market was the former social and business mecca of Savannah. Since the late 18th century, it has known fires and various devastations, including a threatened demolition. But in a major move, the city of Savannah decided to save the district. Today, once-decaying warehouses are filled with restaurants and shops, offering everything from antiques to various collectibles, including many Savannah-made products. Everything from seafood and pizza to French and Italian cuisine is served in the restaurants. Live music often fills the nighttime air—some of the best jazz in the city is presented here in various clubs.

Victorian District   The Victorian District lies south of the Historic District, holding some of the finest examples of post–Civil War architecture in the Deep South. The district is bounded by Martin Luther King Jr. Blvd., East Broad, and Gwinnett and Anderson streets. Houses here are characterized by gingerbread trim, stained-glass windows, and imaginative architectural details. In all, the district encompasses an area of nearly 50 blocks, spread across some 165 acres. The entire district became listed in the National Register of Historic Places in 1974. Most of the two-story homes are

Savannah is a beautiful woman with a dirty face.

—Lady Astor (1946)

wood frame, and were constructed in the late 1800s on brick foundations. The district, overflowing from the historic inner core of the city, became the first suburb of Savannah.

2 Getting Around

Although many points of interest outside the Historic District can be reached by bus, your own wheels will be much more convenient, and they're absolutely essential for sightseeing outside the city proper.

All major car-rental firms have branches in Savannah and at the airport, and it pays to shop around for those with the best basic rate and unlimited mileage. Try **Hertz** (☎ **800/654-3131** or 912/964-9595 at the airport); **Avis** (☎ **800/831-2847**), with offices at 422 Airways Ave. (☎ 912/964-1781) and at 2215 Travis Field Rd. (☎ 912/964-0234); and **Budget** (☎ **800/858-5377**), with offices at 7070 Abercorn (☎ 912/966-1771).

To take the local city buses, you'll need exact change for the $1 fare, plus 5¢ for a transfer. For route and schedule information, call **Chatham Area Transit** (CAT) at **912/233-5767.**

The grid-shaped Historic District is best seen on foot, and in fact, the real point of your visit is to take leisurely strolls with frequent stops in the many squares. The base rate for taxis is 60¢, with a $1.20 additional charge for each mile. For 24-hour taxi service, call **Adam Cab Co.** at **912/927-7466.**

FAST FACTS: Savannah

Airport See "Arriving," earlier in this chapter.

American Express **American Express Travel Service** is at 5500 Abercorn St., Suite 22 (☎ **912/351-0770**).

Camera Repair **Shutter-bugs,** 115 E. River St., in the River Street Inn on the second floor (☎ **912/233-4418**), sells cameras, film, batteries, and disposable cameras. The shop also rents camcorders and repairs cameras.

Car Rentals See "Getting Around," earlier in this chapter.

Climate See "When to Go," in chapter 1.

Dentist   Call **Savannah Dental Association,** 413 W. Duffy St. (☎ **912/234-5000**), for complete dental care and emergencies.

Drugstore   Drugstores are scattered throughout Savannah. One with longer hours is **Revco,** 11607 Abercorn St. (☎ **912/925-5568**), open Monday through Saturday 8am till midnight and Sunday 10am to 8pm.

Emergencies   Dial 911 for police, ambulance, or fire emergencies.

Eyeglass Repair   Eyeglasses can be repaired at **Lenscrafters,** 7804 Abercorn St., in the Oglethorpe Mall (☎912/351-0137), open Monday through Friday 9am to 8pm and Sunday noon to 5:30pm.

Hospitals   There are 24-hour emergency room services at **Candler General Hospital,** 5353 Reynolds St. (☎ **912/356-6037**), and **Memorial Medical Center,** 4800 Waters Ave. (☎ **912/350-8390**).

Information   See "Visitor Information," earlier in this chapter.

Maps   Maps are available at the Savannah Visitor Center (see "Visitor Information," earlier in this chapter).

Newspapers   The *Savannah Morning News* and *Savannah Evening Press* are both dailies filled with information about local cultural and entertainment events.

Police   Call 911.

Post Office   Post offices and sub-post offices are centrally located and open Monday through Friday 7am to 6pm and Saturday 9am to 3pm. The main office is located at 2 N. Fahn St. (☎ **912/235-4653**).

Safety   Although it is reasonably safe to explore the Victorian and Historic Districts during the day, the situation changes at night. The clubs along the riverfront, both bars and restaurants, report very little crime. However, muggings and drug dealing are common in the poorer neighborhoods of Savannah. Wander in those neighborhoods at night only with great caution.

Taxes   The city of Savannah adds a 2% local option tax to the 4% state tax.

Time Zone   Savannah is on eastern standard time.

Transit Information   Call **Chatham Area Transit** at **912/233-5767.**

Weather   Call **912/964-1700.**

3   Accommodations

The undisputed stars here are the small inns in the Historic District, most in restored old homes that have been renovated with modern conveniences, while retaining every bit of their original charm. Book into one of these if you want to experience Savannah graciousness firsthand.

Only Charleston has more historic inns than Savannah. After a burst of hotel openings, Savannah's hotel scene seems to have quieted down. Of course, those who don't want the charm of the restored homes will find such big names as the Hyatt and Marriott still going strong. The cheapest lodgings remain the chain hotels and motels on the periphery of the Historic District, although most of these are without distinction and could be along the road of any major artery leading into any insignificant American town.

Because many of the historic inns of Savannah are in former converted residences, price ranges within an individual hotel can vary greatly. A very expensive hotel might have some smaller and more moderately priced rooms because of the architectural layout of the building, for instance.

Advance reservations are absolutely necessary in most cases, since many of the best properties are quite small.

ALONG THE RIVERFRONT
EXPENSIVE

Hyatt Regency Savannah

2 W. Bay St., Savannah, GA 31401. ☎ **800/228-1234** or 912/238-1234. Fax 912/944-3678. 318 rms, 28 suites. A/C TV TEL.$99–$190 double, $221–$849 suite. AE, DC, DISC, MC, V. Parking $7–$9.

You should have heard the outcry among Savannah's historic preservation movement when this place went up in 1981. Boxy and massively bulky, it stands in unpleasant contrast to the restored warehouses that flank it on either side along the legendary banks of the Savannah River. Today, it's grudgingly accepted as the biggest and flashiest hotel in Savannah, the one best-suited for corporate conventions, and the one most clearly modeled after international, big-city models. There's a soaring atrium as in Hyatts everywhere, and glass-sided elevators. Bedrooms are comfortable, international and modern in their feel, many with balconies overlooking the atrium. The prices of bedrooms vary according to their views—and the ones without views are quite a bargain.

Dining/Entertainment: There's a stylish bar, and two restaurants with a big-city feel and views over the river.

Facilities: A health club, an indoor swimming pool, and a small fitness room.

Olde Harbour Inn

508 E. Factors Walk, Savannah, GA 31401. ☎ **800/553-6533** or 912/234-4100. Fax 912/233-5979. 24 suites (each with kitchenette). A/C TV TEL. $125–$155 suite. Rates include continental breakfast. AE, DISC, DC, MC, V.

The neighborhood has been gentrified, and the interior of this place is well-furnished and comfortable, but you still get a whiff of riverfront seediness as you approach it from Factors Walk's eastern end. Built in 1892 as a warehouse for oil, its masonry bulk is camouflaged with shutters, awnings, and touches of wrought iron. Inside, a labyrinth of passages lead to small but comfortably furnished suites, many of which show the building's massive timbers and structural iron brackets, and many of which offer views of the river. Each unit contains its own kitchen—a useful option for anyone in town for an extended stay. Some decors feature the original brick, painted white. Despite the overlay of chintz, there's a constant sense of the building's thick-walled bulk.

Savannah Marriott Riverfront Hotel

100 General McIntosh Blvd., Savannah, GA 31401. ☎ **800/228-9290** or 912/233-7722. Fax 912/233-3765. 338 rms, 46 suites. A/C TV TEL. $109–$129 double; $169–$379 suite. Children under 18 stay free in parents' room. AE, CB, DC, DISC, MC, V. Free parking.

At least the massive modern bulk of this place lies far enough from the 19th-century restored warehouses of River Street to not clash with them aesthetically. Parts of this place need renovation, despite its relatively recent construction as a Radisson Hotel in the early 1990s. Towering eight stories, with an angular facade sheathed in orange and yellow brick, it doesn't quite succeed at being a top-rated luxury palace, but nonetheless attracts lots of corporate business and conventions. Among local hotels of this type, we prefer the Hyatt, but this would be an acceptable backup choice, with comfortable modern rooms. The soaring atrium contains an awkwardly positioned indoor swimming pool loaded with children, whose water antics are partially concealed behind a barricade of plants.

Dining/Entertainment: The restaurant (T.G.I. Friday's) within the lobby suffers from a claustrophobically low ceiling and has a faux-Victorian decor with a kaleidoscope of stained-glass lamps.

Savannah Accommodations

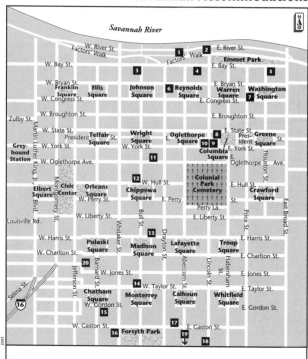

Ballastone Inn **11**

Bed & Breakfast Inn **15**

Courtyard by Marriott **19**

DeSoto Hilton **13**

East Bay Inn **4**

Eliza Thompson House **14**

Fairfield Inn by Marriott **19**

Foley House Inn **12**

Gastonian **18**

Hyatt Regency Savannah **3**

Jesse Mount House **20**

Kehoe House **8**

Lion's Head Inn **17**

Magnolia Place Inn **16**

The Mulberry (Holiday Inn) **5**

Olde Harbour Inn **2**

Planters Inn **6**

Presidents' Quarters **10**

River Street Inn **1**

St. Julian St. B&B **7**

17 Hundred 90 **9**

MODERATE
✪ River Street Inn

115 E. River St., Savannah, GA 31401. ☎ **800/253-4229** or 912/
234-6400. Fax 912/234-1478. 44 rms. A/C MINIBAR TV TEL. $79–$139
double. Children under 18 stay free in parents' room. Rates include breakfast. AE, DC, MC, V. Free parking.

When cotton was king, and Liverpool-based ships were moored on
the nearby river, this building stored massive amounts of cotton pro-
duced by upriver plantations. After the boll weevil decimated the
cotton industry, it functioned as an ice house, a storage area for fresh
vegetables, and—at its lowest point—the headquarters of an insur-
ance company, and a disco pulsating to the sounds of Jimi Hendrix.
Its two lowest floors, built in 1817, were made of ballast stone
carried in the holds of ships from faraway England; its three brick-
built upper floors were added a few decades later.

In 1986, a group of investors poured millions into its development as one of the lynchpins of Savannah's River District, adding
a well-upholstered colonial pizzazz to public areas, and converting
the building's warren of brick-lined storerooms into some of the
most comfortable and well-maintained bedrooms in town. There
are many plusses to staying here, including its position near a
slew of bars, restaurants, and nightclubs. Breakfast is served within
the separately recommended Huey's Restaurant (see "Dining,"
below).

IN THE HISTORIC DISTRICT
VERY EXPENSIVE
✪ Ballastone Inn

14 Oglethorpe Ave., Savannah, GA 31401. ☎ **800/822-4553** or 912/
236-1484. Fax 912/236-4626. 17 rms, 4 suites. A/C TV TEL. $95–$200
double; $145–$185 suite. Rates include continental breakfast. AE, MC, V.
Free parking.

This is one of the most glamorous inner-city B&Bs in Savannah. Set
within a dignified 1838 building separated from the Juliette Gordon
Low house (original home of Girl Scouts of America) only by a well-
tended formal garden, it's richly decorated with all the hardwoods,
elaborate draperies, and antique furniture you'd expect from one of
Savannah's premier inns. It was named for the stones carried as ballast in the holds of sailing vessels, which, when unloaded to make
room for cotton crops at Savannah, were then recycled as the
building's foundations. For a brief period (only long enough to add
a hint of spiciness), the place functioned as a bordello *and* a branch

office for the Girl Scouts organization (now next door) between bouts as an upper-class residence.

Former occupants included at least three prominent warriors for the Confederacy, one of whom hired a Boston-based architect (William Gibbons Preston) to rebuild and redesign the place after the end of the Civil War. In 1987, in a real-estate swap that has become legendary for its savviness, the building was acquired by a Chicago-based entrepreneur, Richard Carlson, and his partner Tim Hargus.

Oddities within abound: There's an elevator, unusual for Savannah B&Bs; no closets (they were taxed as extra rooms in the old days and therefore never added); many truly unusual furnishings noted for their comfort and dignified style; cachepots filled with scented potpourri; art objects that would thrill the heart of any decorator; and a full-service bar area tucked into a corner of what was originally conceived as a double parlor. The four suites, incidentally, are contained within a separate building, a clapboard-sided townhouse within a 5-minute walk, which is staffed with its own live-in receptionists.

✪ The Gastonian

220 East Gaston St., Savannah, GA 31401. ☎ **800/322-6603** or 912/ 232-2869. Fax 912/232-0710. 10 rms, 3 suites. A/C TV TEL. $125–$200 double; $250–$285 suite. Rates include continental breakfast. AE, MC, V. No children under 12.

This elegant place is proof of what good taste, historical antecedents, and lots of money can do. Known as one of the two or three most posh B&Bs in Savannah, it incorporates a pair of Italianate Regency buildings, both constructed in 1868 by the same (unknown) architect as a pair of private homes. (The larger of these was owned by the Champion family, proprietors of a chain of grocery stores.) Hard times began with the stock market crash of 1929, and the buildings were chopped into apartments for the payment of back taxes. In 1984, visitors from California (the Lineberger family) saw the place, fell in love with it, and poured $2 million into restoring its severely dignified premises.

Everything today is a testimonial to Victorian taste and charm except for a skillfully crafted serpentine bridge that interconnects the two buildings and curves above a verdant semi-tropical garden. Afternoon tea is served in a formal, English-inspired drawing room where Persian carpets and a grand piano add the luster of the good life of another era. Rooms are appropriately plush.

✪ The Kehoe House

123 Habersham St., Savannah, GA 31401. ☎ **800/820-1020** or 912/
232-1020. Fax 912/231-0208. 13 rms, 2 suites. A/C TV TEL. $150–$210
double; $225–$250 suite. Rates include full breakfast. AE, DC, DISC,
MC, V.

Kehoe House was built in 1892 by the owners of an iron foundry
as a testimonial to their wealth. Caught up in the salesmanship of
their product, they ordered that the building's trim, window case-
ments, columns, and soffits be cast in iron and bolted into place. In
the 1960s, after the place had been converted into a funeral parlor,
it became the most scandalous building in Savannah when its owners tried to tear down the nearby Davenport House (see "Attractions") for use as a parking lot. The resultant outrage eventually led
to the salvation of most of the neighborhood's remaining historic
buildings.

Today, the place functions as a spectacularly beautiful and opulent B&B, the finest in Savannah, with a collection of fabrics and
furniture that are almost forbiddingly valuable and tasteful. However, it lacks the warmth and welcome of the Ballastone Inn. This
is not a place for children: The ideal client will tread softly on floors
that are considered models of historic authenticity and flawless taste.
Breakfast and afternoon tea are part of the ritual that has seduced
such former clients as, among others, Tom Hanks, who stayed in
room 301 during the filming of parts of *Forrest Gump*.

Magnolia Place Inn

503 Whitaker St., Savannah, GA 31401. ☎ **912/236-7674** or 800/
238-7674 outside Georgia. Fax 912/236-1145. 13 rms. A/C TV TEL. $100–
$195 double. Rates include continental breakfast. AE, MC, V.

It was begun in 1878 on a desirable plot of land overlooking Forsyth
Square, and completed 4 years later by a venerable family who had
been forced off their upriver plantation after the Civil War for
non-payment of taxes. An ancestor of theirs had represented South
Carolina at the signing of the Declaration of Independence, and as
such, the Second Empire ("steamboat Gothic") house was designed
to be as grand and accommodating as funds would allow. The result includes the most endearing front steps in town (Nieman
Marcus is said to have asked to display them as a backdrop for one
of their catalogues), front verandas worthy of a Mississippi steamer,
and an oval skylight (an "oculus") that illuminates a graceful staircase ascending to the dignified bedrooms. New owners acquired the
place in 1994 and have molded it into their own individualized

vision. About half the rooms contain Jacuzzi-style whirlpool baths, and 11 have fireplaces.

EXPENSIVE

DeSoto Hilton

15 E. Liberty St. (P.O. Box 8207), Savannah, GA 31412. ☎ **800/445-8667** or 912/232-9000. Fax 912/232-6018. 245 rms. A/C TV TEL. $115–$140 double. AE, DC, MC, V.

Originally built in 1890 in what was at the time Savannah's showcase commercial neighborhood, this hotel functioned for many generations of Savannahians as the city's grandest hotel. Thousands of wedding receptions, Kiwanis club meetings, and debutante parties later, the venerable building was demolished and rebuilt in a bland modern format in 1967, and has ever since grasped at the vestiges of antique glamour its name still manages to evoke. Today, it's a clean, well-managed commercial hotel, fully renovated by new owners in 1995. Bedrooms are conservatively modern, and are reached after registering in a stone-sheathed lobby whose decor was partly inspired by an 18th-century colonial drawing room. Despite the absence of antique charm, many guests like this place for its polite efficiency and modernism.

Dining/Entertainment: On the premises is The Lion's Den bar (formerly a famous club known as Mercers, whose new format at press time was still unclear), a coffeeshop (Knickerbocker's), and a more formal restaurant, The Pavillion.

Foley House Inn

14 West Hull St., Savannah, GA 31401. ☎ **800/647-3708** or 912/232-6622. Fax 912/231-1218. 19 rms. A/C TV TEL. $85–$190 double. Children under 12 stay free. Rates include continental breakfast. AE, MC, V.

Small scale, and decorated with all the care of a private home, this B&B was established in 1982 within a five-story brick house built in 1896. Two years later, its size was doubled, when the owners managed to acquire the simpler, white-fronted house next door, whose pedigree predates its neighbors by a half-century. The staff will regale you with tales of the original residents of both houses, the older of which had functioned as a dentist's office for many years, the other of which was the site of one of Savannah's most notorious turn-of-the-century suicides.

Breakfast and afternoon hors d'oeuvres, tea, and cordials are served in a large verdant space in back, formed by the interconnected expanse of the two houses' original gardens. Bedrooms each contain

their own fireplaces or wood-burning stoves, four-poster beds, and
enough antiques to evoke the graciousness of old-time Savannah.
Those on the ground floor are more rustic, with exposed brick and
ceiling beams, than the more formal ones upstairs.

✪ Jesse Mount House

209 W. Jones St., Savannah, GA. 31401. ☎ **800/347-1774** or 912/
236-1774. Fax 912/236-2103. 5 suites. A/C TV TEL. $135 suite for two with-
out kitchen, $160 suite for two with kitchen. AE, DISC, MC, V.

Conceived in 1856 as a brick-fronted double townhouse, this building rises in severe dignity on one of the most prestigious streets in
Savannah. Its design might remind you of a sea captain's house in
Nantucket, but inside, its West Coast owner, Sue Dron, managed
to create one of the most dramatic and stylish decors in the New
World. It is far more glamorous than the Foley House Inn. Perfect
Victorian moldings and jewel-toned colors complement the antiques
and modern art she acquired during the years she spent living
in Africa and Spain. Our favorite accommodation is a deliberately
whimsical homage to Africa, a cellar-level suite, whose theme evokes
a safari in Kenya.

The Mulberry (Holiday Inn)

601 East Bay St., Savannah 31401. ☎ **800/465-4329** or 912/238-1200.
Fax 912/236-2184. 96 rms, 21 suites. A/C TV TEL. $125 double; $150 suite.
Children under 18 stay free in parents' room. AE, DC, DISC, MC, V. Park-
ing $5.

Local residents point with pride to this hotel as a sophisticated
adaptation of what might have been a derelict building into a
suprisingly elegant hotel. Originally built in 1868 as a stable and cotton warehouse, it was converted in the early 1900s into a bottling
plant for Coca-Cola. In 1982, it was re-converted into a simple
hotel, and in the 1990s, received a radical upgrade and a gloss of
decorator-inspired Chippendale glamour. Today, its lobby looks like
that of a grand hotel in London, and its bedrooms, although small,
have a formal decor (think English country house with a Southern
accent). The hotel's brick-covered patio, with its fountains, trailing
ivy, and wrought-iron furniture, evokes New Orleans.

Dining/Entertainment: On the premises is a bar (Sergeant
Jasper's Lounge) and two restaurants (The Café for breakfast and
dinner, The Mulberry for more formal dinners).

Facilities: A pool provides a cool dip on a hot day, and there's
access to a nearby health club.

👪 Family-Friendly Hotels

The Mulberry (Holiday Inn) *(see page 130)*   Right in the heart of the Historic District, this hotel lets kids under 18 stay free if sharing a room with their parents. Children enjoy the pool, and cribs are provided free.

Foley House Inn *(see page 129)*   This is one of the few upscale B&Bs that caters to families. Kids under 12 stay free in their parents' room, and cribs are provided free.

River Street Inn *(see page 126)*   The best bet for families with children along the riverfront is a converted cotton warehouse from 1817. Large rooms make family life easier, and children under 18 stay free. There's also a game room, and many fast-food joints are just outside the door of the inn.

Presidents' Quarters

255 E. President St., Savannah, GA 31401. ☎ **800/233-1776** or 912/233-1600. Fax 912/238-0849. 16 rms. A/C TV TEL. $107–$167 double. Rates include continental breakfast. AE, DC, DISC, MC, V. Free parking.

There are many unique aspects to this hotel, the most appealing of which are rooms that are among the largest and most comfortable of any inn or B&B in Savannah. It manages to simultaneously combine the charm of a B&B with the efficiency of a much larger hotel, and do it within a family atmosphere that has appealed to guests as diverse as the former president of Ireland and goodly numbers of Hollywood actors and actresses. Until its restoration in 1986, the 1855 building was a derelict ruin, used as a backdrop for the filming of one of the scenes in the television epic "Roots." Its saviour was Mrs. Muril Broy who, with two intelligent daughters, whipped the property into an appealing small inn. Each accommodation is named after a U.S. president who visited Savannah during his term in office, with memorabilia and framed testimonials to his accomplishments.

Facilities include an outdoor whirlpool/Jacuzzi, a brick-covered patio where continental breakfasts and afternoon teas are served, and a parking lot (rare in the historic heart of Savannah).

MODERATE

East Bay Inn

225 E. Bay St., Savannah, GA 31401. ☎ **800/500-1225** or 912/238-1225. Fax 912/232-2709. 28 rms. A/C TV TEL. $79–$129 double. AE, DC, MC, V.

The inn lies beside the busiest (and least attractive) expanse of Bay Street, but although the views from the windows are uninspired, its location is convenient to the bars and tourist attractions of the nearby riverfront. It was built of brown brick in 1853 as a cotton warehouse. Today, green awnings and potted geraniums disguise the building's once-utilitarian design. A cozy lobby, carved out of the bulky warehouse's street level, contains Chippendale furnishings and elaborate moldings. Bedrooms have queen-size four-poster beds, reproductions of antiques, and coffeemakers. In addition to individual clients, the hotel frequently houses tour groups from Europe and South America. In the cellar is **Schyler's** (☎ **912/232-3955**), an independently managed restaurant specializing in European and Asian cuisine.

Eliza Thompson House

5 W. Jones St., Savannah, GA 31401. ☎ **800/348-9378** or 912/236-3620. Fax 912/238-1920. 23 rms. A/C TV TEL. $89–$109 double. Rates include full breakfast. AE, MC, V.

About half the rooms of this stately home lie within the 1847 original core. The other half are within a gracefully converted carriage house in back. Both were the domain of Eliza Thompson, a socially conscious matriarch whose husband (a cotton merchant) died shortly after the building's foundations were laid in 1846. Developed in 1979 by a team of entrepreneurial antiques dealers (their acquisitions still fill the public areas and the bedrooms of this place), it was bought by new owners in 1995. Bedrooms are comfortable and elegant.

Breakfast is usually a lavish affair, featuring sausage casserole, assortments of muffins, and croissants. During nice weather, it's usually served on the brick terrace of the garden patio which separates the two components of this historic inn.

Lion's Head Inn

120 E. Gaston St., Savannah, GA 31401. ☎ **800/355-LION** or 912/232-4580. Fax 912/232-7422. 4 rms, 2 suites. TV TEL. $85–$110 double; $125 suite. AE, MC, V.

It was originally built in 1883 as a four-story, free-standing Victorian house, something of an oddity in a neighborhood otherwise filled with much smaller 19th-century row houses. A wraparound veranda accents a terra-cotta bas-relief of a lion's head, after which the hotel was named. In October of 1992, a Michigan lawyer, John Dell'Orco, and his wife, Christy, bought the place and furnished it with a collection of antiques that are probably finer than anything the house originally contained. On the premises is a video library, plus 12 fireplaces. Ceilings soar 13 feet above the elegant hardwood floors below them. At any of the afternoon wine and cheese parties, ask about the (empty) coffin the owners discovered during their renovation of one of the bedrooms.

Planters Inn

29 Abercorn St., Savannah, GA 31401. ☎ **800/554-1187** or 912/232-5678. Fax 912/232-8893. 52 rms, 4 suites. A/C TV TEL. $89–$109 double; $125–$200 suite. Rates include continental breakfast. AE, DC, MC, V. Parking $4.50.

This small European-style inn is more businesslike than the average Savannah B&B. Built adjacent to Reynolds Square in 1912 as a seven-story brown brick tower, it boasts a lobby with some of the most elaborate millwork of any commercial building in Savannah, a scattering of Chippendale reproductions, and an honor bar (sign for whatever drink you consume). Bedrooms are comfortably outfitted with four-poster beds and flowery fabrics; they're rather dignified and formal. The Planter's Inn is not associated with the well-recommended Planters' Restaurant (which stands next door, and which is separate).

St. Julian Street B&B

501 E. St. Julian St., Savannah, GA 31401. ☎/fax 912/236-9939. 3 rms (1 with bath). A/C TV. $75–$85 double without bath; $100 double with bath. AE, DISC, MC, V.

Set in a small residential pocket in the commercial heart of town, this B&B is a refreshingly simple alternative to the many grandiose historic inns of Savannah.

The house was built in 1901 at the height of the "golden oak" period, as a quick view of the trim in the living and dining room inside will show. Don't expect glamour here: The place is as homey and modern-day as you'll get, with a loquacious charm provided by Bill and Judy Strong, their dogs, and their son Eric. Bedrooms contain a combination of modern and antique furniture, and all phone calls are made from shared facilities in the hall. Nightlife owls appreciate this place's convenience to Market Square.

Ⓢ 17 Hundred 90

307 E. President St., Savannah, GA 31401. ☎ **800/487-1790** or 912/236-7122. Fax 912/236-7123. 14 rms. A/C TV TEL. $99–$149 double. AE, MC, V.

A severely dignified brick and clapboard-sided house, this place will remind you of the low-ceilinged antique houses you'd have expected along an 18th-century street in New England. It's the oldest inn in Savannah, permeated with conversation and laughter from the basement-level bar and restaurant (see separate listing) and also with the legends of the ghost who haunts the place. (The daughter of the building's first owner threw herself off one of the balconies when the German-born sailor she loved abandoned her for a life at sea.) Accessible via cramped hallways, bedrooms are small but charming, and outfitted with the colonial trappings appropriate for an inn of this age and stature. About a dozen contain fireplaces and small refrigerators.

INEXPENSIVE

Bed and Breakfast Inn

117 W. Gordon St. (at Chatham Square), Savannah, GA 31401. ☎ 912/238-0518. Fax 912/233-2537. 14 rms (7 with bath). A/C TV TEL. $49 double with shared bath; $74 double with private bath. Rates include full breakfast. AE, DISC, MC, V.

Set adjacent to Chatham Square, in the oldest part of historic Savannah, this is a dignified, stone-fronted, four-story townhouse originally built in 1853. Guests climb a gracefully curved front stoop to reach the cool, high-ceilinged interior, which is outfitted with a combination of antique and reproduction furniture. Some accommodations contain refrigerators. No smoking.

Courtyard by Marriott

6703 Abercorn St., Savannah, GA 31405. ☎ **800/321-2211** or 912/354-7878. Fax 912/352-1432. 144 rms, 12 suites. A/C TV TEL. Mon–Fri $82 double, Sat–Sun $67 double; from $102 suite all week. Children under 16 stay free in parents room. Senior discounts available. AE, DC, DISC, MC, V. From I-16, take exit 34A to I-516 East, and turn right on Abercorn Street.

Built around a landscaped courtyard, this is a three-story building and one of the more recommendable motels bordering the Historic District. Many Savannah motels, although cheap, are quite tacky, but this one has renovated bedrooms with separate seating areas, oversize work desks, and private patios or balconies. Family-friendly, it offers a coin laundry and free cribs. The hotel has both a pool and a whirlpool. The restaurant serves an à la carte and a buffet breakfast. Exercise equipment includes weights and bicycles.

Fairfield Inn by Marriott

2 Lee Blvd. (at Abercorn Rd.), Savannah, GA 31405. ☎ **800/228-2800** or 912/353-7100. Fax 912/353-7100. 135 rms. A/C, TV, TEL. $54 double. Children under 18 stay free in parents' room. AE, DC, DISC, MC, V. From I-16, take exit 34A to I-516 East, then turn right on Abercorn Street and go right again onto Lee Boulevard.

Not quite as good as Marriott's other recommended motel (The Courtyard by Marriott), this reliable budget hotel offers standard but comfortably appointed bedrooms, with in-room movies and a large, well-lit work desk. The big attraction of this three-story motel is its outdoor pool. Health-club privileges are available nearby, as are several good and moderately priced restaurants.

4 Dining

ALONG THE WATERFRONT

EXPENSIVE

The Chart House

202 W. Bay St. ☎ **912/234-6686.** Reservations recommended. Main courses $14.50–$29.95; early-bird special (5:30–6:30pm) $14.95. AE, MC, V. Sun–Thurs 5:30–10pm, Fri–Sat 5:30–11pm. STEAK/SEAFOOD/PRIME RIB.

Overlooking the Savannah River and Riverfront Plaza, "the home of the mud pie" is part of a nationwide chain—and it's one of the better ones. It's housed in a building that dates prior to 1790, reputed to be the oldest masonry structure in the state of Georgia and once a sugar and cotton warehouse. You can enjoy a view of passing ships on the outside deck, perhaps ordering an appetizer and drink before dinner. The bar is one of the most atmospheric along the riverfront. As in all Chart Houses, the prime rib is slow roasted and served au jus, or else you can sample one of the steaks from corn-fed beef. Steaks are aged and hand-cut on the premises before being chargrilled. The most expensive item on the menu is lobster, or you might prefer one of the fresh catches of the day.

MODERATE

The Boar's Head

1 N. Lincoln St. (at River Street). ☎ **912/232-3196.** Reservations recommended. Lunch $5–$9; dinner main courses $12–$25. AE, MC, V. Tues–Sun 11:30am–10:30pm. CONTINENTAL/AMERICAN.

One of the most popular waterfront eateries since the 1960s, this restaurant places its tables to take advantage of the view of the Savannah River. The spot is said to be Savannah's oldest restaurant on River Street, a former cotton warehouse some 250 years ago. The stone walls, original brick, and wooden ceiling beams are intact, and the effect is that of a faux-medieval pub. Hanging baskets of greenery and soft candlelight create a cozy, intimate mood. You've probably dined on more fabulous fare in your lifetime, but what you get here isn't bad. There's the usual array of seafood, beef, chicken, veal, lamb, and pasta dishes. A continuous exhibition of paintings is for sale.

✪ Huey's

115 E. River St. ☎ **912/234-7385.** Reservations recommended. Main courses $8.95–$15.95; lunch sandwiches $5.25–$6.99. AE, DISC, MC, V. Mon–Thurs 7am–10pm; Fri 7am–11pm; Sun 8am–10pm. CAJUN/CRÉOLE.

This casual eatery on the ground floor of the River Street Inn overlooks the Savannah River. There's not much here to make this place look different from the other restored warehouses along the water. But you'll discover that it's special when you taste the food, created under the direction of Louisiana-born Mike Jones. He even manages to please visitors from New Orleans—and that's saying a lot. The place is often packed, doing the highest turnover of business on this bustling street. Breakfast might start your day with a Créole omelet; midday might find you munching on an oyster po'boy. But the kitchen really shines at dinner, turning out dishes such as jambalaya with andouille sausage, crawfish etoufée, and crab and ship au gratin, made with Louisiana crabmeat and Georgia shrimp. Soups are homemade, and appetizers are also distinctive. A jazz brunch is featured on Saturday and Sunday from 8am to 3pm. The bar next door offers live entertainment.

River House

125 W. River St. ☎ **912/234-1900.** Reservations recommended. Jacket and tie required at dinner. Lunch main courses $5–$12; dinner main courses $9–$22. AE, MC, V. Mon–Thurs 11am–10pm; Fri–Sat 11am–11pm; Sun noon–10pm. SEAFOOD.

At the point where the S.S. *Savannah* set sail on its maiden voyage across the Atlantic in 1819, this converted riverfront cotton warehouse excels in fresh seafood, the menu depending on the catch of the day. Overlooking River Street with its boat traffic, and lying just down from the Hyatt, this is one of the best dining choices along the river. Appetizers include a seafood strudel made with shrimp, crabmeat, and feta cheese, along with creamed spinach baked in phyllo leaves. Main courses range from deviled crab to charbroiled swordfish. Steaks, chops, chicken, and even pizzas appear on the menu. Sam Harris, the pastry chef, bakes from scratch cookies, pastries, and sourdough French bread in a bakery inside the restaurant. Georgia pecan pie is a house specialty.

Savannah Dining

Billy Bob's ❶

Bistro Savannah ❾

The Boar's Head ❺

The Chart House ❼

Clary's Café ⓰

The Exchange Tavern ❸

45 South at
the Pirate's House ❻

Garibaldi's ❾

Huey's ❷

Il Pasticcio ⓫

Mrs. Wilke's
Boarding House ⓯

Nita's Place ⓬

The Olde Pink House
Restaurant ❿

The Pirate's House ❻

River House ❽

17 Hundred 90 ⓭

Shrimp Factory ❹

606 East Café (Cow Patio) ❾

Wall's ⓮

ⅱ Family-Friendly Restaurants

The Boar's Head *(see page 135)*   One of the best places along the waterfront for families with children is this long-established eatery in a former cotton warehouse. The menu's so wide ranging that even hard-to-please kids usually find something they like.

Mrs. Wilkes' Boarding House *(see page 142)*   Since your kid didn't grow up in the era of the boarding house, here's a chance to experience a long-faded American dining custom. It's an all-you-can-eat type of family-style place. Your little ones might balk at the okra and collards, but go for the corn-on-the-cob and the barbecued chicken.

The Pirates' House *(see page 140)*   It doesn't serve the best food in Savannah, but it's still a hit with kids because of its swashbuckling style, conjuring up memories of *Treasure Island* and other legendary exploits. Stories of shanghaied sailors and ghosts, and rooms with names such as The Black Hole and The Jolly Roger, are guaranteed to grab their interest.

INEXPENSIVE
⑤ Billy Bob's

21 E. River St. ☎ **912/234-5588.** Reservations not necessary. Main courses $5.95–$16.95. AE, DISC, MC, V. Sun–Thurs 11am–10pm, Fri–Sat 11am–11pm. BARBECUE.

Its decor was modeled after a barn somewhere on the panhandle of Texas, with an emphasis on indestructibility (lots of stainless steel tabletops and thick timbers). Recorded music reminds you of the country-western tunes they play at this place's namesake (Billy Bob's) in Houston. Barbecues here are succulent and tender, having been slowly marinated and spicily flavored. Examples include baby back ribs, barbecued chicken, shrimp, and beefsteaks. Appetizers feature a warm crab and artichoke dip, "Miss Kitty's topless oysters," and steaks and seafood include grilled swordfish, battered shrimp platters, and at least five kinds of Angus beef.

The Exchange Tavern

201 E. River St. (east of Bull St.). ☎ **912/232-7088.** Main courses $7.95–$18.95; child's plate $2.95. AE, DC, MC, V. Sun–Thurs 11am–11pm, Fri–Sat 11am–1am. SEAFOOD/LOW COUNTRY.

A local favorite, this 1790s cotton warehouse has been turned into a much-frequented waterfront eatery east of Bull Street, opening onto the riverfront. Surely the chefs make no pretense about their food. Everything is hale and hearty rather than gourmet. Your best bet is the ocean-fresh seafood, served grilled, broiled, or fried. Handcut grilled ribeye steaks are a specialty, along with Buffalo-style wings, shrimp, oysters, and well-stuffed sandwiches served throughout the day. Since 1971 this place has been dispensing its wares, including shish kebabs, fresh salads, and homemade soups. It's also a good place for a drink.

Shrimp Factory

313 E. River St. (2 blocks east of the Hyatt). ☎ **912/236-4229.** Reservations not accepted. Lunch main courses $10.90–$13.90; dinner main courses $15.90–$23.90. AE, MC, V. Mon–Thurs 11am–10pm, Fri–Sat 11am–11pm, Sun noon–10pm. SEAFOOD.

In a king-cotton warehouse, circa 1850, the exposed old brick and wooden plank floors form a setting for a harborview dining venue. Lots of folks drop in before dinner to watch the boats pass by, perhaps enjoying a Chatham Artillery punch in a souvenir snifter. Yes, the place is touristy, never more so than when it welcomes tour buses. A salad bar rests next to a miniature shrimp boat, and fresh seafood comes from local waters. Over a period of a year, 24 different varieties of fresh fish are offered. A specialty, "pine bark stew," is served in a little iron pot with a bottle of sherry on the side; it's a potage of five different seafoods simmered with fresh herbs—but minus the pine bark today. Other dishes include peeled shrimp, shucked oysters, and various fish filets. Live Maine lobsters and sirloin steaks are also featured.

THE HISTORIC DISTRICT
VERY EXPENSIVE
✪ 45 South at the Pirates' House

20 E. Broad St. ☎ **912/233-1881.** Reservations required. Jacket advised for men. Main courses $18.50–$24.50. AE, MC, V. Mon–Sat 6–10pm. INTERNATIONAL.

Elegant and ritzy, recommended by such magazines as *Food & Wine, Southern Living,* and even *Playboy,* this upscale restaurant stands next door to the much more famous Pirates' House, to which it is infinitely superior. Moved to the site in the Pirates' House complex in 1988, this former southside restaurant is small and stylish, done in the "decadent" tones of mauve and green so evocative of Savannah. The ever-changing gourmet Southern menu is likely to feature smoked North Carolina trout, rack of lamb flavored with crushed sesame seeds, grilled venison with a gratin of sweet potatoes, chicken breast with a truffled pâté, or sliced breast of pheasant with foie gras. Appetizers might include everything from South Carolina quail to crab cakes. Perhaps the most expensive restaurant in Savannah, it is softly lit with elegantly set tables and a cozy bar. Service is impeccable.

EXPENSIVE

✪ The Olde Pink House Restaurant

23 Abercorn St. ☎ **912/232-4286.** Reservations recommended. Main courses $17.95–$18.95. AE, MC, V. Daily 6–10:30pm. SEAFOOD/ AMERICAN.

Built in 1771, this place literally glows with a shade of pink (its antique bricks show through the protective covering of stucco). This venerable old house has functioned as a private home, a bank, a tea room, and headquarters for one of Sherman's generals. Today, its interior is outfitted with a severe kind of dignity, with stiff-backed chairs, bare wooden floors, and an 18th-century aura reminiscent of Williamsburg, Virginia. (According to local legend, many of the dinner guests who dined here in the early 1770s plotted the overthrow of the British government in what were at the time the American colonies.)

Today, the restaurant's cuisine is richly steeped in the age-old traditions of the Low Country, and include crispy scored flounder with apricot sauce; steak au poivre; black grouper stuffed with blue crab and drenched in Vidalia onion sauce; and grilled tenderloin of pork crusted with almonds and molasses. You can have your meal in the candlelit dining rooms, or in the basement-level piano bar (described later in this chapter under "Savannah After Dark").

The Pirates' House

East Broad and Bay Street. ☎ **912/233-5757.** Reservations recommended. Lunch buffet $5.95–$8.95; dinner main courses $15.95–$18.95; Sun brunch $14.95. AE, DC, MC, V. Mon–Sat 11:30am–2:30pm, Sun 11am–3pm; Daily 5:30–9:15pm. SEAFOOD/LOW COUNTRY.

Arguably, this is the most famous restaurant in Georgia. It is certainly a Savannah legend. A labyrinth of low-ceilinged dining rooms, the Treasure Island bar, a gift shop, and a small museum share this 1754 Bay Street Inn, once a rendezvous for pirates and sailors. Robert Louis Stevenson used the place as a setting in *Treasure Island,* and it's listed as an authentic house museum by the American Museum Society. You'll want to explore all its many dining rooms.

Time was, we used to veer way out of our way on drives between New York and Florida just to dine here. But sadly, that's not the case anymore. The restaurant has become touristy and the food is often bland—not at all what it used to be. Some dishes are better than others, though, including the sautéed shrimp with an herb Créole sauce and the honey-pecan fried chicken. But a recent sampling of the okra gumbo and a small plate of the Low Country jambalaya proved disappointing. Bring the kids, though. They may love the place, unless they're a future Julia Child or James Beard in the making.

17 Hundred 90

307 E. President St. ☎ **912/236-7122.** Reservations recommended. Lunch main courses $5.50–$8.95; dinner main courses $14.95–$20.75. AE, MC, V. Mon–Fri noon–2pm, daily 6–10pm. INTERNATIONAL.

Set in the brick-lined cellar of the oldest inn in Savannah, this place evokes a seafaring tavern along the coast of New England. Many visitors opt for a drink at the woodsy-looking bar, set within a separate room in back, before heading down the slightly claustrophobic corridor to the cozy, nautically inspired dining room. Students of paranormal psychology remain alert to the ghost that is rumored to wander through this place, site of Savannah's most famous 18th-century suicide.

Lunch might include a simple array of such dishes as quiche of the day with salad; southern-style blue crab cakes; and a choice of salads and sandwiches. Dinners are more formal, featuring crab bisque, snapper parmesan, steaks, and bourbon-flavored chicken. Cookery is of a high standard.

MODERATE

Il Pasticcio

2 E. Broughton St. (corner of Bull and Broughton). ☎ **912/231-8888.** Lunch pastas $6.95–$8.95; main dinner courses $10.95–$23.50; pizzas $7.95–$10.95; Sun brunch $19.95. AE, DC, V. Daily 11:30am–2:30pm; Mon–Fri 6–10pm; Sat–Sun 6–11pm. ITALIAN.

This combination restaurant, bakery, and gourmet market is one of the city's newest dining selections. In a postmodern style, with big windows, a high ceiling, and a location in the commercial heart of town, it has a definite big-city style. A wood-burning pizza oven and a rôtisserie turn out specialties. Adjacent to the dining room is a market showcasing Italian specialties, including cold cuts and breads. The market also sells deli sandwiches. Many locals come here just for the pasta dishes, all of which are homemade and served with savory sauces. Begin with carpaccio (thinly sliced beef tenderloin) or else a tricolor salad of radicchio, endive, and arugula. Main dishes are likely to feature a mixed grilled seafood platter or grilled fish steak with tricolor sweet roasted peppers. The Sunday brunch buffet features live jazz.

INEXPENSIVE
⑤ Clary's Café
404 Abercorn St. (at Jones Street). Breakfast specials $4.50–$7.95; main dinner courses $6.95–$10.95. AE, DC, DISC, MC, V. Mon–Fri 6am–4pm; Sat 8am–4pm; Sun 8am–3pm; Sun–Thurs 5–10pm; Fri–Sat 5–11pm. AMERICAN.

Clary's Café has been a Savannah tradition since 1903, although the aura today—under the devilish direction of Michael Faber—is decidedly in the '50s. The place was famous long before it was featured in *Midnight in the Garden of Good and Evil*. The author, John Berendt, is still a frequent patron, as is the fabled Savannah drag queen, Lady Chablis, who was featured in the novel. A former drugstore, the café has long attracted the regulars of the Historic District, including the eccentric flea-collar inventor. Begin your day with the classic Hoppel Poppel (scrambled eggs with chunks of kosher salami, potatoes, onions, and green peppers) and go on from there. Fresh salads, New York–style sandwiches, and stir-fries along with grandmother's homemade chicken soup and flame-broiled burgers are served throughout the day, giving way to specials of the evening, likely to include chicken pot pie, stuffed pork loin, or planked fish (a fresh filet of red snapper, either broiled, grilled, or blackened).

⑤ Mrs. Wilkes' Boarding House
107 W. Jones St. (west of Bull Street). ☎ **912/232-5997.** Reservations not accepted. Breakfast $5; lunch $8. No credit cards. Mon–Fri 8–9am and 11:30am–3pm. SOUTHERN.

Remember the days of the boarding houses, when everybody sat together and belly-busting food was served in big dishes in the center of the table? Mrs. Selma Wilkes has been serving locals and travelers in just that manner since the 1940s. Charles Kuralt and David Brinkley are among the long list of celebrities who have dined here. You won't find a sign ("It would look so commercial, not at all like home," according to Mrs. Wilkes), but you probably will find a long line of people patiently waiting for a seat at one of the long tables in the basement dining room of an 1870 gray brick house with curving steps and cast-iron trim. Mrs. Wilkes believes in freshness and plans her daily menu around the seasons. Your food will be a reflection of the cuisine Savannah residents have enjoyed for generations—fried or barbecued chicken, red rice and sausage, black-eyed peas, corn-on-the-cob, squash and yams, and other traditional Southern dishes such as okra, cornbread, and collard greens.

🅢 Nita's Place

140 Abercorn St. ☎ **912/238-8233.** Lunch $6.65; dinner $7.65–$8.65. No credit cards. Mon–Sat 11:30am–2:30pm; Wed–Sat 5–8pm. SOUTHERN.

In its way, it's one of the most popular restaurants in Savannah, a local institution favored by a broad cross-section of diners. Outfitted with formica-clad tables and chairs that look straight out of a bowling alley lounge, it occupies cramped, no-frills quarters about a block from Oglethorpe Square, within a building dominated by the black community's most visible Mama, Nita Dixon. Survivor of such earlier jobs as a chef at Burger King, and veteran of years of cooking for teams of construction workers in the field, she established her stake in the early 1990s with a $2,000 inheritance left to her by her father.

You'll be greeted with a broad smile from Nita or her designated representative (any of a squadron of loyal friends); then follow in line to a steam table where simmering portions of Southern food wait delectably to be selected and eaten. They'll include crab cakes, crab balls, meatloaf, fried chicken, collards, pork or beef ribs, several different preparations of okra, butterbeans, yams, and hoecakes, many of whose recipes were handed down from generation to generation through Nita's long line of maternal forebears. Past clients have included Meg Ryan and *The People's Court*'s Judge Wopner.

🅢 Wall's

515 E. York Lane (between York St. and Oglethorpe Ave.). ☎ **912/232-9754.** Reservations not accepted. Main courses $3.60–$5.75. No credit cards. Wed 11am–5pm; Thurs 11am–10pm; Fri–Sat 11am–11pm. BARBECUE.

This is the first choice for any good ol' boy seeking some of the best barbecue in Savannah. Southern barbecue aficionados have inbuilt radar to find a place like this. Once they see the plastic booths, bibs, Styrofoam cartons, and canned drinks from a fridge, they'll know they've found home. Like all barbecue joints, the place is aggressively casual. Spareribs and barbecue sandwiches star on the menu.

Deviled crabs are the only nonbarbecue item, although a vegetable plate of four nonmeat items is also served.

IN & AROUND THE CITY MARKET
MODERATE
Bistro Savannah

309 W. Congress St. ☎ **912/233-6266.** Reservations recommended. Main courses $10.95–$17.95. AE, MC, V. Sun–Thurs 6–10:30pm, Fri–Sat 6pm–midnight. INTERNATIONAL/COASTAL.

Near the City Market, this is probably the most self-consciously artsy restaurant in Savannah, with a staff dressed in the style of a Lyonnais bistro in long aprons and white shirts, and a selection of paintings on exhibit from local art galleries. The decor includes long, uninterrupted expanses of reddish-gray Savannah brick, a reminder of the space's days as a commercial building in the late 1800s. (The staff isn't shy about telling you about the building's role, long ago, as a bordello.)

Menu items feature an eclectic mix of Low Country and international cuisine, and might include a seafood platter, crabmeat-stuffed shrimp, potato-crusted salmon, a savory version of meatloaf made from veal and wild mushrooms, pecan-crusted chicken with blackberry sauce, and onion-crusted red snapper with Madeira sauce.

Garibaldi's

315 W. Congress St. ☎ **912/232-7118.** Reservations recommended. Main courses $6.25–$15. AE, MC, V. Sun–Thurs 6–10:30pm, Fri–Sat 5:30pm–midnight. ITALIAN.

Many of the city's art-conscious students appreciate this Italian café because of the fanciful murals that adorn its walls. (Painted by the owner's daughter, their theme is defined as "The Jungles of Italy.") If you're looking for a quiet, contemplative evening, you'd be well-advised to go elsewhere—the setting is loud and convivial during the early evening, and even louder as the night wears on. Originally designed as a fire station (The Germania) in 1871, it boasts the original pressed-tin ceiling, whose ornate designs seems to reverberate the sound through the room.

Menu items include roasted red peppers served with goat cheese croûtons on a bed of wild lettuces, crispy calamari, artichoke hearts with aïoli, about a dozen kinds of pasta, and a repertoire of Italian-inspired chicken, veal, and seafood dishes. Daily specials change frequently, but sometimes include duck Garibaldi, king-crab fettuccine, and a choice of lusciously fattening desserts.

INEXPENSIVE

606 East Café (Cow Patio)

319 W. Congress St. ☎ **912/233-2887.** Salads, burgers, sandwiches $3–$6.50; platters $6.50–$12.95. AE, MC, V. Mon–Wed 11am–10pm, Thurs–Sat 11am–11pm, Sun 11am–9pm. AMERICAN.

It reigns without competition as the most eclectic, offbeat, irreverent, and good-natured restaurant in Savannah, the almost aggressively whimsical creation of former flower child Sandi Baumer, owner and muralist. A self-described "hater of plain white walls," she combined carloads of 1950s kitsch with pink leopardskin and tongue-in-cheek testimonials to the proud but passé days of psychedelic rock.

Scion of a New Jersey–based family of pizza parlor magnates, and survivor of several years residency in a bus surrounded by an organic farm in Montana, she arrived in Savannah in the mid-1980s with a baby daughter, a beat-up car, and very little money, determined to survive in the restaurant trade.

Food and drinks are served by Cyndi Lauper look-alikes in short, crinoline skirts, and live music is usually featured on a side terrace outfitted like a New Orleans courtyard as viewed through a purple haze. Vegetarian lasagna, burgers, pasta primavera, shrimp tempura, and an "amazing" meatloaf sandwich are included in the bill of fare.

THE VICTORIAN DISTRICT

VERY EXPENSIVE

✪ Elizabeth on 37th

105 E. 37th St. ☎ **912/236-5547.** Reservations required. Main courses $21.50–$25.50. AE, DC, DISC, MC, V. Mon–Thurs 6–9:30pm; Fri–Sat 6–10:30pm. MODERN SOUTHERN.

It reigns in Savannah as the restaurant most frequented by business and media moguls from faraway Atlanta, Los Angeles, and New York. It's the most glamorous, upscale, and conspicuously elegant choice in town, located in a palatial building reminiscent of a neoclassical villa in Monaco. Ringed with semi-tropical landscaping and cascades of Spanish moss, it was built in 1900 as a copy of a house the original owner—a cotton broker—had admired in Boston.

Since 1980, the place has been a restaurant run by Savannah's most successful culinary team, Elizabeth Terry and her husband, ex-attorney Michael, the chef and wine steward, respectively. Elizabeth won the 1995 James Beard best chef award for the Southeast.

Menu items change frequently and with the season, and manage to retain their gutsy originality despite their elegant presentation. Depending on the night of your visit, they're likely to include roast quail with mustard and pepper sauce and an apricot-pecan chutney; herb-seasoned rack of lamb; or broiled salmon with a mustard-garlic glaze. You might begin with grilled eggplant soup, a culinary first for many diners. There's also an impressive wine list, and on Thursday all wines are sold by the glass. Desserts are the best in Savannah. Yes, they are worthy of getting *Gourmet* magazine on the phone.

NEARBY

⑤ Bryan's Pink Pig

Hwy. 170-A, Levy, S.C. ☎ **803/784-3635.** Reservations not necessary, but a phone call for directions is advisable. Barbecue platters $3.85–$7.50. No credit cards. Tues–Wed 11am–7pm; Thurs–Sat 11am–8pm. BARBECUE.

It's so eccentric that despite its location 5 miles northeast of town (across the South Carolina border, en route to Hilton Head), many Savannahians head here for informal and often raucous dinners. It's hard to miss. Its genteel owners, extended members of the Bryan family, used farmland their forebears farmed as the site of a tidy cinderblock building they designed and erected themselves.

Why is it different from other greasy spoons scattered across the state? It's painted in pinks and Day-Glo purples that range from soothing to lurid, and scattered throughout with tongue-in-cheek depictions of pigs, swine, hogs, and piglets, all playing and cavorting like cherubs across a trompe-l'oeil ceiling from the Renaissance.

And what do you get as a reward for your trek out to pig-land? A friendly greeting from one of the most hip and charming staffs of any barbecue joint in the Southeast, and oak- and hickory-smoked barbecue that is positively sublime, made according to recipes perfected by many generations of dedicated barbecue gourmands. Everyone's favorite seems to be the chopped pork sandwiches, although Brunswick stew, coleslaw, ribs, chicken, and burgers are also popular. No beer or liquor is sold, but most locals compensate by bringing in large thermos jugs of tequila or beer.

Johnny Harris Restaurant

1651 Victory Dr. (Hwy. 80). ☎ **912/354-7810.** Reservations recommended. Jacket for men required Sat night in main dining room. Lunch main courses $4.95–$7.95; dinner main courses $7.95–$18.95. AE, CB, DC, DISC, MC, V. Mon–Thurs 11:30am–10:30pm; Fri–Sat 11:30am–midnight. AMERICAN.

Started as a roadside diner in 1924, Johnny Harris is Savannah's oldest continuously operated restaurant. The place today has a lingering aura of the '50s. It also features all that great food so beloved back in the days of Elvis and Marilyn: barbecues, charbroiled steaks, and seafood. The barbecue pork is especially savory, and the prime rib tender. Colonel Sanders never came anywhere close to equaling the fried chicken here. Guests can dine in the "kitchen" or the main dining room, and dance under the "stars" in the main dining room on Friday and Saturday nights when live entertainment is provided. This place will make you nostalgic.

The River's End

3122 River Dr. ☎ **912/354-2973.** Reservations required on Fri–Sat nights. Full dinners $10.95–$24.95. AE, DC, MC, V. Mon–Thurs 5–10pm; Fri–Sat 5–11pm. SEAFOOD. Go 5¹/₂ miles east on U.S. 80 to Victory Drive, then ¹/₂ mile south on River Drive.

At Tassie's Pier next door to the Thunderbolt Marina on the Intracoastal Waterway, this is the preferred place to relax and watch shrimp boat and pleasure boat traffic outside. To the sounds of grand piano music, you can begin with either oysters Rockefeller or Savannah she-crab soup. Charbroiled seafood items include salmon, swordfish, grouper, and tuna. Specials of the day are also recited by the waiter. Fish isn't the only item served. You can try chicken Alfredo, charbroiled steaks, even succulent lamb and duck à l'orange. Desserts range from fresh key lime pie to Georgia bourbon pecan pie.

5 Seeing the Sights

Suggested Itineraries

If You Have 1 Day

Don't put foot outside the Historic District—even at that, you won't see it all. Go to the Savannah Visitors' Center for general orientation, where you can view a 15-minute video presentation to acquaint yourself with the city. Pick up a free map before going to an adjacent building to see the Savannah History Museum. Walk through the museum. Take a guided tour via trolley or bus and later relax and enjoy a harbor cruise.

If You Have 2 Days

See Day 1 above. Spend the second day exploring historic River Street, a nine-block plaza facing the Savannah River, with shops, restaurants, galleries, and pubs. Take our walking tour that encompasses the City Market with its City Market Arts Center, home of some 30 working artists.

If You Have 3 Days

Spend Days 1 and 2 as recommended above. On the third day, stroll the Bull Street corridor with its shops, galleries, museums, and beautiful squares, and pay a visit to some of the elegant historic inns, all uniquely different, perhaps deciding where you'd like to stay on your next visit to Savannah. Sit back and enjoy a leisurely horse-and-carriage tour (perhaps take an evening ghost tour) to see Savannah in a different light. You'll especially enjoy this tour in the evening as the lights are coming on in the houses.

HISTORIC HOMES

Davenport House Museum

324 E. State St. (on Columbia Square). ☎ **912/236-8097.** Admission $4 adults, $3 children 6–18; free for children 5 and under. Mon–Sat 10am–4pm, Sun 10am–4:30pm. Closed major holidays.

This is where those seven determined women started the whole Savannah restoration movement in 1954. They raised $22,500, a tidy sum back then, and purchased the house, saving it from demolition and a future as a parking lot. They established the Historic Savannah Foundation, and the city was spared. Constructed between 1815 and 1820 by master builder Isaiah Davenport, it's one of the truly great Federal-style houses in this country, with delicate ironwork and a handsome elliptical stairway.

Green-Meldrim Home

14 W. Macon St. (on Madison Square). ☎ **912/233-3845.** Admission $4 adults, $2 children. Tues and Thurs–Sat 10am–4pm.

This impressive house was built for cotton merchant Charleston Green. But its moment in history came when it became the Savannah headquarters of General William Tecumseh Sherman at the end

Impression

To His Excellency President Lincoln Washington, D.C. I beg to present you as a Christmas gift the city of Savannah, with one hundred and fifty heavy guns and plenty of ammunition, also about twenty-five thousand bales of cotton.

— W.T. Sherman, Major-General, December 22, 1864

Downtown Savannah Attractions

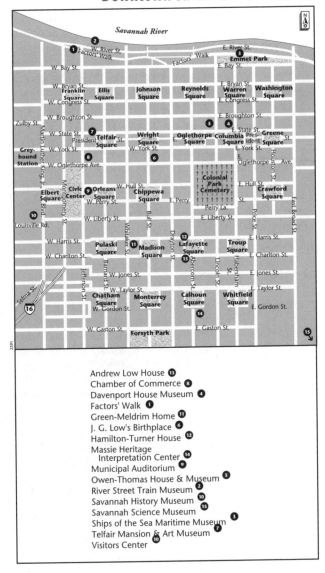

Andrew Low House ⑬
Chamber of Commerce ⑧
Davenport House Museum ④
Factors' Walk ❶
Green-Meldrim Home ⑪
J. G. Low's Birthplace ⑥
Hamilton-Turner House ⑫
Massie Heritage
  Interpretation Center ⑭
Municipal Auditorium ⑨
Owen-Thomas House & Museum ⑤
River Street Train Museum ❷
Savannah History Museum ⑩
Savannah Science Museum ⑮
Ships of the Sea Maritime Museum ❸
Telfair Mansion & Art Museum ⑦
Visitors Center ⑩

of his March to the Sea in 1864. It was from this Gothic-style house that the general sent his now infamous (at least in Savannah) Christmas telegram to President Lincoln, offering him the city as a Christmas gift. Now the Parish House for St. John's Episcopal Church, the house is open to the public. The former kitchen, servants' quarters, and stable are used as a rectory for the church.

Juliette Gordon Low's Birthplace

142 Bull St. (at Oglethorpe Avenue). ☎ **912/233-4501.** Admission $5 adults, $4 children 18 and under. Tues–Thurs 10am–4pm; Sun 12:30–4:30pm. Closed some Sun in Dec–Jan and major holidays.

The founder of the Girl Scouts lived in this Regency-style house that is now maintained both as a memorial to her and as a National Program Center. The Victorian additions to the 1818–21 house were made in 1886, just before Juliette Gordon married William Mackay Low.

The Andrew Low House

329 Abercorn St. ☎ **912/233-6854.** Admission $5 adults, $3 students, $2 children 6-12, free for children 5 and under. Mon–Wed and Fri–Sat 10:30am–4pm, Sun noon–4pm. Closed major holidays.

After her marriage, Juliette Low lived in this house built in 1848, and it was here that she actually founded the Girl Scouts. She died here in 1927. The classic mid-19th-century house is of stucco over brick with elaborate ironwork, shuttered piazzas, carved woodwork, and crystal chandeliers. William Makepeace Thackeray visited here twice (the desk at which he worked is in one bedroom), and Robert E. Lee was entertained at a gala reception in the double parlors in 1870. It faces Lafayette Square.

Telfair Mansion & Art Museum

1212 Bernard St. ☎ **912/232-1177.** Admission $2 adults, $1 students, 50¢ children 6–12; free for children 5 and under. Tues–Sat 10am–5pm, Sun 2–5pm.

The oldest public art museum in the South, housing a collection of both American and European paintings, was designed and built by William Jay in 1818. He was a young English architect noted for introducing the Regency style in America. The mansion was constructed for Alexander Telfair, son of Edward Telfair, the governor of Georgia. A sculpture gallery and rotunda were added in 1883, and Jefferson Davis, former president of the Confederacy, attended the formal opening in 1886. William Jay's period rooms have been restored, and the Octagon and Dining Rooms are particularly

★ Frommer's Favorite Savannah Experiences

Breakfast at Clary's Café. At this former soda fountain, the insider crowd of Savannah shows up—not only John Berendt, author of *Midnight in the Garden of Good and Evil*, but some of the characters in the book as well, including the notorious drag queen, Lady Chablis. This joint also serves the best breakfast in town.

A Night in a Historic Inn. Savannah has some of the most sumptuous inns in the Deep South, and you can find one that suits your dreams—perhaps sleeping in the same bed where Tom Hanks slept when he was in the city filming *Forrest Gump*. To wander into the gardens, parlors, breakfast rooms, and eventually to sleep in the bedrooms of these restored mansions is reason enough to come to Savannah.

Wandering the Squares of the City. Savannah boasts some of the loveliest squares in America, and you can explore them at your leisure, perhaps finding your own bench to tell a stranger the story of your life, as Forrest Gump did. Your best bet is to walk Bull Street, stretching south from the river and named for Col. William Bull, an aide to General Oglethorpe. It holds five of the loveliest squares of Savannah, including Johnson Square, between Bryan and Congress streets, followed by Wright Square, between York and State. Other squares include Chippewa Square, Madison Square, and Monterey Square, all leading to Forsyth Park. The cast-iron fountain here is a focal point for Savannah residents, who sit on its railing, feeding pigeons and listening to strolling musicians.

outstanding. Adapted from the original slave quarters and stable, the Carriage House Visitors' Center opened in 1995.

Owen-Thomas House & Museum

124 Abercorn St. ☎ **912/233-9743.** Admission $5 adults, $3 students, $2 children 6–12; free for children 5 and under. Tues–Sat 10am–5pm, Sun 2–5pm.

Famed as the place where Lafayette spent the night in 1825, this jewel box evokes the heyday of Savannah's golden age. It was designed in 1816 by English architect William Jay, who captured the grace of Georgian Bath in England's county of Avon, and the splendor of Regency London. You can visit not only the bedchambers and kitchen, but the garden and the drawing and dining rooms where gilded entertainment once occurred. Lafayette addressed the people from a balcony on the side of the building.

The Hamilton-Turner House & Ghost House

330 Abercorn St. ☎ **912/233-4800.** Admission $5. Tours daily 10am–4:30pm.

Constructed by a former mayor of Savannah, this is the only Victorian house open to the public in Savannah, and it's said to be haunted. Featured in the novel *Midnight in the Garden of Good and Evil,* it was once described as "the finest furnished home in the South." *A Field Guide to American Houses,* published by Alfred A. Knopf, cites it as a prime example of the Second Empire style, popular in America from 1855 to 1885. The house, once a setting for countless cotillions, debuts, receptions, and weddings, is furnished with museum-quality antiques from the 17th and 18th centuries.

NEARBY FORTS

About 2¹/₂ miles east of the center of Savannah via Islands Expressway stands **Old Fort Jackson,** 1 Fort Jackson Rd. (☎ **912/232-3945**), the oldest standing fort in Georgia, with a 9-foot-deep tidal moat around its brick walls. In 1775 during the Revolutionary War, an earthen battery was built on the future site of Fort Jackson. The original brick fort was begun in 1808 and was manned during the war of 1812. The fort was enlarged and strengthened between 1845 and 1860, and saw its greatest use as the headquarters for the Confederate river defenses during the Civil War. Sherman arrived to conquer it in 1864. Its arched rooms, designed to support the weight of heavy cannon mounted above, hold 13 exhibit areas. The fort is open daily from 9am to 5pm, and charges $2.50 for adults and $2 for seniors and children 6–18, free for 5 and under.

Fort McAllister, Richmond Hill, 10 miles east of U.S. 17 (☎ **912/727-2339**), on the banks of the Great Ogeechee River, was a Confederate earthwork fortification. Constructed in 1861–62, at the beginning of the Civil War, it withstood nearly 2 years of al-most constant bombardment from the sea before it finally fell on December 13, 1864, in a bayonet charge that culminated General Sherman's infamous March to the Sea across Georgia. Sherman remarked that the taking of Fort McAllister was "the handsomest thing I have seen in this war." There's a visitors' center with historic exhibits, and also walking trails and campsites. Hours are Tuesday through Saturday from 9am to 5pm and on Sunday from 2 to 5:30pm. Admission is $2 for adults and $1 for children.

Fort Pulaski (☎ **912/786-5787**), a national monument, stands 15 miles east of Savannah off U.S. 80 on Cockspur and McQueen islands at the very mouth of the Savannah River. It cost $1 million and took 25 tons of brick and 18 years of toil to finish. Yet it was captured in just 30 hours by Union forces. Completed in 1847 with walls $7^1/_2$ feet thick, it was taken by Georgia forces at the beginning of the war. However, on April 11, 1862, defense strategy changed worldwide when Union rifled cannon, firing from more than a mile away on Tybee Island, first overcame a masonry fortification. The effectiveness of rifled artillery—firing a bullet-shaped projectile with great accuracy at long range—was clearly demonstrated. The new Union weapon marked the end of the era of masonry fortifications. The fort was pentagonally shaped, with casemate galleries and draw-bridges crossing the moat. You can still see shells from the 1862 battle imbedded in the walls. There are exhibits of the fort's history in the visitors' center. Hours are daily except Christmas, from 8:30am to 5:15pm. Admission is $2 for adults and free to those 16 and under, with a $4 maximum per car.

LITERARY LANDMARKS

Long before "the book" (the local reference to *Midnight in the Garden of Good and Evil*), there were other writers who were associated with Savannah.

Chief of these was Flannery O'Connor (1925–64), author of such novels as the 1952 *Wise Blood* and the 1960 *The Violent Bear It Away.* She was also known for her short stories, including the collection *A Good Man is Hard to Find* (1955). She won the O. Henry Award three times for best short story, and her portraits of the South have earned her much acclaim. Between October and May, an association dedicated to her holds readings, films, and lectures about her and other Southern writers. You can visit the **Flannery O'Connor Childhood Home** at 207 E. Charlton St. (☎ **912/ 233-6014**). From June through August the house is open only on Saturday from 1 to 4pm. The rest of the year it is open Friday through Sunday from 1 to 4pm. Admission is free.

Conrad Aiken (1889–1973), the American poet, critic, writer, and Pulitzer Prize winner, was also born in Savannah. He lived at 228 and also at 230 E. Oglethorpe Ave. The first home helped launch the revitalization of Savannah's Historic District. No. 228

Searching for Forrest Gump

No sooner do visitors get off the plane or arrive by car than they ask the big question of locals: "Where's the bench?"

At least until the millennium, that question can mean only one thing: Where is the bench that Tom Hanks sat on to spin the adventures of Forrest Gump?

In spite of the mayor's protestations, there is no Forrest Gump bench at Chippewa Square, where scenes from the blockbuster film were shot. Paramount removed the bench, which was a movie prop (not City of Savannah property) when the film was completed.

Visitors react in despair when they learn there is no bench once warmed by Tom Hanks. Even Meg Ryan, Hanks' co-star in *Sleepless in Seattle,* was visibly disappointed when she couldn't find the bench while visiting Savannah.

On Chippewa Square, visitors can see a statue of Gen. James E. Oglethorpe, founder of Georgia. It was because of this early colonial that the mayor lost her bid to have a bronze of Hanks placed on the square, sitting on the bench with a box of chocolates. Local reaction was expressed in this news article, "Gump is not real history and has not the credentials to share Chippewa Square with General Oglethorpe." *Entertainment Tonight* and *People* magazine argued on the side of the mayor for the Gump bench and Hanks bronze, but the idea was squelched.

Paramount actually created four look-alike Savannah park benches to use during filming, since there never was a real-life bench on the spot where Forrest began to spin his tales. Two were rejected as "not authentic looking," and weren't used. One was lost in the bowels of a Paramount warehouse. The fourth bench was appropriated by a member of the film crew, and shipped to his home in North Carolina. That bench is today in private hands and, as one commentator said, "might become as significant as Marilyn's white dress or Dorothy's red shoes."

Paramount has provided Savannah with a fiberglass replica of the bench, and the city has installed it in the Visitors' Center along with a real-life twin taken from Forsyth Park. Visitors can have their pictures taken on the city bench, as the fiberglass can't stand up to heavy use.

Buy your own box of chocolates before heading for the bench to be photographed.

was Aiken's home for the first 11 years of his life. He lived at no. 230 for the last 11 years of his life. In *Midnight in the Garden of Good and Evil,* Mary Hardy and its author sipped martinis at the bench-shaped tombstone of Aiken in Bonaventure Cemetery.

The **Mercer-Wilder House,** 429 Bull St., which Jacqueline Onassis tried to purchase for $2 million, is one of the most fabled and scandalous homes of Savannah, although not open to the public. It's been called "the envy of Savannah," and thousands of visitors stop by to photograph it. This splendid Italianate mansion, where the song-writer Johnny Mercer grew up, was the home of Jim Williams, the rich, gay Savannah antiques dealer. It was in this house that Williams was said to have shot the male hustler Danny Hansford, that "walking streak of sex." Williams was tried four times for murder but was acquitted each time, dying finally of a heart attack, no doubt induced by all his courtroom trauma. This shooting formed the basis of John Berendt's *Midnight in the Garden of Good and Evil.* Today the house is occupied by Dorothy Kingery, sister of Jim Williams.

MUSEUMS

Savannah History Museum

303 Martin Luther King Jr. Blvd. ☎ **912/238-1779.** Admission $3 adults, $1.75 senior citizens and students. Daily 8:30am–5pm.

Housed in the restored train shed of the old Central of Georgia Railway station, behind the visitors' center at Liberty Street and Martin Luther King Jr. Boulevard, this museum is a good introduction to the city. In the theater, the Siege of Savannah is replayed. In addition to the theatrics, there's an exhibition hall displaying memorabilia from every era of Savannah's history.

Savannah Science Museum

4405 Paulsen St. ☎ **912/355-6705.** Admission to museum and planetarium, $3 adults, $2 senior citizens and children 12 and under. Tues–Sat 10am–5pm, Sun 2–5pm. Closed major holidays.

Lying one mile east of downtown Savannah, this museum features hands-on exhibits in natural history, astronomy, and science. Reptiles and amphibians of Georgia are also featured, and planetarium shows realistically re-create night skies every Saturday at 1pm. There are ramps for wheelchair access.

Ships of the Sea Maritime Museum

503 East River St. ☎ **912/232-1511.** Admission $4 adults, $2 children 7–12, free for children 6 and under. Daily 10am–5pm. Closed major holidays.

Located in a renovated waterfront building, it has intricately constructed models of seagoing vessels from Viking warships right up to today's nuclear-powered ships. In models ranging from the size of your fist to 8 feet in length, you can see such famous ships as the *Mayflower* or the S.S. *Savannah,* the first steamship to cross the Atlantic. There are more than 75 ships in the museum's Ship-in-a-Bottle collection, most of them constructed by Peter Barlow, a retired British Royal Naval Commander.

ESPECIALLY FOR KIDS

River Street Train Museum

315 W. River St. (4 blocks west of the Hyatt). ☎ **912/233-6175.** Admission $1.50, 50¢ ages 5–12; free for children under 5. Mon–Sat 11am–6pm; Sun 1–6pm.

To everyone who was given a set of model trains as a child, this museum evokes memories. And it's sure to delight kids of today. Peggy and Tom Spirko operate this family business, which includes both die-cast and plastic-coated models. Toy train displays from the 1930s are featured, and there is also a gift shop.

Massie Heritage Interpretation Center

207 E. Gordon St. ☎ **912/651-7022.** Free admission, but $1.50 donation requested. Mon–Fri 9am–4pm.

Here's a stop in the Historic District for the kids. Geared to school-age children, the center features various exhibits about Savannah, including such subjects as the city's Greek, Roman, and Gothic architecture; the Victorian era; and a history of public education. Other exhibits include a period-costume work room and a 19th-century classroom, where children can experience a classroom environment from days gone by.

BLACK HISTORY SIGHTS

Savannah boasts the First African Baptist Church in North America. It's the **First African Baptist Church** at 23 Montgomery St. (☎ 912/233-6597). Morning worship is at 11:30am daily. It was established by George Leile, a slave whose master allowed him to preach to other slaves when they visited plantations along the Savannah River. Leile was granted his freedom in 1777, and later raised some $1,500 to purchase the present church from a white congregation relocating to Chippewa Square. The black congregation rebuilt the church brick by brick, and it became the first brick building in Georgia to be owned by African-Americans. The church also houses the oldest pipe organ in Georgia, dating from 1888. The pews on either side of the organ are the work of African slaves.

The **Savannah Civil Rights Museum,** 460 Martin Luther King Jr. Blvd. (☎ **912/231-8900**), close to the Savannah Visitors' Center, opened in 1996. It is dedicated to the life and service of African-Americans and the civil-rights movements in Savannah. The museum is a catalyst for educating the public on the rich heritage of African-Americans in Savannah. Call for hours and price of admission.

WALKING TOUR
Historic Savannah

Start: River Street
Finish: Chippewa Square
Time: 2¹/₂ hours
Best Times: Monday to Saturday 9am to 5pm, when most of the stores and attractions are open.
Worst Times: Monday to Saturday after 5pm, when traffic is heavy. On Sunday, there's little life except on the riverfront.

Begin your walk almost where Savannah began at the port opening onto River Street. (Ramps lead down from Bay Street.) The cobblestones came from ballast left behind by early sailing ships coming up the Savannah River.

1. **River Street** runs along the Savannah River. In the mid-19th century, the present brick buildings were most often warehouses holding king cotton.

   On your left is the **John P. Rousakis Plaza.** A multi-million-dollar restoration has revived the riverfront, now a nine-block area ideal for strolling and ship watching. Some 80 boutiques, galleries, restaurants, pubs, and artists' studios line the riverfront today. All of the old cotton warehouses have been restored to a rustic beauty. If you happen to be there on the first Saturday of any month, you'll be swept up in a River Street festival, with live entertainment, street vendors, and sidewalk artists and craftspeople hustling their achievements.

   Near the end of the walk you reach Morrell Park, the site of the:

2. **Waving Girl Statue,** a tribute to Florence Martus (1869–1943), at the foot of the East Broad Street ramp. The statue depicts a young girl waving toward the ships in the harbor. Florence, or so

it is said, fell in love with a sailor. She promised to greet every ship until he returned to marry her. For 44 years, she waved a white cloth by day and a lantern by night to every ship entering the harbor past the Elba Island Light, where she lived with her brother. Greatly loved and looked for eagerly by seamen, she never missed an arriving ship (she said she could "feel" them approaching), and assisted in at least one heroic rescue. Her own sailor never returned.

At the end of the eastern end of the park, take a sharp right and begin your stroll along:

3. **Factors Walk,** lying between River Street and Bay Street. In the 19th century, Factors Walk was named for the factors or brokers who graded the cotton for its quality. Now restored, the walk is filled with specialty shops, often antique. Buildings rise two or three floors above the bluff. The lower floors were cotton and naval warehouses. Connecting bridges lead to upper-level offices opening onto Bay Street.

On your right you'll pass the:

4. **Ships of the Sea Maritime Museum,** 503 E. River St. Artists and models trace the evolution of ships from the Vikings who may have discovered North America before Columbus up to nuclear-powered vessels. You can either visit the museum now or save it for later.

Also on your right is one of the best places to:

☕ TAKE A BREAK F.G. Goodfellows, 115 E. River St. (☎ 912/233-5288), which offers you a choice of eating and drinking inside or out. We prefer the waterfront deck. Sandwiches, seafood dishes, and prime rib are the featured fare. You can also drop in for drinks. It opens at 11am daily and closes when business wanes in the early hours of the morning.

After your refueling stop, climb the brick stairs up to Bay Street, exiting at the River Street Inn. You will be at Old City Exchange Hill, site of the:

5. **Savannah Cotton Exchange,** which today houses the Solomon's Lodge Number 1 of the Free Masons. When it was built in 1887, it was the major center for cotton trading. An example of the Romantic Revival period, it became one of the first buildings in America to use "air rights" and was erected completely over a public street. Its wrought-iron railing honors famous writers and politicians.

Continue to walk down the street, heading west until you reach:

6. **City Hall,** dating from 1905. The stone bench to the left commemorates the landing of Oglethorpe, founder of Georgia, on Feb. 12, 1733. The two floors of this building open onto the spot where, on May 22, 1819, the S.S. *Savannah* set sail. It became the first steamship to cross the Atlantic.

Continue along Bay Street, going left onto Whitaker. Go down Whitaker until you reach Congress Street at which point you turn right, passing the City Market Art Center on your right. This complex in a restored former feed and seed warehouse today houses the working studios of some three dozen of Savannah's finest artists, including photographers, stained-glass designers, sculptors, painters, woodcarvers, and fiber artists.

Congress Street opens onto Ellis Square, site of the:

7. **City Market,** occupying four blocks in the Historic District. Renovated to capture the atmosphere of the past, it is today filled with specialty shops, restaurants, bars, and open-air jazz clubs, along with many theme shops, especially those specializing in crafts, accessories, and gifts.

When you reach the end of the City Market at Franklin Square, turn left onto Montgomery Street and walk down to:

8. **Liberty Square,** lying between York and State streets. It was laid out in May 1799, and was named to honor the "Sons of Liberty," who fought against the British during the Revolutionary War.

From Liberty Square, cut east along President Street to:

9. **Telfair Square,** between York and State streets. Originally it was called St. James' Square, but was renamed for the Telfair family in 1883. Modern Federal buildings are on two sides of the square, and it is also home to the Telfair Academy of Arts and Sciences, which was the site of the Royal Governor's residence from 1760 until the end of the Revolutionary War. Today it's a museum of the arts.

Continue east along President Street until you come to:

10. **Wright Square,** named for Sir James Wright, the third and last colonial governor of Georgia. A large boulder marks the grave of Tomochichi, the Yamacraw Indian chief who befriended Oglethorpe's colonists. A monument here honors William Washington Gordon I, early Georgia financier and founder of the Central Georgia Railway.

East from the square (still on President Street) takes you to:

11. **Oglethorpe Square** between State and York streets. Mapped out in 1742, it, of course, honors General James Edward Oglethorpe, founder of Georgia.

From Oglethorpe Square head south along Abercorn until you reach:

12. **Colonial Park Cemetery,** on your left, which was opened to burial from 1750 to 1850. It became the second public burial ground of Old Savannah, and many famous Georgians were buried here, including Button Gwinnett, a signer of the Declaration of Independence, and Edward Green Malbone, the famous miniature painter. Visitors can wander among the grounds, exploring the inscriptions on the old tombstones.

From the cemetery, go west this time along East McDonough until you reach:

13. **Chippewa Square** along Bull Street, between Perry and Hull streets. The bronze figure in the square immortalized General Oglethorpe and is by Daniel Chester French, dean of American sculptors. The square is visited today by hordes of tourists not wanting to see Georgia's founder but to sit on the bench where Tom Hanks sat in *Forrest Gump.* The actual movie bench isn't there, unfortunately, but plop yourself down somewhere on the square anyway.

6 Organized Tours

A delightful way to see Savannah is by horse-drawn carriage. An authentic antique carriage carries you over cobblestone streets as the coachman spins a tale of the town's history. The one-hour tour ($13 for adults, $6 for children) covers 15 of the 20 squares. Reservations are required; contact **Carriage Tours of Savannah** (☎ 912/236-6756).

Colonial Tours (☎ 912/233-0083) operates tours of the Historic District, with pickups at most downtown inns and hotels ($14 for adults, $6 for children under 12), as well as a one-hour **Haunted History tour** detailing Savannah's ghostly past (and present). Call to reserve for all tours.

Gray Line Savannah Tours (☎ 912/236-9604) have joined forces with **Historic Savannah Foundation Tours** (☎ 912/ 234-TOUR) to feature narrated bus tours of museums, squares, parks, and homes. Reservations must be made for all tours, and most have starting points at the visitors' center, and pickup points at various hotels and motels. Tours cost $18 for adults and $7 for children under 12.

The **Negro Heritage Trail Tour,** 502 E. Harris St. (☎ **912/234-8000**), offers organized tours ($10 adults, $5 children) from an African-American perspective. The trail is sponsored by the King-Tinsdell Cottage Foundation.

Savannah Riverboat Cruises are offered aboard the *Savannah River Queen* operated by River Street Riverboat Co., 9 East River St. (☎ **800/786-6404** or 912/232-6404). You get a glimpse of Savannah the way Oglethorpe saw it back in 1733, as you sit back and listen to a narration of the river's history. You'll see the historic cotton warehouses lining River Street and the statue of the "Waving Girl" the way the huge modern freighters see it today as they arrive at Savannah port daily. Lunch and bar service are available. Adults pay $8.50, and children under 12 are charged $6.

"Ghost Talk Ghost Walk" takes you through colonial Savannah on a journey filled with stories and legends based on Margaret Debolt's book, *Savannah Spectres and Other Strange Tales.* A guide, Jack Reynolds, unfolds these stories of hauntings, howlings, and habitations. If you're not a believer at the beginning of the tour, perhaps you will be at the end. The tour begins at Reynolds Square. For information, call Jack Richards at New Forest Studios, 127 E. Congress St. (☎ **912/233-3896**). Hours for tour departures can vary. The cost is $10 for adults and $5 for children.

Tours by BJ, Inc., departing from Madison Square (☎ **912/233-2335**), walks "the book"—*Midnight in the Garden of Good and Evil,* of course—every Sunday (call for reservations and times). The cost is $12.50 per person, and the tour begins at Monterey Square. You can also join a storyteller for a 90-minute "Spirited Stroll" daily, lasting $1^{1}/_{2}$ hours and costing $12.50. That tour departs at twilight from Madison Square, and reservations are necessary.

Low Country River Excursions, a narrated nature cruise, is available at Bull River Marina, 8005 Old Tybee Rd. (Hwy. 80 East). For information, call **912/898-9222.** Passengers are taken on a 1993 38-foot pontoon boat, *Nature's Way,* for an encounter with the friendly bottle-nose dolphin. Both scenery and wildlife unfold during the 90-minute cruise down the Bull River. Trips are possible daily at 2pm, 4pm, and sunset spring through fall, weather permitting. Adults pay $12, seniors $10, and children under 12 $8. There's a 30-passenger limit.

7 Outdoor Activities

A 10-minute drive across the river from downtown Savannah delivers you to the wild even though you can see the city's industrial and port complexes in the background. The **Savannah National Wildlife Refuge,** which overflows into South Carolina, is a wide expanse of woodland and marsh, ideal for a scenic drive, a canoe ride, a picnic, and most definitely a look at a variety of animals.

From Savannah, get on U.S. Hwy. 17A, crossing the Talmadge Bridge. It's about 8 miles to the intersection of Hwys. 17 and 17A, where you turn left in the direction of the airport. You'll see the refuge entrance, marked Laurel Hill Wildlife Drive, after going some 2 miles.

The refuge draws naturalists, botanists, canoeists, birders, and just plain visitors—it's like visiting a zoo without the cages. Inside the gate to the refuge is a visitors' center, distributing maps and leaflets.

Laurel Hill Wildlife Drive goes on for 4 miles or so. It's also possible to bike this trail. Mainly people come here to spy on the alligators; spottings are almost guaranteed. However, other creatures in the wild abound, including the bald eagle or perhaps an otter.

Hikers can veer off the drive and go along Cistern Trail leading to Recess Island. As the trail is marked, there is little danger of getting lost.

Nearly 40 miles of dikes are open to birders and backpacking hikers, among others. Canoeists float along tidal creeks, which are "fingers" of the Savannah River. Fishing and hunting are allowed in special conditions and in the right seasons. Deer and squirrel are commonplace. Rarer is the feral hog known along coastal Georgia and South Carolina. The refuge was once the site of rice plantations in the 1800s.

Visits are possible daily sunrise to sunset. For more information, write Savannah National Wildlife Refuge, U.S. Fish & Wildlife Service, Savannah Coastal Refuges, P.O. Box 8487, Savannah, GA 31412 (☎ **912/652-4415**).

BIKING

Of course, it's always dangerous to ride bikes in any city, but Savannah does not usually have a lot of heavy traffic except during rush hours. Therefore, you can bicycle up and down the streets of the Historic District, visiting as many of the green squares as you wish. There is no greater city bicycle ride in all of the state of Georgia.

Impressions

For me, Savannah's resistance to change was its saving grace. The city looked inward, sealed off from the noises and distractions of the world at large. It grew inward, too, and in such a way that its people flourished like hothouse plants tended by an indulgent gardener. The ordinary became extraordinary. Eccentrics thrived. Every nuance and quirk of personality achieved greater brilliance in that lush enclosure than would have been possible anywhere else in the world.
—John Berendt, *Midnight in the Garden of Good and Evil* (1994)

The **Wheelman Bicycle Shop,** 103 W. Congress St. (☎ 912/ 234-0695), will provide a map and tips on the city's most scenic routes with each rental, costing $5 per hour and $25 per day.

CANOEING

White's Canoe Rentals, Route 4, Bush Rd. (☎ 912/748-5858), charges $35 per hour for canoes. Rentals include drop-off at the Ogeechee River and I-80 by a staff member and, at a predetermined time, pickup downstream at Morgan's Bridge. Open daily 6am till dark.

DIVING

The **Diving Locker–Ski Chalet,** 74 W. Montgomery Cross Rd. (☎912/927-6604), offers a wide selection of equipment and services for various watersports. Scuba classes cost $230 for a series of weekday evening lessons, and $245 for a series of lessons that run from Friday evening through Sunday. A full scuba-gear package, including buoyancy-control device, tank, and wet suit, goes for $38. You must provide your own snorkel, mask, fins, and booties. Open Monday through Friday 10am to 6pm and Saturday 10am to 5pm.

FISHING

Amicks Deep Sea Fishing, 6902 Sand Nettles Dr. (☎ 912/ 897-6759), offers daily charters featuring a 41-foot 1993 custom-built boat. The rate is $65 per person and includes rod, reel, bait, and tackle. Bring your own lunch, although beer and sodas are sold on board. Reservations are recommended, but if you show up 30 minutes before scheduled departure, there may be space available. Daily departures from Bull River Marina on Hwy. 80 are at 7am, with returns at 6pm.

Another possibility is Captain George Patterson's **Escapade Charters,** Hogan's Marina (☎ **912/897-9569**). Options include inland, near coastal, snapper banks, and Gulf Stream fishing, as well as sightseeing runs. Specializing in blue marlin fishing, Escapade offers half-day off-shore charters for $360 and full-day for $550. Rates include rod, reel, and tackle, but you must supply your own food and beverages. Full-day bottom fishing from the Gulf costs $850. Call for reservations and charter times.

GOLF

Bacon Park, Shorty Cooper Dr. (☎ **912/354-2625**), is a 27-hole course with greens fees costing $11.75 Monday through Friday and $13.75 Saturday and Sunday for an 18-hole round. Carts can be rented for an additional $9.50 per round. Golf facilities include lighted driving range, putting greens, and pro shop. Open daily 6:30am to 8:30pm.

Henderson Golf Club, 1 Henderson Dr. (☎ **912/920-4653**), includes an 18-hole championship course, lighted driving range, PGA professional staff, and golf instruction and schools. The greens fees are $27.56 Monday through Friday and $34.98 Saturday and Sunday. Open daily 7:30am to 10pm.

Another option is the 9-hole **Mary Calder,** West Congress St. (☎ **912/238-7100**), where the greens fees are $8 per day Monday through Friday and $10 per day Saturday and Sunday. Carts rent for $3.50 for a 9-hole round. Open daily 7:30am to 7pm.

IN-LINE SKATING

At **Diving Locker–Ski Chalet** (see "Diving," above), 4-hour skate rentals cost $12 and full-day $20 with a Friday to Monday rental going for $35.

JET SKIING

At **Bull River Marina,** 8005 Old Tybee Rd., Hwy. 80 East (☎ **912/898-9222**), you can rent one-, two-, and three-seater jet skis. The one- and two-seaters go for $30 per half hour and $50 per hour, with the three-seaters renting at $35 per half hour and $60 per hour. Open daily 9am to 6pm. Reservations are recommended.

JOGGING

"The most beautiful city to jog in"—that's how the president of the Savannah Striders Club characterizes Savannah. He is correct. The historic avenues provide an exceptional setting for your run.

The Convention and Visitors Bureau can provide you with a map outlining three of the Striders Club's routes: Heart of Savannah YMCA Course, 3.1 miles; Symphony Race Course, 5 miles; and the Children's Run Course, 5 miles.

NATURE WATCHES

Explore the wetlands with **Palmetto Coast Charters,** Lazaretto Creek Marina, Tybee Island (☎ **912/786-5403**). Charters include trips to the Barrier Islands for shell collecting and watches for otter, mink, birds, and other wildlife. The captain is a naturalist and a professor so he can answer your questions. Palmetto also features a dolphin watch usually conducted daily from 4:30 to 6:30pm, when the shrimp boats come in with dolphins following behind. Times of the charters depend on the weather and the tides; therefore you must call ahead for an appointment. A minimum of 2 hours is required, costing $100 for up to six people and $50 for each additional hour.

RECREATIONAL PARKS

Bacon Park (see "Golf," above and "Tennis," below) includes 1,021 acres with archery, golf, tennis, and baseball fields.

Daffin Park, 1500 East Victory Dr. (☎ **912/355-7964**), features playgrounds, soccer, tennis, basketball, baseball, a swimming pool, a lake pavilion, and picnic grounds. Both of these parks are open daily from May through September 8am to 11pm, and from October through April 8am to 10pm.

Located at Montgomery Cross Road and Sallie Mood Drive, **Lake Mayer Park** (☎ **912/652-6780**) consists of 75 acres featuring a multitude of activities, such as public fishing and boating, lighted jogging and bicycle trails, playground, and pedal-boat rentals.

The public school system operates **Oatland Island Education Center,** 1711 Sandtown Rd. (☎ **912/897-3773**), set on 175 acres with a marsh walkway, observatories, compass trails, marine-monitoring station, and trails to 10 animal habitats. Admission is a minimum 50¢ donation per person. Open from May through August and October through March, Monday through Friday 8:30am to 5pm, and every second Saturday 10am to 5pm.

SAILING

Sail Harbor, 618 Wilmington Island Rd. (☎ **912/897-2896**), features the Precision 21 boat, costing $90 per half-day and $120 per day with an additional day costing $80. A Saturday and Sunday outing goes for $200. Open Tuesday through Saturday 10am to 6pm, and Sunday 12:30 to 5:30pm.

TENNIS

Bacon Park (see "Golf," above; ☎ 912/351-3850) offers 14 lighted courts with operating hours of Monday through Thursday 9am to midnight, Friday 9am to 5pm, and Saturday 9am to 1am. **Forsyth Park,** at Drayton and Gaston streets (☎ 912/351-3852), has four courts that are open daily 7am to 9pm. Both parks charge $1.75 per hour during the day and $2.25 per hour after 5pm. The use of the eight lighted courts at **Lake Mayer Park,** at Montgomery Cross Road (see "Recreational Parks," above), costs nothing. Courts are open daily 8am to 11pm.

8 Shopping

River Street is a shopper's delight, with some nine blocks (including Riverfront Plaza) of interesting shops, offering everything from crafts to clothing to souvenirs. The **City Market,** between Ellis and Franklin squares on West St. Julian Street, has art galleries, boutiques, and sidewalk cafés along with a horse-and-carriage ride. Bookstores, boutiques, and antique shops are located between Wright Square and Forsyth Park.

ANTIQUES

Alex Raskin Antiques

441 Bull St. (in the Noble Hardee Mansion), Monterey Square. ☎ 912/232-8205.

This shop offers a wide array of antiques of varying ages. The selection includes everything from accessories to furniture, rugs, and paintings. Open Monday through Saturday 10am to 5pm.

J.D. Weed & Co.

102 W. Victory Dr. ☎ 912/234-8540.

This shop prides itself on providing "that wonderful treasure that combines history and personal satisfaction with rarity and value." If you are looking for a particular item, just let the staff know and they will try to find it for you. Open Monday through Friday from 8am to 4:30pm, and Saturday from 9am to 3pm.

Memory Lane

230 W. Bay St. ☎ 912/232-0975.

More than 8,000 square feet of collectibles can be found here. The specialty of the house is a collection of German sleds and wagons.

You'll also find glassware, furniture, and pottery. Open Monday
through Saturday 10am to 5pm, and Sunday 11am to 4pm.

ART
Bull Street Gallery
248 Bull St. ☎ **912/233-4307.**

This gallery features the works of more than 80 artists. Pieces include
hand-thrown pottery, metalwork, paintings, prints, woodworks, jewelry, and glass, including hand-blown and leaded. Open Monday
through Saturday 10am to 6pm.

Gallery 209
209 E. River St. ☎ **912/236-4583.**

Housed in an 1820s cotton warehouse, this gallery displays two
floors of original paintings by local artists, sculpture, woodworking,
fiber art, gold and silver jewelry, enamels, photography, batiks,
pottery, and stained glass. You'll also find a wide selection of limited-edition reproductions and note cards of local scenes. Open
Monday through Saturday 10:30am to 5:30pm, and Sunday noon
to 5:30pm.

Guess What? II
24 Drayton St. ☎ **912/236-8644.**

This gallery features a large selection of artifacts by artists from
around the country. From the hand-blown glass to the pottery and
kaleidoscopes, you'll be sure to find just the right gift item. Open
Monday through Friday 10am to 5pm, and Saturday 11am to 2pm.

John Tucker Gallery
5 West Charlton St. ☎ **800/350-1401** or 912/231-8161.

This gallery offers museum-quality pieces by local artists as well as
those from around the world, including Haitian and Mexican
craftspeople. Located in a restored 1800s home, the gallery features
19th- and 20th-century landscapes, marine-art painting, portraits,
folk art, and still life. Open Tuesday through Saturday 10am to
5:30pm.

Village Craftsmen
223 W. River St. ☎ **912/236-7280.**

This collection of artisans offers a wide array of handmade crafts,
including hand-blown glass, needlework, folk art, limited-edition
prints, restored photographs, and hand-thrown pottery. Open daily
10am to 6pm.

BOOKS

Book Warehouse

8705 Abercorn St. ☎ **912/354-1441.**

This store offers more than 75,000 titles, including fiction, cookbooks, children's books, computer manuals, and religious tomes. Prices begin at less than a dollar, and all proceeds are donated to Emory University for cancer research. Open daily 10am to 9pm.

E. Shaver, Bookseller

326 Bull St. ☎ **912/234-7257.**

Book aficionados will love this shop. Housed on the ground floor of a Greek Revival mansion, E. Shaver features 12 rooms of tomes. Specialties include architecture, decorative arts, regional history, and children's books, as well as 17th-, 18th-, and 19th-century maps. Open Monday through Saturday 9am to 6pm.

CANDIES

River Street Sweets

13 E. River St. ☎ **800/627-6175** or 912/234-4608.

Begun more than 20 years ago as part the River Street restoration project, this store offers a wide selection of candies, including pralines, bearclaws, fudge, and chocolates. Included among the specialties are more than 30 flavors of taffy made on a machine that dates back to the early 1900s. Top-quality ingredients with no preservatives go into making this candy, most of which is made on the premises. Open Monday through Thursday 9:30am to 10pm, and Friday through Sunday 9:30am to 9pm.

Savannah's Candy Kitchen

225 E. River St. ☎ **800/242-7919** or 912/233-8411.

Chocolate-dipped Oreos, glazed pecans, pralines, and fudge are only a few of the delectables to be found at this confectionery. While enjoying one of the candies or ice creams, you can watch the taffy machine in action. Staff members are so sure that you'll be delighted with their offerings that they offer a full money-back guarantee if not satisfied. Open Monday through Saturday 9:30am to 11pm, and Sunday 9:30am to 10pm.

CANDLES

River Street Candle Factory

121 W. River St. ☎ **912/231-9041.**

Ann Marie and Chuck Jones own this candle-making establishment. You can watch a candle being made from beginning to end in about

15 minutes at demonstrations held throughout the day. All the personnel train for roughly one year before they can create their own pieces. Open Monday through Saturday 10am to 9pm.

DISCOUNT SHOPPING
Savannah Festival Factory Stores
Abercorn at I-95. ☎ **912/925-3089.**

Thirty manufacturer-owned factory-direct stores offer savings up to 70%. Shops feature national brand names of shoes, luggage, gifts, cosmetics, household items, toys, and clothing, including T-Shirts Plus and the Duckhead Outlet. Open Monday through Saturday 9am to 9pm, and Sunday 11am to 6pm.

FASHION
CHILDREN'S
Kidswear Outlet
1 W. Broughton Rd. ☎ **912/233-4354.**

Specializing in clothes for children up to age 16, this store sells national name brands with discounts up to 50% off department store prices. The selection includes more than 25,000 items for infants, girls, and boys. Open Monday through Saturday 9:30am to 6pm.

Punch and Judy
4511 Habersham St. ☎ **912/314-JUDY.**

Specializing in children's clothes since the mid-1940s, this store carries a large selection of brand-name clothing, in sizes for newborn up to pre-teen girls, and boys size 20. Other items offered include items for the nursery, from furniture down to accessories. Open Monday through Saturday 9:30am to 6pm, and Sunday 12:30 to 5pm.

MEN'S & WOMEN'S
Land & Sea Wear
209 West River St. ☎ **912/232-9829.**

Billed as "casual wear with a nautical flair," the inventory here covers everything you'll need for a day at sea. Offerings include T-shirts, souvenir sweatshirts, sportswear from PCH, and some of the hippest boating attire around. Open daily 10am to 10pm.

FLEA MARKETS
Keller's Flea Market
5901 Ogeechee Rd. ☎ **912/927-4848.**

With more than 400 booths, this market is touted as "the largest flea market in the coastal empire." You'll see a 1920 Fairbanks and

Morse diesel engine, antique farm equipment, a cane mill, and syrup cooker. Included on the property is Janie Arkwright's Kitchen and Snack Bar, serving dishes such as barbecue, popped pork pellets, corndogs, and burgers. Open Saturday and Sunday 8am to 6pm.

FOOD

Plantation Sweet Vidalia Onions
Route 2, Cobtown. ☎**800/541-2272.**

On the way to Savannah, check out the Vidalia onion specialties offered by the Collins family for more than 50 years. Try one of the relishes, dressings, gift items, as well as the world famous sweet onions. Call for directions. Open Monday through Friday 8am to 6pm.

GIFTS

Charlotte's Corner
1 W. Liberty St. (at the corner of Bull Street). ☎ **912/233-8061.**

Specializing in local items, this shop offers a wide array of gifts and souvenirs. The selection includes children's clothing, a few food items, Sheila houses, and Savannah-related books, including guide books and Southern cookbooks. Open daily 10am to 6pm.

The Checkered Moon
422 Whitaker St. ☎ **912/233-5132.**

Located in the Historic District, this shop features more than 40 artists from throughout the Southeast. You'll find wall hangings, pottery, jewelry, clothing, furniture, and sculptures. Open Monday and Wednesday through Saturday 10:30am to 5pm, and Sunday noon to 3pm.

D&B Collection
408 Bull St. ☎ **912/238-0087.**

You'll find a mixed bag of items from around the world, as well as pieces from estate collections and local craftspeople. Lamps, art, mirrors, pillows, pedestals, boxes, bowls, sculpture, and furniture are just a few of the items on sale. Open Monday through Saturday 10am to 6pm.

Elizabeth's Fancy
311 Bull St. ☎ **912/234-8937.**

Victorian specialties abound in this shop. From the reproduction jewelry to antique home accessories, everything smacks of the

Victorian era right down to the laces, including Heritage and Battenburg. Open Monday through Saturday 10am to 5pm.

HAMMOCKS

The Hammock Company

20 Jefferson St. (at the City Market). ☎ **800/344-4264** or 912/232-6655.

Here you can learn about the history and tradition of the more than century-old world-famous Pawleys Island Rope Hammock. Other items featured include plantation rockers, Audubon guides, wind chimes, garden supplies, and a multitude of other nature gifts. Open Monday through Saturday 9am to 9pm, and Sunday 10am to 7pm.

JEWELRY

Levy Jewelers

4711 Waters Ave. ☎ **912/238-2125.**

Located downtown, this boutique deals mainly in antique jewelry. It offers a large selection of gold, silver, gems, and watches. Among its other offerings are crystal, china, and gift items. Open Monday through Saturday 10am to 5:30pm.

MALLS

Oglethorpe Mall, at 7804 Abercorn St., has more than 100 specialty shops and four major department stores, as well as restaurants and fast-food outlets. The **Savannah Mall,** 14045 Abercorn St., is Savannah's newest shopping center, offering two floors of shopping. Included on the premises is a food court with its own carousel. The anchor stores include J.B. White, Montgomery Ward, Parisian, and Belk.

SCULPTURE

The Greek Festival

143 Bull St. ☎ **912/234-8984.**

Many of the clients of this unusual store consider it a valuable resource for the creation of stage or movie sets, fashion displays, or dramatic living spaces. Co-owner Kelli Johnson acquires the molds for pieces of ancient Greek and Roman sculpture, Baroque or Victorian wall brackets, carved animals, and fanciful coffee tables (everything from Chinese Foo dogs to giant tortoises bearing tufted cushions for use as coffee tables). The selection is delightful, and the fact that everything is cast in reinforced plaster or concrete makes the price a fraction of what it would have been if objects had been carved individually. The store can arrange shipping to virtually anywhere, and if what you want isn't in stock, you can order from a voluminous catalogue showing dozens of additional models and designs. Open Monday through Saturday 10am to 5pm.

SILVER

Simply Silver

14-A Bishop's Court. ☎ **912/238-3652.**

The specialty here is sterling flatware, from today's designs to discontinued items from yesteryear. The inventory includes new and estate pieces along with a wide array of gift items. Open Monday through Saturday 10am to 5:30pm.

TOYS

Enchantments

311 Bull St. (at Madison Square). ☎ **800/330-9345** or 912/231-9323.

If you collect bears or dolls, this store has a "pet" for you. Among its other selections is an array of quality toys and collector pieces. Open Monday through Saturday 10am to 5:30pm.

9 Savannah After Dark

River Street, along the Savannah River, is the major venue. Many night owls stroll the riverfront until they hear the sound of music they like, then they go inside.

In summer, concerts of jazz, big band, and Dixieland music fill downtown Johnson Square with lots of foot-tapping sounds that thrill both locals and visitors. Some of Savannah's finest musicians perform regularly on this historic site.

THE PERFORMING ARTS

The **Savannah Symphony Orchestra** has city-sponsored concerts in addition to its regular ticketed events. To spread a blanket in Forsyth Park and listen to the symphony perform beneath the stars, or to be on River Street during the 4th of July when the group sends rousing strains echoing across the river, is to be transported.

The Orchestra is one of two fully professional orchestras in the state of Georgia, and its regular nine-concert masterworks series is presented in the Savannah Civic Center's Johnny Mercer Theater at Orleans Square, which is also home to ballet, musicals, and Broadway shows. Call **800/537-7894** or 912/236-9536 to find out what's being presented when you visit. Tickets range from $9 to $39.

The **Savannah Theater,** Chippewa Square (☎ **912/233-7764**), presents contemporary plays, drama, and comedy. Tickets are usually $13 for regular admission, $11 for seniors and students.

September brings the 5-day **Savannah Jazz Festival,** with nationally known musicians appearing at various venues around the city. For more information, call **912/232-2222.**

THE CLUB & MUSIC SCENE
JAZZ & DIXIELAND
The Crossroads

219 W. St. Julian St. ☎ **912/234-5438.** Cover $3 Fri–Sat.

This club features live entertainment from 10pm to 2am, showcasing the blues. Try your hand at singing on Tuesday's open-mike night. Open Monday through Friday 5pm to 3am, and Saturday 7pm to 3am.

✪ Hannah's East

The Pirates' House, 20 E. Broad St. ☎ **912/233-2225.** $3 cover Fri–Sat after 9pm.

This club—the most popular in Savannah—is the showcase for jazz great Ben Tucker and also for Emma Kelly, "The Lady of 6,000 Songs," who was one of the foremost characters in John Berendt's *Midnight in the Garden of Good and Evil. Gourmet* magazine hailed the club as offering "the best music in the South." Emma holds forth from 6 to 9pm Tuesday through Sunday, and Ben Tucker and his friends entertain with toe-tapping classical jazz Friday and Saturday. Ben has recorded with such stars as Duke Ellington. A Monday night special features authentic Dixieland and New Orleans–style jazz, beginning at 6pm. The club opens nightly at 6pm. Closing times vary, 11pm most nights, but likely to remain open until 3am on Friday and Saturday.

Hip Huggers

9 W. Bay St. ☎ **912/233-6999.** Cover $6 for men, $3 for women.

Nostalgia is the catch phrase here, with this disco offering dance music from the 1970s and '80s. On Thursday night, there's a free buffet. Open Monday through Saturday 7:30pm "until."

✪ Planters Tavern

In the Olde Pink House, 23 Abercorn St. ☎ **912/232-4286.**

It's probably the most beloved tavern in Savannah, graced with a sprawling and convivial bar area and a pair of symmetrically positioned fireplaces that cast a welcome glow over a decor of antique bricks and carefully polished and darkened hardwoods. Because it's located in the cellar of the Olde Pink House restaurant (which is separately recommended under "Dining"), many folks ask for their platters of food to be served at a table in the tavern. Otherwise, you can sit, drink in hand, listening to the melodies emanating from the sadder-but-wiser pianist who warbles away the evening with   the remembered nostalgia of yesteryear. Foremost among the divas who perform is the endearingly elegant Gail Thurmond, one of Savannah's most legendary songstresses. The tavern is open nightly from 5pm till at least 1am, although food service is likely to stop at 10:30pm.

The Zoo

121 W. Congress St. ☎ **912/236-6266.** Cover $3, 21 and over; $10 under 21.

The Zoo is actually three clubs in one. The three dance floors offer top 40, alternative bands, and acid rock. The 25-screen video wall is one of the largest in the Southeast. Open Monday through Saturday 9pm to 3am.

THE BAR SCENE

✪ Club One

1 Jefferson St. ☎ **912/232-0200.** Cover (after 9:30pm only) $10 for 18–20 year olds; $5 for customers 21 and older.

It defines itself as the premier gay bar in a town which prides itself on a level of decadence that falls somewhere between that of New Orleans and Key West. But no one in Savannah caters much to facile definitions of sexuality, and as such, the place is the hottest, hippest, and most amusing nightspot in town. You might meet a coterie of lesbians and gay men from the coastal islands; visiting urbanites from Atlanta, New York, and Los Angeles (including such celebs as Demi Moore and Bruce Willis); and cast and crew members of whatever film is being shot in Savannah at the time. There's also likely to be a healthy dose of voyeuristic readers of *Midnight in the Garden of Good and Evil,* including local suburbanites who come to see the stage where Lady Chablis still occasionally reasserts her status as Savannah's top diva.

Here's how it works: Pay your admission at the door, showing ID if the attendant asks for it. Wander through the street-level dance bar, trek down to the basement-level video bar for a change of (less noisy) venue, and if your timing is right, climb one floor above street level for a view of the drag shows. There, a bevy of *artistes* lip-synch the hits of such oft-emulated stars as Tina Turner, Gladys Knight, and the divine Marilyn Monroe herself.

Open Monday through Saturday 5pm to 3am, Sunday 5pm to 2am; shows nightly at 10:30pm and 1am.

The Crystal Beer Parlor
301 W. Jones St. ☎ **912/232-1153.**

This historic haunt west of Bull Street opened its doors in the Depression days of 1933 and sold huge sandwiches for a dime. Prices have gone up since then, but local affection for this plain, unpretentious place has diminished not one whit. Try to go earlier or later than peak lunch or dinner hours (if you get there at noon, you'll be in for a lengthy wait). Inside, you can order draft beer in a frosted mug, and owner Conrad Thomson still serves up fried oysters and shrimp salad sandwiches, crab stew, and chili. The seafood gumbo is one of the best in the Southern Atlantic region, in our opinion. Plates cost $4.95 to $13.95, and the beer is reason enough to visit. Open Monday through Saturday 11am to 9pm. There's ample parking in the lot off Jones Street.

Kevin Barry's Irish Pub
117 W. River St. ☎ **912/233-9626.**

The place to be on St. Patrick's Day, this waterfront pub rocks all year. Irish folk music will entertain you as you choose from a menu featuring such Irish fare as beef stew, shepherd's pie, and the predictable corned beef and cabbage. Seafood and sandwich platters are also sold. Many folks come here just to drink, often making a night of it in the convivial atmosphere. Open Monday through Friday 4pm to 3am, Saturday and Sunday 11am to 3pm.

Six Pence Pub
245 Bull St. ☎ **912/233-3156.**

This is considered the most authentic-looking English pub in Savannah. You can drop in for a selection of pub grub, including English fare along with homemade soups, salads, and sandwiches. On Sunday an ale-and-mushroom pie is featured. Drinks are discounted during happy hour Monday through Friday from 5 to 7pm. On Friday and Saturday live music is offered, ranging from beach music to contemporary to jazz. Open Sunday 12:30 to 10pm, Friday and Saturday from 11:30am to 1am, and Monday through Thursday 11:30am to midnight.

The Rail

405 W. Congress St. ☎ **912/238-1311.**

Opened in 1995, this place isn't as aggressively noisy as the above-mentioned Club One, but with an enviable grace and ease, it manages to be as sophisticated and welcoming of diverse lifestyles. Its name is an acknowledgment of the 19th-century day laborers who, for many decades, congregated near the site every morning in hopes of being hired that day by the foremen of the region's railway crews. Today, you can "work the rail" in much more comfortable circumstances, positioning yourself within the brick-lined confines of a warm, convivial, and endlessly indulgent watering hole patronized by some of Savannah's most engaging writers, eccentrics, and artists. Tavern meisters Trina Marie Brown (from Los Angeles) and Melissa Swanson (from Connecticut) serve snacks (black-bean salsa, cold pistachio-pasta salad, pesto pizzas, and chili), but most people come just to drink and chat. Open Sunday 11:30am to 10pm, Tuesday and Wednesday 11:30am to 1am, and Thursday through Saturday 11:30am to 3am.

Wet Willie's

101 E. River St. ☎ **912/233-5650.**

There's a branch of this bar in Florida, but it can't be more popular than its Savannah cousin. The sign behind the bar suggests "Attitude Improvement," whereas another says they'll call a taxi when it's time to go home. Wet Willie's is rather like a Dairy Queen with liquor on tap. The specialty drinks are tasty and colorful—sort of a rum and sherbert in a glass. Among the ever-changing favorites are Bahama Mama, Blue Hawaiian, Jungle Juice, Monkey Shine, and Sex on the Beach. Open Monday through Saturday from 11am to 2am, and Sunday from 12:30pm to 1am.

DINNER CRUISES

The *Savannah River Queen,* a replica of the boats that once operated on the Savannah River, is a 350-passenger vessel that departs from Savannah's River Street, behind City Hall; it's operated by **River Street Riverboat Co.,** 9 E. River St. (☎ **912/232-6404**). It offers a 2-hour nightly cruise with a prime rib or fish dinner and live entertainment. Reservations are necessary. The fare is $30.95 for adults and $19.95 for children under 12. Departures are usually daily at 7pm, but the schedule might be curtailed in the colder months.

10   A Side Trip to Tybee Island

For more than 150 years, Tybee Island has lured Savannahians who wanted to go swimming, sailing, fishing, and picnicking. Pronounced Tie-*bee*, an Euchee Indian word for "salt," the island offers 5 miles of unspoiled sandy beaches, just 14 miles east of Savannah. From Savannah take Hwy. 80 until you reach the ocean.

The **Tybee Island Visitors' Center** (☎ **800/868-BEACH** or 912/786-4043) provides complete information if you're planning to spend some time on the island, as opposed to making a day trip from Savannah.

If you're interested in daily or weekly rentals of a bedroom condo or beach house (one or two bedrooms), call **800/755-8562** or 912/786-8805, or write to **Tybee Beach Rentals,** P.O. Box 1440, Tybee Island, GA 31328.

Consisting of 5 square miles, Tybee was once called "the Playground of the Southeast," hosting millions of beach-loving visitors from across the country. In the 1880s, it was a popular dueling spot for the gentlemen of South Carolina.

In the early part of the 1900s, Tybrisa Pavillion on the island's south end became one of the major summer entertainment pavilions in the south. In its time it attracted some of the best-known bands, including Benny Goodman, Guy Lombardo, Tommy Dorsey, and Cab Callaway. It burned down in 1967, and was never rebuilt.

Over Tybee's salt marshes and sand dunes have flown the flags of pirates and Spaniards, the English and French, and the Confederate States of America. A path on the island leads to a clear pasture where John Wesley, founder of the Methodist church in the colonies, knelt and declared his faith in the new land.

Fort Screven on the northern strip of the island began as a coastal artillery station and evolved into a training camp for countless troops in both world wars. Remnants of the wartime installations can still be seen all over Fort Screven.

Also in the area of this fort is the **Tybee Museum,** housed in what was one of the fort's batteries. On display is a collection of photographs, memorabilia, artwork, and dioramas depicting Tybee from the time the Native Americans inhabited the island through World War II.

Across the street is the **Tybee Lighthouse,** originally built in 1742 and the third oldest lighthouse in America. It is 154 feet high, and if you're fit you can climb 178 steps to the top. From the

Isle of Hope

About 10 miles south of downtown Savannah is that nostalgic community, Isle of Hope. First settled in the 1840s as a summer resort for the wealthy, it's now a showcase of rural antebellum life. To reach Parkersburg (as it was called in those days), citizens traveled by steamer down the Wilmington River or by a network of suburban trains. Today, however, visitors to Savannah can reach Isle of Hope by driving east along Victory Drive to Skidaway Road. At Skidaway, go right and follow it to LaRoche Avenue. Here, take a left and follow LaRoche until it dead-ends on Bluff Drive.

This is the perfect place for a lazy afternoon stroll. The short path is home to authentically restored cottages and beautiful homes, most enshrouded with the Spanish moss that cascades from the majestic oaks lining the bluff. A favorite of many local landscape artists and Hollywood directors, Bluff Drive affords the best views of the Wilmington River.

As you head back toward Savannah, drive down Skidaway Road. On your left stands **Wormsloe Plantation,** at 7601 Skidaway Rd. (☎ 912/353-3023). Wormsloe, the home of Noble Jones, is not much more than a ruin, and as you enter the gates, you pass down an unpaved oak-lined drive. The ruins lie less than a half-mile off. Dr. Jones, who constructed Wormsloe as a silk plantation, was one of Georgia's leading citizens during colonial times and a representative to the Continental Congress. Because of its strategic location, Wormsloe has also been home to forts and garrisons during the Civil and Spanish-American wars. It's open Tuesday to Saturday from 9am to 5pm, and on Sunday from 2 to 5:30pm. Admission is $2 for adults, $1 for students 6 to 18, and children 5 and under are admitted free.

When you leave Wormsloe, continue down Skidaway Road. When you hit Victory Drive, head east through Thunderbolt and over the bridge. Take your first left and stop at **Desposito's** (☎912/987-9963). This funky crab shack is the real thing, complete with newspaper on the tables. Here you can sample a variety of fresh seafood straight from the river, listen to oldies by Guy Lombardo or Dean Martin on the jukebox, and wash it all down with a cold Red Dog beer. Open Tuesday to Thursday and Sunday from noon to 10pm, and on Friday and Saturday from noon to 11pm.

panoramic deck you get a sense of "the length and breadth of the marshes," as captured in the Sidney Lanier poem, "The Marshes of Glynn." For information about the museum and lighthouse, call **912/786-5801.** Hours for both the museum and the lighthouse are April through September daily from 10am to 6pm; off-season, Monday and Wednesday through Friday noon to 4pm, and Saturday and Sunday from 10am to 4pm. It is closed Tuesday. Adults pay $2.50, seniors 62 and older $1.50, and children 6–12 75¢; ages 5 and under enter free. There are picnic tables at the lighthouse, and there is easy access to a beach.

Tybee Marine Center, in the 14th Street parking lot (☎ **912/786-5917**), has aquariums with species indigenous to the coast of southern Georgia. Also on display are the usual cast of marina mammals, sharks, and other creatures. Hours are 9am to 4pm daily. Admission is free but donations are accepted.

Tybee Island is a favorite destination for families, the major activity centering around the **Tybee Amusement Park,** 16th Street (☎ **912/786-8806**). Children's rides are available, as are a small roller coaster, a merry-go-round, and a ferris wheel, among other attractions. In summer hours are Monday through Friday from 6 to 11pm, Saturday and Sunday 2 to 11pm. Off-season the place is open only on Saturday and Sunday from 6 to 10:30pm. Admission is free, although each ride requires a ticket.

WHERE TO STAY

Fort Screven Inn Bed-and-Breakfast

24 Van Horne St. (P.O. Box 2511), Tybee Island, GA 31328. ☎ **912/786-9255.** 3 suites. TV. $85–$95 double. Rates include breakfast and a tour of the local museum. AE, MC. V.

Set at the northernmost tip of Tybee Island, Fort Screven was originally conceived in 1897 as a bulwark against the hostilities that led to the Spanish-American War. When it was decommissioned in 1945, its cluster of officers' quarters, hospitals, and gun embankments were parceled off to homeowners, one of whom, Gary Smith, maintains his as a B&B. Set within the southern annex of what used to function as a hospital, the building has heart-pine floors, a large porch, and an atmosphere permeated with respect for the military traditions of both North and South. Many clients here hail from Atlanta, and share an interest in the nearby beaches with an avid devotion and respect for Army and maritime history of the surrounding forts and military strongholds.

WHERE TO DINE

⊗ Crab Shack at Chimney Creek

40 Estill Hammock Rd., Tybee Island. ☎ **912/786-9857.** Main courses $8.95–$19.95. MC, V. Daily 11am–10pm. SEAFOOD.

This place advertises itself as "where the elite eat in their bare feet." At least they're right about the bare feet part! Even if you're wearing shoes, the down-home cookery is likely to be good. Your lunch or dinner might have arrived just off the boat, having been swimming happily in the sea only an hour or so ago. Fat crab is naturally the specialty. It's most often preferred in cakes, or else it can be blended with cheese and seasonings; boiled shrimp is another popular item. Kids delight in selecting their crabs from a tank, although this custom always struck us as a bit ghoulish. A Low Country boil (a medley of seafood) is a family favorite, and the jukebox brings back the '50s.

Palmer's Seafood House

80 Wilmington Island Rd., Wilmington Island, just off Johnny Mercer Boulevard. ☎ **912/897-2611.** Main courses $7.95–$18.99. AE, DC, MC, V. Mon 5–10pm, Tues–Sat 11am–10pm, Sun 11am–9pm. SEAFOOD.

A long-time favorite on Wilmington Island (before your approach to Tybee), Palmer's opens onto a view of Turner's Creek. It is the leading choice for seafood on the periphery of Savannah. A family favorite and wheelchair-accessible, it gets you going with a cup or bowl of seafood gumbo, made with more tomatoes here than in the Bayou country of Louisiana. Red snapper is often served, perhaps lightly grilled and covered with shrimp and scallops. Sautéed and steamed fish and seafood are the most favored items, especially the oyster and shrimp combo. Shellfish platters, including snow crab, crab claws, and rock shrimp, are also served. Blue crab appears in season. Of course, the usual array of burgers, chicken fingers, and such appears on the menu. If you don't like fish, you might opt for the charred rib-eye steak. Service is attentive, if a bit rushed at times.

Index

HILTON HEAD